WILL ROGERS

Reflections and Observations

WILL ROGERS

Reflections and Observations

Compiled and Edited by
Bryan B. Sterling
and
Frances N. Sterling

Crown Trade Paperbacks
New York

Published by Crown Trade Paperbacks, 201 East 50th Street,
New York, New York 10022. Member of the Crown Publishing
Group.

Random House, Inc. New York, Toronto, London, Sydney,
Auckland

CROWN Trade Paperbacks and colophon are trademarks of
Crown Publishers, Inc.

Manufactured in the United States of America

Library of Congress Cataloging-in-Publication Data

Rogers, Will, 1879–1935.
   A Will Rogers treasury.

   "A Lou Reda book."
   Includes index.
   1. Sterling, Bryan B.   II. Sterling, Frances N.
III. Title.
[PN6161.R66435   1986]   814'.52   86-23298

Design by Joanna Nelson

ISBN 0-517-88021-0

10 9 8 7 6 5 4 3 2 1

First Paperback Edition

To the memory of
  PAULA MCSPADDEN LOVE
  curator, 1938–1973
  and
  ROBERT WILLARD LOVE
  manager, 1938–1975
  Will Rogers Memorial
  Claremore, Oklahoma

  Their dedication and tireless industry
preserved and organized the legacy of Will
Rogers.
  We had the good fortune to know them,
and to learn from them. Through the years
of our friendship, we came to appreciate
and love Will Rogers' Oklahoma, as they
did.
  We surely miss them.

        Frances and Bryan Sterling

Contents

Contents

Contents

WILL ROGERS

Reflections and Observations

Introduction

On Friday, December 7, 1917, Will Rogers briskly entered the New Amsterdam Theatre on West Forty-second Street and made his way to his dressing room. Under his arm he carried a roll of the latest editions of New York's numerous newspapers. It was still fifteen minutes before curtain time, more than enough for Will to change and be ready for the evening performance of the Ziegfeld Follies. But first he had to read the latest news items to get his act ready.

He dropped the bundle of papers on one of the two straight, ladder-back chairs, settled himself on the other and, oblivious to the surrounding plainness, began to read. Except for the two chairs, the room was quite bare. When Betty Rogers had first seen her husband's dressing room, she was distressed by its simplicity. She went to one of the large department stores and bought a comfortable chaise longue, two deep, soft armchairs, lamps, drapes and curtains for the single window, and an Oriental rug for the floor. When she had finished, the room had been transformed into a most relaxing parlor.

That evening Will Rogers was surprised, and he pretended to be pleased. A few days later Betty returned, expecting to find Will resting on the chaise longue, but found him sitting cross-legged on the floor. It was the only really comfortable place he had found. Betty sent the furnishings back to the store and never again attempted to decorate one of Will's dressing rooms. The two chairs were just what Will wanted, simple and functional.

There was a timid knock on the door. Will called out. A young man stuck his head into the room and identified himself as a reporter for *The American Magazine.* Will told him to enter. The young man looked around the room, the floor now littered with discarded sections of newspapers. There was no place for him to sit, so the reporter stood, uncomfortably leaning against the wall, his pad and stubby pencil ready.

Will looked at him, his blue eyes twinkling. "I have observed," he said, "that a reporter takes down notes just to show you how different they can write a thing in the article from what you told them."

"Mr. Rogers," the reporter began. He cleared his throat nervously, and began again. "Mr. Rogers, did you really come from the West?"

"No," Will smiled kindly, enjoying his own answer. "I'm from New Jersey, but don't you tell anybody."

The next question was one Will expected. "How did you get on the stage?"

"Say, anything can get on the stage. It's keeping 'em off that's hard. A fellow can be a champion soup eater, and if he can locate a manager that will set him up behind a bowl of soup, and tell him to go to it—if he can keep the audience amused, and the soup holds out, why, he is on the stage."

The question that followed was the one most often asked by people who met Will Rogers for the first time. "Who writes your stuff?"

"Why, the newspapers write it! All I do is get all the papers I can carry, and then read all that's going on. I use only one set method in my little gags, and that is to try and keep to the truth. Of course you can exaggerate it, but what you say must be based on truth. Personally I don't like jokes that get the biggest laughs, as they are generally as broad as a house and require no thought at all. I like one where, if you are with a friend and you hear it, it makes you think and you nudge your friend and say, *he is right about that!* I would rather have you do that than to have you laugh—and then forget the next minute what it was you laughed at."

The interview was duly published. And there, for all to see, lay revealed the secret of Will Rogers' successful career.

It was indeed a most successful career, which took him to the top of every field he entered. He was a star roper, performing tricks with the lasso that are still unequaled today. He traveled with the circus, and later in vaudeville, as a favorite performer. He starred in the most prestigious of all Broadway presentations, the *Ziegfeld Follies.* When his best friend, musical comedy star Fred Stone, was almost fatally injured in an airplane crash, Will stepped into Fred's role in a

Broadway musical that was about to open. He starred as Nat Miller in Eugene O'Neill's only comedy, *Ah, Wilderness!*—the one time Will had to deliver lines just as they had been written. Will was the foremost radio commentator of his day. Many an American family might not go to church on a Sunday morning, but to miss Will Rogers' broadcast on a Sunday evening was unthinkable. When he announced that he would give up his radio chore, the entire United States Senate sent him a petition asking that he reconsider. He did.

Will was the country's most widely read columnist, with more than 40 million readers at a time when the entire population of the United States totaled 120 million. He was the top male motion picture box office attraction during the last three years of his life, 1933 to 1935. As Will said: "I did everything in the circus, Wild West shows, the Follies, the movies, and even a play by O'Neill. There is only one other amusement line I haven't been in, and that's to go to the U.S. Senate. But I ain't going to try that, I've got some pride left."

Will could have been elected senator, or governor, from almost any state he chose. He was approached many times to enter politics, and at the Democratic conventions of 1924 and 1928 his name was placed in nomination for the presidency.

He was that rarest of all phenomena, a philosopher with honor in his own country and in his own time. He could portray a hobo or cavort on the screen in a nightgown, lassoing a rat, and still remain a most powerful influence.

The mainstream of American humor has traditionally flowed from the countryside to the city. Historically, humor served those who had nothing against those who had much; those who were the Outs against those who were the Ins. It would show how the wily rustic could best the city slicker. Henry Wheeler Shaw's character, Josh Billings, was such a popular, exaggerated New England rustic. Charles Farrar Browne's famous character, Artemus Ward, gained countrywide recognition though he spoke in strange regional idioms and could not spell. David Ross Locke's character, Petroleum V. Nasby, was supposedly a stupid, prejudiced man. Finley Peter Dunne's character, Mr. Dooley, spoke with a thick Irish brogue.

Will Rogers, too, came from the country—the Indian Territory, before it became the state of Oklahoma. But here comparisons end, except perhaps that he, too, had trouble with his spelling. Will Rogers was neither a sophisticated actor donning the disguise of a simple cowboy nor a character invented by a brilliant writer. He was essentially what he seemed—a country boy who had come to the big city. He had observed the city's ways, and he had become successful.

But he was a success—as he was the first to recognize—because he had remained a country boy.

He made millions laugh, but he was not a clown; he was something far more rare and important—he was a jester, making millions laugh while telling the unflattering truth. People never laughed at him, nor with him. Will made them think, and they ended up laughing at themselves. Yet his audiences never resented having their weaknesses and shortcomings revealed, for Will was one of them. These were his weaknesses and shortcomings, too. They loved him for it, and they trusted him. He was not merely a distant voice on the radio or some movie star to be viewed on a screen on Saturday night, but their close, personal friend.

If America's wisest men had gathered to locate the single most stable fulcrum to help Americans weather the tragic years of World War I and the unemployment that followed it, to help keep a sense of balance and reason during the Roaring Twenties, and to keep hope alive during the hunger-filled years of the Great Depression and the Dust Bowl, they could not have found a more steadfast man than Will Rogers. It was Rogers, more than any single elected official, who represented the people. It was his voice that spoke for those too timid to come forward. His were the statements each American would have made had he been offered the platform.

When Will Rogers ridiculed the federal airplane program by stating that so far it had turned out more air than planes, an immediate investigation was ordered. When he called for help for the 1927 Mississippi flood victims, hundreds of thousands donated their time and funds.

Once, Will casually mentioned in a broadcast that while flying, pilots often had difficulties identifying small towns, and that it would be a good idea to paint the names of towns on the roofs of houses. Almost as an aside, he conceded that it could become a financial hardship to certain small towns and suggested that in such cases the bill for the paint be sent to him. Hundreds of towns and villages followed his suggestion and made identification from the air possible. Only a minute number submitted invoices—which Rogers paid.

When Rogers mentioned that it might be a good idea to let Congress know how the country felt about certain legislation then under consideration, well over a million letters flooded Capitol Hill.

The power and influence entrusted to Will Rogers, a private citizen elected to no office, is unequaled in American history. No other man was ever so universally believed. Such power in the hands of a lesser man could easily have been abused.

In his writings and speeches, Will mirrored his times, as indeed the times forged Will Rogers. When World War I broke out, he was at first most hesitant to criticize the efforts of the government. But when President Woodrow Wilson not only laughed at Will's chides but quoted them frequently, Rogers continued to observe history in his own whimsical style.

Warren G. Harding was probably the least amused president Rogers joked about. In fact, Harding sent emissaries asking that Will go easy on him. When the *Ziegfeld Follies* played Washington, D.C., Will was quite hurt when President Harding snubbed the *Follies* and attended some second-rate theatrical performance instead. Will was not hurt for himself—honors and recognitions meaning little to him—but that because of his joshing, his fellow performers had been denied the honor of a presidential visit.

One could not possibly conjure up two more unlikely friends than dour Calvin Coolidge and gregarious Will Rogers, but that was the case. Will was invited several times to the White House, spent the night there, and frequently reported directly to the president. Yet Rogers continued to joke about Silent Cal. On one occasion, Will, who was an excellent mimic, imitated President Coolidge in a nonsensical State of the Union message on a coast-to-coast radio hookup. Mrs. Coolidge complimented Will but insisted that she could imitate the president even better. "I believe it," conceded Will, "but look what you had to go through to learn it."

After the economic collapse following the stock market crash of 1929, Will once again changed his style of humor. It was obvious to him that what was needed most was optimism—not the optimism of a politician running for office, but optimism in the realm of reality. His contention was never that "prosperity is just around the corner!" Actually, he maintained that "war is closer around the corner than prosperity." When severe critics pounced on President Herbert Hoover as the single cause for the Depression, Rogers pointed out the illogic of such a belief: "The way some people are talking, you'd think that Mr. Hoover got up one morning, looked out the window, and said: This looks like a nice day for ruining the country, I think I'll do it today."

Will came to the defense of the Republican party, blamed for everything from the stock market crash to massive unemployment— albeit in typical Rogers style: "Don't blame all the things that have been happening to us lately on the Republican Party. They are not smart enough to have thought 'em up!"

Franklin D. Roosevelt realized early the importance of Will Rogers. After Will's first trip to Russia in 1926, Roosevelt publicly commented on Will's report: "Mr. Rogers' account was not only more amusing, it was more accurate than any I have read."

After Roosevelt's election to the presidency, Rogers was often invited to the White House. The president read Will's columns and listened to his broadcasts. As Postmaster General James A. Farley said, "Everybody else was doing it, why shouldn't the president?"

But the importance of Will Rogers is not merely that he was a film star, or that he was a friend of the powerful, or that he threw velvet-tipped harpoons at the pompous, or even that he was loved by millions. This book intends to show Will Rogers the chronicler. From 1922 to 1935, Rogers, more impartially than any other observer, recorded the life and times, not only of the United States but of other countries. In that period Will Rogers wrote some 660 weekend feature articles, a score of magazine reports, and more than 2,800 daily squibs, keeping in fact a day-by-day public diary. He reported on events, important and unimportant, on prominent men and women, their deeds and misdeeds, on dramas and blunders.

Here is an era exactly as it was, seen with humor and love, but not blind love, through the tolerant eyes of a completely nonpartisan participant. He not only observed an age, he lived it and even helped to make it bearable. He injected sanity where there was none, and humor where there was only folly. Will Rogers makes it great fun— but don't let him fool you, for he is also food for thought.

1922

America is a nation of more than 110 million, most of whom hum, whistle, plunk, or strum tunes like "Yes, We Have No Bananas," "Chicago," "'Way Down Yonder in New Orleans," and "Toot, Toot, Tootsie, Goo' Bye." Pulitzer Prizes go to Eugene O'Neill for *Anna Christie* and to Booth Tarkington for his novel *Alice Adams*. The play *Abie's Irish Rose* premieres on Broadway and will run for 2,327 consecutive performances.

The major films of the year are: *The Prisoner of Zenda*, with Lewis Stone and Alice Terry; *Robin Hood*, with Douglas Fairbanks and Wallace Beery; *Blood and Sand*, with Rudolph Valentino; *Orphans of the Storm*, with Dorothy and Lillian Gish.

Radio inflicts the first advertising commercial on its listeners. Radio pioneer Lee De Forest will complain bitterly: "What have you done with my child? You have sent him out on the street in rags of ragtime, to collect money from all and sundry . . . a stench in the nostrils of the gods of the ionosphere."

On the New York Stock Exchange, American Telephone & Telegraph sells for as high as 128¼, General Motors is 14⅞, Standard Oil of New Jersey hovers all year around 39, while New York Central is 94⅛. On the New York Curb (now the American Stock Exchange), Reo Motors sells for 14, but Radio Corporation can be had for 3¼. A brand-new Hupmobile, touring car model, can be bought for $1,115, FOB Detroit—revenue tax extra.

Because of Prohibition, the usually popular New Year's pledge "I promise never to drink another drop!" has been paraphrased to "I promise never to drop another drink!"

In baseball the New York Yankees, American League champions, are easily defeated in the subway World Series by the National League champions, the New York Giants.

An eighteen-year-old boy from Chicago's Illinois Athletic Club sets the swimming world on its ear by amassing records. His name is John Weissmuller and he is to become an Olympic champion, and the most famous movie Tarzan of them all.

A fifteen-year-old girl from New York's Women's Swimming Association easily captures the freestyle outdoor championship in the 220- and 440-yard races. Her name is Gertrude Caroline Ederle, and she will become the first woman to swim the English Channel.

1922 is also the year in which the first diabetic patient is treated with insulin.

In Washington, D.C., the Great War, the war to end all wars, has at last officially ended by a joint resolution of Congress. Not settled at this time, and a hotly debated political issue for years to come, is the debt of more than ten billion dollars, plus interest of more than one billion, incurred during the war by America's allies. Without these huge loans, allied European countries would have collapsed economically prior to U.S. entry into the war. Much external and internal pressure will be brought to bear on Washington to cancel these loans. But as a positive nod toward the future, a multipower conference on the limitation of armament is in session.

The Lincoln Monument along the Potomac River is dedicated after seven years of construction.

Congress collectively criticizes Michigan's Senator Truman H. Newberry for his extravagant campaign expenditure of $195,000. Though Congress allows him to be seated, Senator Newberry resigns ten months later because of the continuing public outrage at such excessive campaign spending.

When Georgia's Senator Thomas Watson dies, Mrs. Rebecca Latimer Felton is appointed to fill his unexpired term, becoming the first woman senator.

The U.S. Supreme Court hands down the decision that Japanese are not eligible for American citizenship. The League of Nations approves the British mandate of Palestine, and on September 11 that mandate is proclaimed in Jerusalem. Just five months earlier, the United States Senate had passed a declaration in favor of the restoration of Palestine as the national home for the Jewish people.

Warren Gamaliel Harding, an "old guard" Republican, is in the

White House, and John Calvin Coolidge is his vice-president. Charles Evans Hughes is secretary of state, and an engineer named Herbert Clark Hoover is secretary of commerce. Secretary of the Interior Albert Bacon Fall leases U.S. naval reserves number 3 (in Teapot Dome, Wyoming)—without competitive bids—to Harry F. Sinclair, who turns it over to Mammoth Oil Company for stock totaling $160 million. Two weeks later, the same Albert Bacon Fall leases the oil reserves number 1 at Elk River, California—again without competitive bids—to Edward L. Doheny, for a personal bribe of $100,000.

Three magazines are published for the first time, and will make quite an impact on America's reading habits: *Reader's Digest, Better Homes and Gardens,* and *True Confessions.*

The aeroplane, which will celebrate only its nineteenth birthday in December, is still the ultimate for heroic exploration. At San Diego, J. A. MacReady and O. G. Kelly set a world endurance record by staying aloft for 35 hours, 18 minutes, and 35 seconds. Brig. Gen. William ("Billy") Mitchell sets a world speed record for airplanes by whizzing past a measured mile at an incredible 224.05 miles per hour. U.S. Army Air Corps Lt. James ("Jimmy") H. Doolittle is the first to fly from coast to coast when he covers the distance between Florida's eastern beach and San Diego in just under 21½ hours.

And with progress comes disaster. On April 7, the first airline collision is recorded when a Farman Goliath, operated by the French airline Grands Express, smashes into a DH-18 of Daimler Airways over Poix, in northern France.

In New York City, two time-honored traditions pass. After ninety-one years, the famed Delmonico's restaurant, the city's foremost eating place, closes its doors. And late in December, the thundering hoofs of horses drawing fire equipment over cobblestone streets is heard no more. The last two fire stations that still used horse-drawn apparatus have been modernized with fire trucks.

In India, the factory act is passed, setting the workweek at sixty hours and raising the minimum age for working children from nine to twelve years. On February 1, the Mahatma Mohandas Karamchand Gandhi sends a letter to the British viceroy threatening massive civil disobedience. On March 10, Gandhi is arrested and charge with sedition.

The IRA (Irish Republican Army) is formally constituted—its purpose to "safeguard the honour and independence of the Irish Republic."

On October 19, Britain's Prime Minister David Lloyd George, who has presided over a coalition government, resigns when that coalition disintegrates. Andrew Bonar Law, Canadian-born leader of the Conservatives, heads the new government.

In Italy, Benito Mussolini, an ex-Socialist, marches with his Fascist supporters on Rome and establishes himself in power.

In Moscow, Russian revolutionist Leon Trotsky declares: "The industrial depression from which revolutionary Russia is now emerging will finally bring about a revolution in Europe, and when this occurs, America, that Babylonian Tower of Capitalism, will fall also!" But until then, America continues to send relief to starving Russia; by year's end the total gift reaches $50 million.

At Thebes, in Upper Egypt, Howard Carter, famous British Egyptologist, uncovers the steps leading down to the entrance gallery of the tomb of mid-fourteenth-century B.C. Pharaoh Tutenkhamon. The exact date of this discovery is November 4, 1922.

On that same day, almost half a world away in New York City, Will Rogers observes his birthday. At age forty-three he has achieved national and international fame.

Born in the Indian Territory that was to become the state of Oklahoma, Will was raised as the only surviving son of a well-to-do and influential rancher. To be properly educated, he was sent to a number of schools, but he liked none and preferred instead to practice with the lariat, roping anything that moved. When Will was ten years old, his mother died; three years later, his father married again. Will's dislike of schooling continued, until finally he was sent to the Kemper Military School in Boonville, Missouri, in the hope that the discipline would settle him down. After less than two years, Will left one night and "quit the school business for life."

He worked as a cowboy, entered rodeos, and finally made his way around the world. He looked after cattle being shipped from the Argentine to South Africa, broke horses, finally joined a Wild West show and "was ruined for life." In New Zealand he worked in a circus, and eventually saved enough to book passage home. In America, he again worked in a Wild West show, performing as a stunt roper. In 1905 he developed a roping act in which he performed stunning catches of a horse galloping across the stage, and he turned to vaudeville. Following the various theater circuits from coast to coast and through Canada, Will Rogers added humor and proved perennially successful.

In 1908, Betty Blake from the small town of Rogers, Arkansas, finally agreed to marry Will. They had first met years before, when Betty had come to visit her sister, the wife of the station master at Oologah, near the Rogers ranch. Will had courted her over the years, mostly by mail. Their honeymoon was taken along the Orpheum theater circuit, as Betty was introduced to the life of vaudeville performers.

By 1915 Will had also appeared in a number of Broadway musicals, most of them short-lived, although his own performances were always singled out by critics.

It was Gene Buck, Florenz Ziegfeld's lyricist, writer, and talent scout, who discovered Rogers and brought him to Ziegfeld's Midnight Frolic. Located atop the multistoried building that housed the New Amsterdam Theatre, where most Ziegfeld's *Follies* were shown, the Midnight Frolic was Ziegfeld's latest experiment. Starting at 11:30 P.M., it catered primarily to an aftertheater crowd. The large room became the forerunner of modern nightclubs, with its elaborate floor shows, big-name entertainment, and huge cast of show beauties. It was unmatched anywhere, featuring dinners, the best in liquors, and dancing.

When Joseph Urban, the genius designer, joined Ziegfeld, he added a movable stage, glass balconies, and crosslighting that created amazing rainbow effects.

As New York's foremost late-night spot—Ziegfeld advertised it as "The Meeting Place of the World"—many of its patrons dined there several times a week. Will realized immediately that his routine would have to be changed daily, and from this time on he relied far less on his famed dexterity with the lariat, switching almost exclusively to comments on the current news. Will Rogers, the astute political commentator, was born.

When Ziegfeld saw Will's drawing power at the Midnight Frolic, he asked him to join the cast of the *Follies,* playing downstairs at the regular theater. Despite an impressive cast, which included W. C. Fields, Ed Wynn, Ina Claire, Leon Errol, Bert Williams, Ann Pennington, and Mae Murray, the show seemed in trouble. Will Rogers proved the right catalyst.

Will had stayed on as Ziegfeld's star through annual new editions of the Follies until 1919. During the years of their association, the two men had no written contract, only a handshake. Will had wanted it that way.

In 1918, Will had starred in the motion picture *Laughing Bill Hyde,* which had been filmed at studios at Fort Lee, New Jersey, just across the Hudson River from New York City. When Sam Goldfish (he had not yet changed his name to Goldwyn) saw the result, he signed Rogers to a lucrative one-year contract, with an option to renew at an even higher salary. The sole stipulation was that all subsequent films would be produced at the California studios. Will consulted Betty, and the two concluded that the move would not only further Will's career but would be beneficial to the children. The family had now grown to three boys and one girl: Will, Jr. (eight), Mary (six), Jimmy (four), and Fred (one). Thus, in 1919, Will said farewell to Ziegfeld and Broadway and moved his whole family west. Tragedy struck the family in 1920, when Fred, just two years old, died during a diphtheria epidemic.

After two years with Sam Goldwyn, Will's contract was not renewed. Trying to produce his own films, Will not only lost all he had managed to save but went deeply into debt. Leaving the family in Los Angeles early in 1922, he went back to star in the Frolic and the *Follies*. Ziegfeld welcomed him with open arms.

Thus, as 1922 comes to an end, Will Rogers is not only Broadway's highest-paid entertainer but also New York's most celebrated after-dinner speaker. His individual style of good-natured irreverence and humor sets a new trend in both fields.

And on December 24, Rogers begins yet another phase in his career. On that date the first of his weekly columns appear in *The New York Times*. A week later, on the last day of the year—December 31, 1922—the first of the nationally and internationally syndicated columns is published. He will write these weekly columns for the rest of his life.

Batting for Lloyd George

I want to apologize and set the many readers of The Times straight as to why I am blossoming out as a weekly infliction on you all.

It seems The Times had Lloyd George signed up for a pack of his memoirs. Well, after the late election in England, Lloyd couldn't seem to remember anything, so they sent for me to fill in the space where he would have had his junk.

You see, they wanted me in the first place, but George came along and offered to work cheaper, and also to give his to charity. That benevolence on his part was of course before England gave him his two weeks notice.

Now I am also not to be outdone by an ex-Prime Minister donating my receipts from my prolific tongue to a needy charity. The total share of this goes to the civilization of three young heathens, Rogers by name, and part Cherokee Indians by breeding.

Now by wasting seven minutes if you are a good reader—and ten to twelve if you read slow—on me every Sunday, you are really doing a charitable act yourself, by preventing these three miniature bandits from growing up in ignorance.

A great many people may think that this is the first venture of such a conservative paper as The Times, in using something of a semi-humorous nature, but that is by no means the case. I am following the Kaiser, who re-wrote his life after it was too late. I realize what a tough job I have, succeeding a man who to be funny, only had to relate the facts.

Please don't consider these as my memoirs. I am not passing out of the picture, as men generally are who write these things. I want to warn you of a few pitfalls into which our poorly paid but highly costing politicians are driving us daily.

We pay an awful lot of dough in the course of a year to get our country run in such a shape that a certain per cent of our citizens can keep out of the poorhouse. The shape we are in now, over and above all the taxes we pay, allows us to hang on to about 8 per cent of our gross earnings.

Now, that's entirely too rich we are getting—too prosperous. So they are talking of lending Europe about a billion and a half, more. I knew there would be something stirring when J.P. Morgan visited Washington last week. He goes down once every year, and lays out the following year's program.

Europe owes us now about eleven billions. Lending them another billion and a half would make it just even 12.5. You see, it's so much easier to figure the interest on 12.5, than on 11. Of course the interest ain't going to be paid, but it's got to be figured.

The government could charge it off on their income tax to publicity. I only hope one thing, and that is, if we make the loan, Europe will appreciate this one.

The Allied Debt Conference broke up last week in London. It's getting harder every day for nations to pay each other, unless one of them has some money. They called that an Economic Conference—and, as we didn't attend, it was. Why don't somebody lend Germany the money so they can pay France what France owes England, so England can pay us the money to lend Germany to pay France? It only takes somebody to start it.

I see they been holding another Peace Conference in some burg called Lausanne. They are having those things now just like Chautauquas—you jump from one to the other. This one must have been somewhere near Italy, as that is the stopping place of the

Ambassador that we sent there. He didn't go officially, as we don't belong to the League of Nations. We only finance it. Well this Ambassador, his name is Child, as I say, he went as a kind of Uninstructed Delegate. He got into the game, but his efforts were more like a cheer leader at a football game—they heard him, but he had no direct effect on the game.

It seems that the Allies—that's, those of them that are speaking to each other—wanted Turkey to promise to protect the minority nations within her territory. Now this Turkey is a pretty foxy nation; she's got her mind on something besides wives and cigarettes.

Turkey said: "We'll agree to give minority nations the same protection that you all give yours."

Well, that was not exactly what the Allies wanted, but they took it as a compromise, and hope at some future time to get full protection for them.

Settling the Affairs of the World

Everybody is writing something nowadays. It used to be just the Literary, or Newspaper men who were supposed to know what they were writing about, that did all the writing. But nowadays, all a man goes into office for is so he can try to find out something, and then write it when he comes out.

Now being in the Ziegfeld Follies for almost a solid year in New York has given me an inside track on some of our biggest men in this country who I meet nightly at the stage door.

So I am breaking out in a rash right here in this paper every Sunday. I will cite an example to prove to you what you are going to get. Last week, there was a mess of Governors here from various provinces. And a good friend of mine brought back to the stage, and dressing room, Governor Allen of Kansas. (Hurry up and print this story, or he won't be Governor).

Well, I stood him in the wings, and he was supposed to be looking at my act, but he wasn't. He was watching what really is the backbone of our show. Anyway, he heard some of my gags about our government, and all who are elected to help misrun it.

So at the finish of my act, I dragged him out on the stage and introduced him to the audience. He made a mighty pretty little speech and said he enjoyed Will's Impertinences—and got a big laugh on that. Said I was the only man in America who was able to tell the truth about our men and affairs. When he finished, I explained to the audience why I was able to tell the truth. It is because I never mixed in Politics. So you all are going from time to time to get the real low down on some of these birds who are sending home the radish seed.

You know, the more you read and observe about this Politics thing, you got to admit that each party is worse than the other. The one that's out, always looks the best. My only solution would be to keep 'em both out one term, and hire my good friend Henry Ford to run the whole thing and give him a commission on what he saves us. I tell you folks, all Politics is apple sauce.

The President gave a luncheon for the visiting Governors, where they discussed, but didn't try Prohibition. It was the consensus of opinion of all their speeches, that there was a lot of drinking going on, and that if it wasn't stopped by January, that they would hold another meeting and try and get rid of some of the stuff.

Senator Curtis of Kansas proposed a bill this week to stop bootlegging in the Senate, making it unlawful for any member to be caught selling to another member while on government property. While the bill was being read, a government employee fell just outside the Senate door and broke a bottle of pre-war stuff (made just before last week's Turkish war). Now they are carpeting all the halls with a heavy material, so in case of a fall, there will be no serious loss.

Well, New Year's is here now and I suppose we will have to hear and read all these big men's New Year's greetings, such men as Charles Schwab, who founded Bethlehem Steel, Gary who is chairman of the board over at U.S. Steel, and John D. Rockefeller, Sr., who founded the Standard Oil Company, and all of them, saying the same old apple sauce, that they are optimistic of the coming year, and everybody must put their shoulder to the wheel and produce more, and they predict a great year. Say, if we had those bird's dough, we could all be just as optimistic as they are. But it's a good joke, and it's got in the papers every year, and I suppose, always will.

Now the Ku Klux Klan is coming into New York, but I guess it couldn't get much of a footing in New York. If there was some man they wanted to take out and tar and feather, they wouldn't know where he lived. People move so often here, their own folks don't know where they live. And even if they found out, the elevator man in the apartment building wouldn't let 'em up.

I see where there is bills in Congress now to change the Constitution all around, elect the President in a different way, and have Congress meet at a different time. It seems the men who drew up this thing years ago didn't know much, and we are just now getting a bunch of real fellows who can take that old parchment, and fix it up like it should have been all these years. It seems it's just been luck that got us by so far.

Now when they get the Constitution all fixed up, they are going to start in on the Ten Commandments—just as soon as they find somebody in Washington who has read them.

Speech for the American Bond and Mortgage Company

You birds are so prosperous looking, one would think you were the buyers of the bonds, instead of the sellers. There ain't a one of you that don't look better than these men who own the company. Not only that, but your mind seems to be more at ease. Why, if a man told people in New York that some of you come from Columbus and Grand Rapids, they wouldn't believe it. But if you ever told them you had men in here that come from the wilds of Rockford and Davenport, it would be unbelievable.

I am the only man that had never heard of what you sell. I had never had anything to mortgage, and never had anything to buy a mortgage with. It had never been my idea of happiness, to make money by having a mortgage on something somebody else was trying to make a living out of.

I only loan to a man who I think will pay it back. If I had to take a mortgage, I wouldn't loan it to him. A man shouldn't be allowed to borrow who wouldn't pay back.

Did you ever figure that banking, loans, mortgages, interests of any kind are the most non-essential industries in the world? Interest eats up half the earnings of the world. Suppose nobody borrowed anything, and if they did, they paid back just what they borrowed. If you live by a neighbor and need a sack of flour, or some potatoes, you borrow from your neighbor and when you pay it back, you pay one sack of flour, not one sack and 8/100th. Now this neighbor only borrows when he needs it, and you only loan him when you have confidence in him. Imagine what would happen if every man owns the business he is in? He don't owe anything on it. No interest to pay. So he don't have to charge as much for his goods. You work, buy what you need, save up, buy just what you can pay for, and no more. Eliminate all business worries.

Don't say it couldn't be done, for two-thirds of the world lives now without receiving a cent in interest. Well, let this other third live, or go to work without receiving any.

Now I am not a-saying anything against you salesmen. You are working hard, trying to get along. It's these capitalists here I am trying to convert. I want to try and get them to turn honest. Now take my graft, it's about the same thing—it's non-essential. I want to get out of it as soon as I can find something else. No man should spend money for amusement, or to see anything funny on the stage. My Lord, ain't there enough funny looking things off the stage, and ain't most of the things that men say funny enough to suit any one?

Now they kidded you fellows, saying, "We are going to take you back east on a trip. We are going to give a lot of you fellows a chance to come to New York. We are going to have a convention!"

Convention—that is the curse of all business, is conventions. That's what makes the overhead on all we poor buy, is the rich holding conventions. The minute a firm gets big enough to hire over two men, why, they call a convention, where they herd you around like a lot of sheep and pin a badge on you and make speeches to you, and tell you what the organization is going to do during the coming year. That you have gypped so many people during the past year, and that by putting your shoulders to the wheel, you should go out this year and gyp more. They tell you what great guys you are, but that next year you are expected to do better. And maybe all the time they are telling you this, they are figuring on some other fellow in a competitor's firm to take your place. Now you know why they brought you here? It's so they could charge it off on their income tax. The company brought you all through some of the smaller towns like Washington, so by the time you got here, you all would be house broke.

I got an invention to get rid of a bond salesman. Some people in small towns have dogs that protect them, but even that is no good as most salesmen are so hard boiled they just got to biting the dogs. For a while people used to say they were broke, then you figured out a plan to sell them on credit. My invention is a highly tuned instrument to carry in your pocket, and when a bond salesman comes in the same block, it rings and gives you warning. That's the time to get away from there.

Address to Traffic Chiefs

I am here to represent what is left of a vanishing race, and that is the pedestrian. Now while you birds have been directing traffic in all of our big cities, I know more about it than the whole mess of you do— I've been dodging it! Why, you even have those traffic towers built up in the air, so you won't get run over yourself.

That I am able to be here tonight, is not any thanks to you. I owe it to a keen eye and a nimble pair of legs. But I know they'll get me some day. I'm not as young as I used to be, and they are missing me closer every day. Just yesterday I had to run into a store and shut the door in a driver's face, to keep him from getting me. Another chased me into a building, and I hopped into an elevator—that's all that saved me. Now in my younger days I could have stayed on the sidewalk and dodged these fellows fairly. Taxi cab drivers nowadays, why, they are the same fellows that run the submarines during the war. They duck down, and don't come up for three or four blocks.

Some towns have the streets all marked up with white lines. It's sort of a game. If the fellow driving the car hits you while you are inside those white lines, it don't count. He got to come back and run over you again.

Before we had traffic officers, there was not near as many people killed outright, as there is now. But there was more hurt; which proves that by having a traffic officer to properly direct you, the driver can finish his victim, where in the old days he could only hurt him. So I think your organization can well report progress.

Prohibition has helped the pedestrian a little, as the drivers are afraid to run over just anybody. It might be a bootlegger, and they would get the tires all cut up.

In New York we just have red and green lights. Some of your towns have a yellow light. I asked the cop what the yellow light was for. I thought one of them had faded. He said it was to get ready. Well, I was ready when I got there. I guess the yellow light is for old men who have been standing there so long, to start limbering up, then, if they are in good condition, maybe they can make the other side. I wanted the cot privileges while the lights was changing.

Here are a few rules which I want you to adopt. Eliminate all right and left turns, make everybody go straight ahead. Rule two: eliminate all street cars from the streets; they only get in people's way who are in a hurry walking home. Third, to speed up traffic have a man hired by the city in each block, to do nothing but crank stalled Ford cars.

Fourth, nobody is allowed to drive on Sunday but just the weekend drivers who don't drive any other day, then all they can hit is each other. Fifth, allow no car on the street that is not fully paid for. That would make playgrounds out of our boulevards overnight. Sixth, have everybody going East go on Monday, everybody going West, go on Tuesday, and so on. That's the only way you will ever make the streets of the United States safe for Democracy. At the present rate, in two years there will be no pedestrians left. So where will you birds' jobs be?

Address to the Bankers' Association

Loan sharks and Interest hounds! I have addressed every form of organized graft in the U.S., excepting Congress. So it's naturally a pleasure for me to appear before the biggest.

You are without a doubt, the most disgustingly rich audience I ever talked to, with the possible exception of the Bootleggers Union, Local 1, combined with the enforcement officers.

Now I understand you hold this convention every year to announce what the annual gyp will be. I have often wondered where the depositors hold their convention. I see your wives come with you. You notice I say "come" not "were brought." I see where your convention was opened by a prayer, and you had to send outside your ranks to get somebody that could pray. You should have had one creditor here, he would have shown you how to pray!

I noticed that in the prayer the clergyman announced to the Almighty that the bankers were here. Well, it wasn't exactly an announcement, it was more in the nature of a warning. He didn't tell the devil, he figured the devil knew where you were all the time.

I see by your speeches that you are very optimistic of the business condition of the coming year. If I had your dough, I would be optimistic, too.

Will you please tell me what you do with all the vice presidents a bank has? I guess that's to get you more discouraged before you can see the president. Why, the United States is the biggest business institution in the world, and they only have one vice president, and nobody has ever found anything for him to do.

I have met most of you, as I come out of the stage door of the Follies every night. I want to tell you that any of you that are capitalized under a million dollars, needn't hang around there. Our girls may not know their Latin and Greek, but they certainly know their Dun and Bradstreet.

You have a wonderful organization. I understand you have ten thousand here, and with what you have in the various federal prisons, that brings your membership up to around thirty thousand.

So, goodbye paupers, you are the finest bunch of shylocks that ever foreclosed a mortgage on a widow's home.

"Nomination" of Henry Ford for President

Democrats are the middle-of-the-road party; Republicans are the straddle-of-the-road party; so I hereby nominate Mr. Henry Ford for president, and christen the party, the all-over-the-road party.

In the first place it is too bad he is so competent, that's the only thing that will beat him. Mr. Ford is a good friend of mine, and years ago he overlooked a suggestion that would have made him immortal. That's when he went over to Europe to stop the war. I wanted him to take the girls we had in the Follies, and let them wear the same costumes as in the shows and march them down between the trenches. Believe me, the boys would have been out before Christmas.

He has made more money than any man in the world by paying the highest wages; yet he don't even manufacture a necessity; neither would you call it a luxury; it just kinder comes under the heading of knick-knacks.

I was in his home last year and happened to ask him that in case of stiff competition just how cheap he could sell his car. He said, "Will, by controlling the selling of the parts, I could give the cars away." He said, "those things will shake off enough bolts in a year to pay for themselves. Why, the second year, that's just clear profit."

People think that Dr. Coue was the originator of auto-suggestion. Mr. Ford is! He originated auto suggestion. He just recently lowered the price fifty dollars. That's done to discourage thievery.

He is the first man that ever took a joke and made it practical. So let's let him take this country, maybe he can repeat. He should make a good political race, he carries two thirds of this country now. There is no reason why there shouldn't be a Ford in the White House; they are everywhere else.

He is the only man that could make Congress earn their salary. He could start a bill through, and give each one something to tack on to it, and when it comes out, it would be ready to use. He is the only man that when Congress started stalling, could pick up the hood and see what was the matter with it. Some are against him because he don't know history. What we need in there is a man that can make history, not recite it.

Now if Mr. Ford will just take another one of my suggestions, he can be elected. If he would just make one speech and say: Voters, if I am elected, I will change the front on them!

Scanning the News

Now all I know is just what I read in the papers. I see where another wife out on Long Island shot her husband. Season opened a month earlier this year. Prohibition caused all that. There is just as many husbands shot as in the old days, but women were missing 'em. Prohibition improved their marksmanship 90 per cent.

Never a day passes in New York, without some innocent bystander being shot. You just stand around this town long enough, and be innocent, and somebody is going to shoot you. One day there was four shot. That's the best shooting ever done in this town. Hard to find four innocent people in New York, even if you don't stop to shoot them. That's why a policeman never has to aim here; he just shoots up a street anywhere. No matter who he hits—it's the right one.

Robberies! Did you ever read about so many robberies? I see where some of our cities and towns are talking about being more strict with these robbers. When they catch 'em from now on, they're going to publish their names.

They've been having every kind of a week here in New York. Smile Week, Apple Week, and one called Don't-Get-Hurt-Week. Taxi cab drivers couldn't hardly wait till the following Monday to run over you.

Everybody is talking about what's the matter with this country, and what this country needs. What this country needs, worse than anything else is a place to park your car. What our big cities need is another orange in these orangeade stands.

I read where a New York society woman is suing her ex-husband again. Claims she can't properly support their child on $50,000 a year alimony. Somebody's been feeding that young one meat.

Lots of people wonder why we left our soldiers in Germany so long. We had to leave them over there, two of them hadn't married yet.

21

I'm off home rule for Ireland from now on. I read an Irish paper the other day, and it says that liquor is 18 cents a quart. Can you imagine a nation wanting more freedom than that?

See where the Ku Klux Klan is coming into New York, Yes Sir. They are. I'm no fool, you ain't going to get me telling jokes about them.

Right now we couldn't go into another war—we haven't got any slogan. Couldn't go into a war, anyhow, we might win it. We can't afford to win another war. I have a plan that will stop all wars. When you can't agree with your neighbor, you move away. If you can't agree with your wife, she either shoots you, or moves away from you. Well, that's my plan, move nations away from each other. Take France and Germany, when they can't agree, take France and trade places with Japan. Let Japan live there by Germany. If those two want to fight— let 'em fight. Who cares.

We don't always agree with Mexico. Well, trade Mexico off with Turkey, harems and all. We got men in this country that would get on great with Turkey. And that would solve the Irish problem. Take England and move them away from Ireland. Take them over to Canada, and let 'em live off their son-in-law. But when you move England away from Ireland, don't you let Ireland know where you're taking 'em, or they'll follow 'em and get 'em.

1923

The Union of Soviet Socialist Republics (Russia, the Ukraine, Belorussia, and Transcaucasia) is established in July. Nikolai Lenin, the "liberator of the proletariat," creates the first Soviet forced-labor camp northwest of Archangel.

French troops occupy the Ruhr basin, as Germany has defaulted on the Versailles peace pact condition calling for specific coal deliveries. Germany's inflation soars. In January, 1 American dollar equals 7,260 German marks. By July, the rate of exchange is 1 million marks for 1 dollar, and by the end of the year, 1 dollar will bring more than 4 trillion marks. Prices rise so fast that workers insist on being paid not only daily but several times during the day.

In Munich, Adolf Hitler stages his beer-hall putsch and, with Gen. Erich Ludendorff, seizes the city government. The coup fails and Hitler is arrested. He will be tried and sentenced to five years in prison. While in jail, he will write *Mein Kampf*, in which he will outline his future actions. After serving nine months in relative luxury, he will be pardoned.

In Japan, an earthquake and the resultant fire kill almost 100,000, with additional thousands missing; three-quarters of a million are injured. Almost half a million houses are destroyed or severely damaged, but the Imperial Hotel in Tokyo, built by American architect Frank Lloyd Wright, remains undamaged.

In America, automobile production reaches a surprising 3.8 million, up 700 percent in ten years. There are more than 13 million automobiles on, or mostly stuck in, muddy roads. Yearly style changes are initiated, so that the staggering cost of such planned obsolescence will force some manufacturers out of the market. In three years more than half of the current one hundred car makers will either have been absorbed or gone out of business. In another decade, ten manufacturers will control the market. A new fuel additive, tetraethyl lead mixed with ethylene dibromide, will eliminate the well-known engine knock, giving rise to the advertising slogan "Not a knock in a tankful!"

Dr. Robert Ernest House, an obstetrician from Ferris, Texas, introduces scopolamine, a drug producing twilight sleep, as a means to determine the truth in criminal cases.

American sugar production statistics seem to indicate a consumption of almost 110 pounds per capita, but actually much of it goes into the manufacture of illegal liquor.

Congress, intent on demonstrating America's appreciation to Great War veterans, had voted a special bonus bill in 1922, but President Harding had vetoed it. But national debate does not cease until Congress will finally pass another bonus bill in 1924, stipulating however that payment be delayed until 1945. President Coolidge will veto the bill, but Congress will override that veto.

On August 2, President Warren Harding suddenly dies in San Francisco. Vice-President John Calvin Coolidge is not sworn in until early the following morning.

In sports, heavyweight Jack Dempsey retains his world championship by beating Argentine's "Wild Bull of the Pampas," Luis Angel Firpo, in two rounds, after being knocked completely out of the ring in the first round.

On April 19, New York's Yankee Stadium—the House that Ruth built—is officially opened. Total cost: $2.5 million. To celebrate, Babe Ruth hits a three-run homer as the Yankees beat the Boston Red Sox, 4 to 1. The Yankees will also win the World Series, defeating the New York Giants, four games to two.

The most popular songs in America are: "Nobody's Sweetheart," "Mexicali Rose," "I Cried for You," and "Who's Sorry Now?" On the musical stage, a smash show called *Running Wild* features in addition to the catchy title song a showstopper: "Charleston," which begins a national dance craze.

Across the country people flock to movie houses to see these silent films: *The Hunchback of Notre Dame,* with Lon Chaney, Erich von Stroheim's *Greed,* Cecil B. DeMille's *The Ten Commandments,* and James Cruze's *The Covered Wagon.*

The Broadway season features George Bernard Shaw's *Saint Joan*, with Winifred Lenihan, but the Pulitzer Prize goes to Owen Davis for *Icebound*.

Kahlil Gibran's *The Prophet* is published, and will eventually sell more than fifty million copies. And while Edna St. Vincent Millay wins the Pulitzer Prize for poetry, Robert Frost writes the memorable "Stopping by Woods on a Snowy Evening."

A new magazine, the brainchild of two Yale classmates, reaches the American market. Recapitulating the week's news, it will present the foremost items in a highly individual style. Its name: *Time*.

On New York City's Park Avenue, the Byzantine-style Saint Bartholomew's Church is completed; in Los Angeles, Aimee Semple McPherson dedicates her Angelus Temple. In December, President Coolidge initiates a tradition by lighting the first White House Christmas tree.

For Will Rogers, 1923 begins on a lonely note. Betty and children are in California, while Will is appearing in the *Ziegfeld Follies* in New York. In addition, Will accepts dozens of invitations to appear at benefits. He will also address almost any group that is prepared to pay his fee—usually one thousand dollars. He has left a substantial debt in California after the ill-fated attempt to produce his own pictures, and he is going to make certain that every dollar is repaid.

In June, Will finally returns to Los Angeles. In his weekly article of June 24, he writes: "I have spoken at so many banquets during the year, that when I get home I will feel disappointed if my wife, or one of the children don't get up at dinner and say: We have with us this evening a man who, I am sure, needs no introduction."

Will is now under contract to Hal Roach to appear in a number of short silent comedies. By year's end three "shorts" are released, for which he also writes the humorous titles, which serve as dialogue.

Will also writes and stars in a highly successful parody on *The Covered Wagon*, the epic film. Claiming to have found two wagons that had not been used in the original film, Will calls his burlesque *Two Wagons—Both Covered*.

The Soldiers' Bonus

Just been reading what both sides have to say for, and against, the Bonus. Now, while nothing I would say would be quoted, as what you say for Humanity doesn't have near the appeal as what you say for political purposes, especially in a presidential election year, still, my opinion on the Bonus question is not issued after first taking the opinion of any constituents, and then stringing with the majority.

My opinion is based on what I heard uttered to soldiers in the days when we needed them, when they were looked on *not* as a political organization with a few votes to cast, but as the pick of one hundred million people, the saviors of civilization. We never looked on a soldier in his uniform but what we who didn't go felt he was worth 10 of us. He went—did more than we ever expected him to, now why is he not just as much to us today? He still looks like 10 to 1 to me, and the same to a lot of others if they will be honest and tell the truth.

You promised them everything but the kitchen stove if they would go to war. Now a lot of our wealthy men are saying: "Oh, I am willing to do anything for the disabled but nothing for the well." It wasn't these boys' fault they didn't get shot. When he went away you didn't tell him he had to come home on a stretcher before you would give him anything, did you?

We promised them everything, and all they got was $1.25 a day and some knitted sweaters and sox. And after examining them, they wore the sox for sweaters, and the sweaters for sox. They deserve a Bonus just for trying to utilize what was sent to them.

They got a dollar and a quarter a day. Out of the millions of bullets fired by the Germans every day, statistics have proven than an average of 25 bullets were fired at each man each day. That figures out at the rate of 5 cents a bullet. Now I am no agitator for an unfair wage, or trying to hold anyone up, but the boys in this Bonus want the salary at least doubled. And I don't think that 10 cents a bullet is an exorbitant price.

At the price things are today, I believe that to offer yourself as a target at 10 cents a shot, is not too much. Some days he worked 24 hours but the pay was just the same. Those Germans would not observe the 8-hour law. Then they are not asking anything extra for gas bombs, air raids and cooties. Those things are accepted gratis.

Now the way to arrive at the worth of anything, is by comparison. Take shipbuilding, wooden ones, for instance. Statistics show that the men working on them got, at the lowest, $12.50 per day, and, by an odd coincidence, statistics show that each workman drove at the rate of 25 nails a day—the same number of nails as bullets stopped or evaded by each soldier per day. That makes 50 cents a nail.

Now I am broadminded enough to admit that there is a difference between the grade of these two employments. But I don't think that there is 45 cents per piece difference. I know that bullet stopping comes under the heading of unskilled labor, and that shipbuilding by us during the war, was an art. But I don't think there is that much difference between skilled and unskilled. That makes the skilled 10 times better than the unskilled, while I claim he is only 5 times as good.

I may be wrong in my estimation of the two jobs. Kareful Kal Koolidge is against me on this. It's the first time he and I have disagreed on one of the big questions. He is new and I want to give him the benefit of the doubt. I realize that our opinions have been formed somewhat by our associations. He has been thrown, especially lately, with the wealthy, while I have, except on very rare occasions, been thrown with the common herd.

Now, as I say, while the soldiers got no overtime, the nail expert got time and a half for overtime, up to a certain time, then double time and salary after that. Of course, he lost some time in the morning, selecting which silk shirt he should nail in that day. And it was always a source of annoyance, as to what car to go to work in.

Now I may be wrong, for these rich men who are telling you that the nail is 10 times harder to handle than the bullet, know, because they made and sold both of them to the government.

Everybody's alibi for not giving the soldiers that Bonus is: "We can't commercialize the patriotism of our noble boys!" "They didn't go to war for money, they went for glory!" Then another pet argument is: "The better element of the returned soldiers are against it themselves!" These wealthy men say: "All for the disabled; nothing for the well!"

Now I have a scheme that I don't think has ever been proposed. Of course, coming from one with no political office to back it up, I doubt if it will be considered. Pay the Bonus to all! Then let the boys who don't want it, give their share to a fund to be added to the disabled ones in addition to their regular share. Everybody wants the disabled to be cared for first and best. This plan would doubly care for them.

I also have a plan of raising the money for this Bonus, which I haven't heard brought up. That is, raise it by a tax on all tax-exempt securities. These boys helped their country in a time of need. Tax-exempt bond buyers knowingly hindered it in a time of need by cheating it out of taxes.

In 1916 there were 1,296 whose income was over $300,000 and they paid a billion in taxes. This year, 1923, there were only 246 whose income was supposed to be over $300,000, and they only paid 153 million in taxes. You mean to tell me that there were only 246 men in this country who made $300,000? Why, say, I have spoken at

27

dinners in New York where there were that many in one dining room, much less the United States.

That old alibi about the country not being able to pay, is all apple sauce. There is no debt in the world too big for this country to pay, if they owe it. If you owed it to some foreign nation you would talk about honor, and then pay it. Now what do you want to beat your own kin out of anything for? You say: "Oh, it's not enough to do him any good, anyway." If it's not enough to do him any good, it's not enough to do you any harm when you pay it! Tax-exempt securities will drive us to the poor house, not soldiers' Bonuses. This country is not broke, automobile manufacturers are three months behind in their orders, and whiskey never was as high in its life.

And don't forget that there are many and many thousands of boys who came back and are not classed as disabled, but who will carry some effect of that terrible war as long as they live. I never met 10 who were not injured in some minor way, to say nothing of the dissatisfaction. I claim we owe them everything we have got, and if they will settle for a Bonus, we are lucky.

Now if a man is against it, why don't he at least come out and tell the real truth! Let him say: "I don't want to spare the money to pay you boys."

I think the best insurance in the world is to take care of the boys who fought in the last one; you may want to use them again.

Congress at Work

Well, they brought our soldiers back from Germany last week. Would have brought them back sooner but we didn't have anybody in Washington who knew where they were. We had to leave 'em over there, so they could get the mail that was sent to them during the war.

Anyhow, since last week an awful lot has happened at the studio in Washington, D.C. You know, out in Hollywood, where they make the movies, the place we make them in, is called the studio. We, and Congress, are a great deal alike in lots of respects. We make what we think will be two kinds of pictures, comedy and drama. Now you take the capitol at Washington. That's the biggest studio in the world. We call ours "pictures" when they are turned out; they call theirs "laws." It's all the same thing. We often make what we think is drama, but when it is shown, it is received by the audience as comedy. So the uncertainty is about equal in both places.

The way to judge good comedy is by how long it will last, and have people talk about it. Now Congress has turned out some that have lived for years and people are still laughing about them. You see, girls win a little state popularity contest that is conducted by some newspaper; then they are put into the movies to entertain 110 million people who they never saw or know anything about. Now that's the same way with members of the Capitol Comedy Company of Washington. They win a state popularity contest backed by a newspaper and are sent to Washington, to turn out laws for 110 million people they never saw.

They have what they call the House of Representatives, or Lower House. That compares to what we call the "Scenario Department." That's where somebody gets the idea of what he thinks will make a good comedy law, and they argue around and put it into shape. Then it is passed along, printed, or photographed, as we call it, then it reaches the Senate, or the Cutting and Titling Department. Now in our movie studios, we have what we call Gag Men, whose sole business it is to furnish some little gag, or Amendment as they call it, which will get a laugh or perhaps change the whole thing around.

Now the Senate has what is considered the best and highest priced Gag Men that can be collected anywhere. Why, they put in so many little gags or amendments that the author of the thing don't know his own story. They consider if a man can sit there in the studio in Washington, and just put in one funny amendment in each bill, or production, that will change it from what it originally meant, why, he is considered to have earned his pay. Take for instance the Prohibition Production! That was introduced in the Congress, or Scenario Department, as a comedy.

Well, when it came up in the Senate, one of the Gag, or Title Men, says: I got an idea; instead of this just being a joke, and doing away with the saloons and bar rooms, why, I will put in a title here that will do away with everything." So they sent around to all the bars in Washington, and got a quorum, and released what was to be a harmless little comedy made over into a tragedy.

And we don't any more than get one of these laws sorter halter broke, and get people kinder used to it, when some judge comes along and says it ain't so. Last week Judge Knox comes out and decides that a doctor in prescribing for the modern American illness. can prescribe any amount of alcohol for "medicinal purposes" he thinks necessary. Now according to the Volstead Law, as passed by Congress, no patient is allowed to get "sick" over a pint's worth every 10 days. So, along comes this judge, and says: "Congress is no doctor (they are all patients). How do they know how sick a man can get? Why, for a pint every 10 days, a man would really not be sick at all; he would just be indisposed." So now, when a fellow comes to see the doctor, the doctor will say: "What's the matter with you?" The patient will say: "Why, about a gallon, Doc."

Or the doctor, after looking over one of his perpetual patients, will say: "Why, you are looking great today; your case has improved from two quarts to one. If you don't look out, you will get well."

Instead of doctors studying at a medical school, as they used to, now he just takes a course in rapid penmanship. It looks like a great year for fountain pens.

Another production put out by the Capitol Comedy Company was called the Non-Taxable-Bond, or "Let the Little Fellow Pay." Well, it had a certain vogue for a while with the rich, but it flopped terribly in the cheaper priced houses.

Another one they put out which a lot of you will remember, is the Sur Tax. The main character in this one was a working man on salary with no capital investment to fall back on, paying more on his income than the fellow who has his original capital, and draws his money just from interest. That production has been hissed in some of the best houses.

Then they started to put on a Big one that everybody in America was looking forward to and wanted them to produce; it was called "The Birth of the Bonus," or "How Could You Forget So Soon?" But on account of finances they couldn't produce that and the Non-Taxable-Bond Production, both, so they let the Bonus go.

They are working on two dandies this week. One is called "Refund, Refund, I am always refunding You." It's principally for British trade. The other is really a serial, as they put it on every year. Everybody in the whole studio is interested in it and gets a share of it. It is really their yearly bonus, in addition to their salary. It's called "I'll Get Mine."

Will Disagrees with England's Chancellor of the Exchequer

This bird, Sir Percy Baldwin, that's visiting over here, made some slighting remark about our Senate and House of Representatives. Now I resent that. The President and I can get vexed at Congress sometimes, but we are all the same family. We resent any foreigner coming in here and knocking our representatives. He said that all they know, is to raise hogs and wheat. He is wrong. They don't even know how to raise hogs and wheat.

The worst thing was, Sir Percy said our Congress was "rural and pastoral." Now I understand Congress not calling him down, because they were like me. They didn't know what this "pastoral" gag meant. But offhand, if I had to give a meaning to it, I would interpret it and say it meant HICK.

Now if Congress won't defend themselves, I will enter a protest. I knock 'em, but I like 'em, and I understand 'em. I know they do wrong sometimes, but they mean well. They just don't know any better.

Truth in Politics?

We have discovered out here in California, a Dr. House of Texas, who has discovered a serum called Scopolamine, a thing that when injected into you will make you tell the truth—at least for a while, anyway. Now, I don't know that the stuff is any good, but he certainly came to the right state to get material to try it on. If he can make us fellows in California tell the truth, his experiment will be a total success.

He only has to ask one question when he has a Californian under his spell. All he has to do is ask him if he don't think it is a very hot day. If the patient says "Yes," why, his experiment is an assured success. But if the patient says "Well, it's warm today, but that is very unusual for this time of year," why, then he might just as well throw his serum in the creek. It is a failure.

They started in by trying it on some convicts in various prisons out here. I don't know on what grounds they reason that a man in jail is a bigger liar than one out of jail. The chances are that telling the truth is what got him in there. Anyway, it has worked wonders; every man they tried it on said he didn't commit the crime. The chances are he would have said the same thing if the injection had been hydrant water, instead of Scopolamine.

Naturally everybody in jail is for it, for they want to prove their innocence. But everybody out of jails is against it, for fear they will get in themselves under its influence. Even ministers are denouncing it now.

But it has done wonders outside the jails, and has proved that it really has magical qualities. They tried it on a male movie star in Hollywood, and he told his right salary, and his press agent quit him. Then they tried it on a female movie staress, and she recalled things back as far as her first husband, and remembered her real maiden name.

Their only failure to date has been a Los Angeles real estate agent. They broke three needles trying to administer the stuff to him and it turned black the minute it touched him, so they had to give him up. He sold Dr. House three lots before he got out of the operating room.

It really is a wonderful thing, and if it could be brought into general use, it would, no doubt, be a big aid to humanity. But Humanity is not yet ready for either real truth, or harmony. And it will not come to pass, for already the politicians are up in arms against it. It would ruin the very foundation on which our political government is run.

If you ever injected truth into politics, you would have no politics.

Will Rogers, Missionary

The way our politicians are now, they are just like a man who thinks he has oil on his farm. He stops all work and just lives on the hope and prospects of this oil. But after they have bored a well and found it dry, and he knows he has no chance of easy money, why, he will settle right down and go to work, and maybe amount to something in the long run. If he strikes oil, he is ruined. He is a total loss to everybody, but the bootlegger.

Now that is the way I claim it is with these old-time parties. If they knew they had no chance of ever getting any easy money by striking oil in Washington after every election, why, the chances are they would be just like the oilless farmer. They might be rescued to decent society and be a help and a comfort to their families.

Right now I am a missionary. I am going to devote my life's work to rescue this country from the hand of the politician, and also rescue the politician to a life of Christianity.

How I Became an Actor

My little old act with the lasso was just put into the Ziegfeld Follies to kill time, while the girls were changing from nothing to nothing. A male actor's monolog in a girl show is just like an intermission. So I tried to make my act attractive by telling a few jokes, and the audiences laugh, and so Mr. Ziegfeld calls me a star.

Telling jokes was all right, but when Ned Wayburn, who so cleverly helps Mr. Ziegfeld stage those numbers, came to me a few weeks ago and said, "Bill, I'm adding a little dramatic sketch to the Follies, and want you to act one of the roles," I said, "Well, if this guy isn't kidding me, I haven't anything to lose because I've got no reputation as an actor. And if I can make a hit, the critics will come out and say I am versatile, and what not." You know what makes a critic—two seats on the aisle—but I kinder calculated I could make these critics sit up when I came before them to do a John Barrymore. But then the blow fell.

At the first rehearsal I learned they wanted me to wear skirts. Now skirts is all right in their proper places. Girls wear them, and sometimes the shortest ones are worn by old ladies. College boys wear them when they indulge in amateur theatricals. But to ask a he-man of the wild and woolly West to wear skirts in a burlesque show kinder flopped me. I thought Wayburn was kidding me, and so—to kid him back—I said "yes."

But the darn fool meant it. He was in earnest. He brought out the manuscript of KOO KOO Nell, and gave me the title role. When I saw I was really expected to play a girl's role, and wear skirts, say, the howling of a prairie dog at midnight was deep silence to what I said. But Wayburn insisted, said I had agreed in front of the whole cast to play the role, and that my contract with Ziegfeld compelled me to play any role for which I was cast—I was roped, tied and thrown—and that's how I got into skirts.

In case you didn't know, our KOO KOO Nell is a take-off on the hit show KIKI at the Belasco Theatre on Broadway, starring Lenore Ulric. So since I had to wear the blamed things, I decided to make up as near like Lenore Ulric as I possibly could, so I saw that little actress at a Thursday matinee, and ordered my costume built just like her first act dress. The audience gets the idea of the burlesque at once, especially since Brandon Tynan as David Belasco, is supposed to be rehearsing the act. I really tried at first to imitate Miss Ulric's voice, which is clear and crisp, but no one could do that, so I imitated her mincing ways and cute little business with the powder puff.

When I went on the first time, I thought the audience would throw things at me, but instead they howled. I didn't know whether they were laughing with me, or agin me, but so long as they laughed and didn't throw things, I had no kick coming.

Now, after playing the darn fool role, I am getting used to the skirts and corset and the plumes on the hat, and I am able to speak my lines without getting rattled. I am now studying the role of Ophelia, and hope to play Juliet next season, when all the other actresses have retired from the combat. Or if Miss Ulric ever gets tired of playing KIKI, I am willing to take her place, if the public will let me. Meanwhile I will keep on throwing the rope, and telling my little jokes in the Ziegfeld Follies, unless someone sends me poisoned candy for playing KOO KOO Nell in our little burlesque. It all goes to show that a real actor must be versatile. I never knew I was a real actor before, but it don't pay to quarrel with the critics, and since some of them called me an actor, I'm beginning to believe I am.

New York's Five Boroughs Celebrate

New York is in the midst of what they call a Silver Jubilee. It's celebrating the 25th anniversary of something, nobody can find out just what. There is no reason to just pick out 25 years and start celebrating it. But I think the reason was that this was as far back as any of them connected with the city could remember. Personally, I think it was to celebrate the starting of the Hat Checking privilege, which originated here and was successfully copied everywhere else, but never with the finesse that it has in the mother lodge here.

Or, on account of being called a Silver Jubilee, it may be celebrating the passing away of all silver coins, as that small denomination vanished entirely here.

They have an exhibit representing progress, showing how much faster we can cross the streets compared to what we used to. Now it's a run, and if you don't make it, and the probabilities are you won't, they show how quick they can get you to the hospital, so you can die there instead of en route, as you used to.

Then they show the modern hearses, which go so fast they have killed more people than they carried. You know, we don't stop to realize it now, but in the old days it was nothing for a man to be late to his own funeral. But now, if you are going to a friend's funeral and happen to be held up in a traffic jam a few minutes, you will arrive there just as his widow is coming out of the church with the next husband, counting the insurance money.

Also, in this exhibition of progress of 25 years, they show the old saloons where you had to walk to the corner to even get a drink. With the modern method it's brought right to your home.

It showed how the city's money was spent for city government. Not all of it, of course, but the 20 per cent which is spent for it, it showed.

It showed police methods years ago compared to now. In the old days they had to hunt till they found the crook. With modern methods they have his fingerprints, so what's the use getting him, if you know who he is. Then, if he ever surrenders, you know if he's telling the truth, or not.

It also showed the art of ticket speculating and its advancement. An Irishman named Louie was the only one in town 25 years ago; now there are hundreds of them in offices where a stranger in the city can go and buy tickets for the last row, without going near the box office.

It showed that 25 years ago they still had a few street cars pulled by horses, but they were up on street level, and were very unsanitary—bad air and everything. Now it shows you how you can be in a nice tunnel under the ground where the air is good. You know it is good because there have been hundreds using it before you got a hold of it.

Then, if you got stuck in old cars, you had to walk to get another car. But now, you can stay right under there, sometimes all day, and read over somebody's shoulder and not get out at all. Oh, I tell you, things do move.

Of course they had a parade. Everything nowadays has to annoy with a parade. They gave all the city employees a day off without pay, and all they had to do was to march 20 miles.

Hold Parades on Sundays

Mussolini said that there was going to be no more celebrations, demonstrations either large or small, or parades of any caliber given on any weekday. That's an inspiration. How many hours have you stood on one side of an avenue in a car, waiting for a parade to pass? Nobody knew who it was for, or what it was about. It looks like parades are formed just to keep people that are in a hurry from getting from one side of town across to the other.

Men will travel days on a train to get to a town to walk 10 miles in a parade, when they haven't walked further from their homes than the barn.

Unrestrained Speeches

There has been an awful lot of fashion shows and their by-products held here in New York. All the out-of-town buyers from all over have

35

been here. So, on behalf of New York City, I had to help welcome them at their various banquets. There was the retail milliners' big fashion show at the Astor Ball Room, where they showed 500 hats and me. Some of the hats were just as funny looking as I was.

Well, I settled the hat and dress business to the satisfaction of everybody but the milliners. So the next night at the Commodore Hotel I mingled with Princes of Brogans, the Leather and Shoe Men, and some time I want to tell you people just how they operate. For we never paid more for our shoes and were nearer barefooted, than we are today, so don't think that I am bought off by those pasteboard highbinders.

Among the events of the week where I had to talk at a banquet, was one at the Astor, given by the entire detective force of New York. Of course, I had to go; in the business of telling you the real truth on certain men, detectives may come in handy to me. All the city officials were there, including Dr. Royal Copeland, who is sentenced to the U.S. Senate, if it ever meets again. And, not that I wish him any hard luck, but there is at least 90 million folks in this country who wouldn't care if the Senate never met. Well, he was trying to stand in with those detectives, too.

A good, conscientious Senator, when he goes to Washington, needs a detective to help him find out what they are doing; and most times, even they couldn't find out. Anyhow, the dinner was quite a success, and it would have been bigger, but most of the detectives couldn't find the Astor Hotel.

A few months ago, there was a New York detective who had been going with a girl for two years, and one night he found out she was married, and had been, all the time. He killed her and himself. He was one of their best detectives. It's too bad that he wasn't one of their ordinary ones, then he would never have found it out.

Then they were holding a convention of Police Chiefs from all over the world here this week, so yesterday, I was asked to address the convention. Although I had never caught a crook, neither had they, so we had a mutual feeling. The first country that catches a crook, gets the next convention.

Now that the police have an organization, it looks like the crooks will have to organize for protection. They could hold their convention at the same time, and in the same town; they would never meet.

I tell you one thing they sure got down pat, and that is that fingerprint thing. They seemed very elated about that. As the president of the convention said, they had the fingerprints of every major crook there is. Now all they got to do is find the fingers.

The big Scotland Yard man from England lost his watch and return ticket the first day in the convention room. New York certainly did entertain them royally, and made them feel at home. They put on robberies and murders for them every day they were here.

Another one of my feeds during the week was a big banquet at the Commodore Hotel; there were eleven hundred rug manufacturers and dealers. There was a fine den to go in amongst, but I was glad, as in building a home, I have encountered two troops of brigands. I thought when I paid the plumbers, the height of highwaymanship had been reached. But boy, when my wife commenced to try to get those floors covered, to try and hide the dirt, I wanted to rush back and kiss the plumbers and apologize. So it was just my good fortune that I should be asked to speak to them. They couldn't find any one else that would say even as much good about them as I did.

Now it's all right to go out and skin a man—that's fair play, but when you take a poor woman who had to chloroform her husband to get enough to buy some floor polish, much less a rug, and those rug ruffians get a hold of her and take an old wool fiber rug and make her believe it is a real antique, a Kabistand, or a Tabreeze, or a Surrook, or any of those names, that's going too far. Even Jesse James never robbed a woman.

I read, before I went over there, in one of their scandal sheets, or rug trade papers, a chart showing that over 50 per cent of all rugs were bought by women between the ages of 18 and 30. A woman will do either one of two things between 18 and 30. She will either get married, or buy a rug; and if she is extra feeble minded, she may do both.

Over in Armenia, the rugs are made by the wives and lady friends of all the men. Over here, they are bought by all the wives and lady friends of the men. Over there, they sometimes take as long as 5 years to make one rug. Over here we sometimes take as long as 10 years to pay for one. Of course, all the foreign rugs, the older they are the more they are worth; but over here, we don't have no old rugs; it never gets a chance to get old in this country—it don't last long enough.

Over there they make the patterns like the Indians used to name their babies, after things that they see. Now can you imagine if that custom was in vogue over here, and the weaver put in what he saw every day? Murder scenes would be the predominant design.

Then imagine naming rugs after towns, and having to take a guest into your living room, and point out: "Here is a Khamokin, Pennsylvania, rug; it's very old, my grandfather bought it on a pilgrimage to

Pittsburgh six months ago. You can see it's aged—look at the holes in it."

The life of these rugs depends on the number of sweepings. You will see a rug advertised to last a year—if you don't sweep it. And these vacuum cleaners, those strong ones that operate from a truck out in the street, they have removed, at one sitting, a cheap rug right out into the truck. They not only clean your rugs, but they clean your floors of rugs.

In investigating their business, I found that there had never been a rug manufacturer that failed. If things look bad, all he had to do was to make another rug and sell it, and open up a branch factory with the profits. It's the only business in the world nobody knows anything about. You don't have to, because your customers don't know either. Their big sales are done by auction, like some second-hand dealer. Their Fall meeting is in April; their Spring auction is in October. I told them, and showed them their whole business was cross-eyed. Can you imagine any other merchant selling overcoats in April and straw hats in October?

And the funny thing about it was they were a fine lot of fellows, and there wasn't a one of them but what could have gone out and made a living in a legitimate business.

But today I want to talk to the ladies. During this reign of indigestion, I was called on to speak at a big banquet at the Waldorf to the Corset Manufacturers. Now that only shows you what a degrading thing this after dinner speaking is. I want to get out of it in a few weeks and back to the movies.

This speaking calls on a fellow to learn something about the articles that a self-respecting man has no business knowing about. So that's why I am going to get away. If a man is called on in a public banquet room, to tell what he knows about corsets, there is no telling what other ladies' wearing apparel he might be called on to discuss next. So get me back to the morals of Hollywood, before it's too late.

I was, at that, mighty glad to appear at a dinner given by an essential industry. Just imagine, if you can, if the flesh of this country were allowed to wander around promiscuously! Why, there ain't no telling where it would wind up. There has got to be a gathering, or a get-together place for everything in this world, so, when our human bodies get beyond our control, why, we have to call on some mechanical force to help assemble them and bring back what might be called the semblance of a human frame.

These corset builders, while they might not do a whole lot to help civilization, are a tremendous aid to the eyesight. They have got what you would call a Herculean Task, as they really have to improve on nature. The same problem confronts them that does the people that run the subways in New York City. They both have to get so many pounds of human flesh into a given radius. The subway does it by having strong men to push and shove until they can just close the door with only the last man's foot out. But the corset carpenters arrive at the same thing by a series of strings.

Now the front lace model can be operated without a confederate. Judiciously holding your breath, with a conservative intake on the diaphragm, you arrange yourself inside this thing. Then you tie the strings to the door knob, and slowly back away. When your speedometer says you have arrived at exactly 36, why, you haul in your lines and tie off.

We have also the side lace model that is made in case you are very fleshy and you need two accomplices to help you congregate yourself. You stand in the middle, and they pull from both sides. This acts something in the nature of a vise. This style has been known to operate so successfully, that the victim's buttons have popped off their shoes.

Of course, the fear of every fleshy lady is the broken corset string. I sat next to a catastrophy of this nature once. We didn't know it at first, the deluge seemed so gradual, till finally the gentleman on the other side of her, and myself, were gradually pushed off our chairs. To show you what a wonderful thing this corsetting is, that lady had come to the dinner before the broken string episode, in a small roadster, and she was delivered home in a bus.

Imagine me being asked to talk at a corset dinner, anyway. Me, who has been six years with the Ziegfeld Follies, and not a corset in the show. Anyhow, men have gone down in history for shaping the destinies of nations, but I tell you this set of corset architects shape the destinies of women and that is a lot more important than some of the shaping that has been done on a lot of nations that I can name offhand. Another thing that makes me so strong for them, if it wasn't for the corset ads in magazines, men would never look at a magazine.

Now, of course, not as many women wear corsets as used to, but what they have lost in women customers, they have made up with men.

I want to also tell you ladies some time about going over to Philadelphia, to talk to the wholesale silk stocking manufacturers at a big luncheon. I had a fellow with me that had a patent to prevent runs, you know, broken threads in stockings. Well, do you know they bought him off, so you will go on having runs in your stockings, and keep on buying them. Now, I did the best I could for you. I tried to get him to sell, but those sox scoundrels got to him first. So don't trust them any more than you would a rug highwayman.

From a Speech to the Allied Leather Association

They used to put your shoes into a cardboard box when you bought them. Now they don't do that. There was a lot of confusion. Customers could not tell when they got home, which was the shoes, and which was the box, as they were both of the same material. A great many claimed the box outwore the shoes. Out in the cattle country, where I live, you pay $1.25 for a cow hide that will make ten pairs of shoes. You put that hide in some machinery, press a lever which stamps them "HAND MADE" and grab a basket and catch 'em as they come out.

1924

Late in January, Nikolai Lenin dies. While Stalin, Trotsky, Kamenev, Zinoviev, and Rykov pretend to cooperate, the struggle for power rages.

Britain's first Labour government takes office under James Ramsay MacDonald, and a week later officially recognizes the USSR. The United States refuses to acknowledge the Soviet regime, and it will be almost a decade before an American government recognizes the Soviet Union.

Italian dictator Benito Mussolini and his Facisti subvert the electoral machinery, and—to no one's surprise—emerge from the April elections with 65 percent of the votes cast.

Under Allied supervision, Germany reorganizes the Reichsbank and ends its exploding inflation. Its tax system is restructured, and the new mark is valued as being equal to one billion old marks. Financial support by the Allies is pledged, with the United States guaranteeing a loan of $110 million.

The giant German chemical firm I. G. Farben starts a program to develop synthetic gasoline, feeling that rising fuel prices will make gasoline extracted from the huge German coal deposits more than competitive.

In the November elections in England, the Labour government is ousted, and Stanley Baldwin now heads the new Conservative government.

Premier Riza Khan Pahlevi of Persia, having subdued most of his opposition, establishes control over the government, and the following year he will be acclaimed shah.

In Paris, the Soviet State Dancers are appearing on tour, and twenty-year-old Georgi Melitonovitch Balanchivadze quits the company and joins Diaghilev's Ballet Russe. Georgi will come to the United States and become its foremost choreographer; he will also change his name to George Balanchine.

The first winter Olympics are held at Chamonix, France; the summer games are at Paris. In tennis, "Big" Bill Tilden and Helen Wills win their respective U.S. singles titles, and the American team defeats Australia for the Davis Cup.

In college football, Notre Dame goes through an entire season undefeated, due principally to a head coach named Knute Rockne, and a backfield that is dubbed "The Four Horsemen." But it is the University of Illinois's halfback Harold "Red" Grange, nicknamed "The Galloping Ghost," who proves the most outstanding player of the year.

There are now only three million radio sets—mostly crystal—in the United States, yet Ford produces two million Model T cars for the second year in a row. Price per car: $290.

Chicago, already notorious for its gang wars, usually followed by funerals with garish floral trimmings, combines both with the gangland execution of rackets boss Dion O'Banion. Al Capone's men kill him in the flower shop he used as his cover. O'Banion's mob is taken over by one Hymie Weiss, who will battle Al Capone and Johnny Torrio for the lucrative illegal liquor trade.

Also in Chicago, two teen-aged students, Nathan Leopold and Richard Loeb, kill fourteen-year-old Robert Franks, just for the thrill. Clarence Darrow, the brilliant defender of "underdogs," manages to save both murderers from execution.

Former President Woodrow Wilson dies in his sleep having never fully recovered from the stroke suffered in 1919. Even the Nobel Peace Prize, awarded him in 1919, had done little to lessen his bitterness at his party's defeat in the presidential election.

The Democratic National Convention, meeting in New York's Madison Square Garden, will irresolutely take 103 ballots trying to break a deadlock between front-runners William Gibbs McAdoo (former U.S. secretary of the treasury, and Woodrow Wilson's son-in-law) and Alfred ("Al") Emanuel Smith, Catholic governor of New York. The convention finally compromises, probably more weary than convinced, and chooses a relatively unknown corporation lawyer, John William Davis.

President Coolidge wins the election on the single promise of Prosperity. His vice-president is Charles Gates Dawes. For the first time women are elected as governors: Nellie Tayloe Ross of Wyoming and Miriam ("Ma") Ferguson of Texas; Mrs. Ross is installed first, and thus becomes the first woman governor in the record books.

On October 5, a new comic strip makes it debut. Drawn by Harold Lincoln Gray, it is called *Little Orphan Annie*.

In Florida, Carl Fisher's publicity and promotion of Florida real estate will result in an inflated land boom, which—naturally—attracts unsavory hucksters who flood the country with fraudulent deals. Thousands of parcels bought "blind" by the gullible are found to be under water.

In Washington, Congress passes a new Immigration Act, which sets limits for most nationalities. The only exception: Asians are completely barred.

In New York City, Macy's famous department store inaugurates the Thanksgiving Day Parade, which officially kicks off the Christmas buying season. And newly opened Saks Fifth Avenue, located just across from Saint Patrick's Cathedral, becomes the first large department store north of Forty-second Street. Its instant claim to fame: On the first day of business, its entire stock of sterling silver hip flasks is sold out.

Edna Ferber wins the Pulitzer Prize for her best-selling novel *So Big*. The children's story *Bambi*, written by Budapest-born Felix Salten, is translated into English by Whittaker Chambers, who twenty-three years later will be involved in the espionage trial of Alger Hiss, and then produce as proof the "pumpkin papers."

The most popular songs include "Tea for Two," by Vincent Youmans; "California Here I Come," by Joseph Meyer; "I'll See You in My Dreams," by Isham Jones; and "Amapola," by James LaCalle.

In Hollywood, Metro-Goldwyn-Mayer is founded by Marcus Loew, while Harry Cohn establishes Columbia Pictures. Among the favorite films of the year: *The Thief of Baghdad* with Douglas Fairbanks; *Beau Brummel* with John Barrymore and Mary Astor; *He Who Gets Slapped* with Norma Shearer, John Gilbert, and Lon Chaney: *Peter Pan* with Betty Bronson; and a teen-aged Swedish actress appears in *Gosta Berling's Saga*, having changed her name from Greta Gustoffson to Greta Garbo.

The New York stage offers a variety of outstanding plays, among them Eugene O'Neill's *Desire under the Elms* and Laurence Stallings and Maxwell Anderson's *What Price Glory*. Among the musicals of the season are *Rose Marie*, by Rudolf Friml; *Lady Be Good*, with Fred and Adele Astaire; and *The Student Prince,* by Sigmund Romberg.

In New York's Aeolian Hall, Paul Whiteman conducts the orchestra in the premiere performance of George Gershwin's *Rhapsody in Blue,* with the composer as the soloist.

On June 24, the latest edition of the *Ziegfeld Follies* opens, starring Will Rogers, Ann Pennington, Evelyn Law, and Vivienne Segal. The book is by Will Rogers and William A. McGuire, and the music by Victor Herbert, Raymond Hubbell, and others.

Will is busy during the first few months of the year making motion pictures for Hal Roach. Before he leaves for the East he will complete ten shorts, which will be released later.

In May, Will visits the family in Oklahoma, then stops off in Cleveland to cover the Republican National Convention, June 9–14. Then he moves on to Washington—or as he calls it at times, The National Joke Factory—for as he claims: "I have no act, so I thought I would run down to Washington to get me some material."

Being in the *Follies* in New York City, Will also suffers through most of the 103 ballots of the Democratic National Convention, having contracted to report on it for national syndication. On election day, November 4, his forty-fifth birthday, Will announces the election returns over radio station WEAF.

England's Prince of Wales, the future Edward VIII, visits America, and Will has a very cordial association with him. They meet at a number of functions, and even play polo together. Will buys one of the prince's polo ponies as a gift for Patty, daughter of Florenz Ziegfeld and his wife, Billie Burke.

Among the speaking engagements in and around New York City is the Alexander Hamilton dinner at Columbia University, with Secretary of the Treasury Andrew Mellon as the guest of honor. Nicholas Murray Butler, president of Columbia University, is Will's personal friend.

Later in September, Will signs a contract with the American Tobacco Company to write special advertisements for Bull Durham, a tobacco sold in a small pouch for those who roll their own cigarettes. Will, who does not smoke, clearly says so. Just as he does when he advertises pianos—claiming simply that this particular make is the best he has ever leaned against.

Year's end sees the publication of the book *Illiterate Digest,* a selection of Will's weekly articles of 1923 and 1924.

Back To Babbitts, Booze, and Bankrolls

I am shaking the dust (of which there is no finer in Southern California) of California's little heralded climate from my feet and am slowly trudging my way via Santa Fe Limited, back across the burning sands to New York City. That city from which no weary traveler returns without drawing again on the home town bank. That city of skyscrapers, where they have endeavored to make the height of their buildings keep pace with their prices. That city of booze and bankrolls, where the babbitts from Butte and Buffalo can pay the speculators $8.80 for a $2.20 show, view the electric signs until 12 o'clock and then write home of the Bacchanalian revels.

In leaving California, this land of perpetual publicity, where a lot on the corner is worth two in the middle, I do so with regret. I know that I am changing the subdivision for the subway, and one single California flea for a billion Long Island mosquitoes.

I am leaving a city where English is the dominant tongue, to return to a city where it is seldom heard, and never understood. I leave from the land where the movies are made, to return to the land where the bills are paid.

I would not have left California, but I do love No. 1 good California oranges and fruit. So I am going back to New York to get them. I have survived for a whole year on culls and seconds. Then things are kinder slowing up out here in the real estate line. A fellow sometimes has to wait until he gets his lot out of escrow before he gets a chance to sell it at a profit. Well, you know that's discouraging. I bought a lot and held it a week and when no offer came, I just said, this is no country for a stable business man. Of course I could have stayed and sued the salesman who sold it to me, as he said I would double my money in three days.

When I started to get Pullman reservations I didn't think it would be any trouble. I had been reading in Los Angeles papers of the thousands coming in by every train, but I had never saw a thing where any one ever left. So when they told me I could not get any seats for days, it was a terrible blow to me. I thought these trains all went back empty. You see, the Californians come out by covered wagon, but they all want to go back by the Limited.

At Albuquerque, New Mexico, they let us get out and walk around.

Fred Harvey runs a restaurant and department store at the depot, and no matter how big a hurry you may be in to get where you are going, he has the train stopped 40 minutes. Everybody that didn't buy a lot in Los Angeles, buys a Navajo blanket at Albuquerque. Those who did buy a lot, can only afford a bow and arrow. I don't know why but they all seem to want to spend their last money for a bow and arrow. I suppose an undertaker meets this train in Kansas City.

I hear the Navajos have struck oil on their reservation. That will give the white man a chance to show his so-called 100 percent Americanism, by flocking in and taking it away from the Indians.

We are now nearing Kansas City, and instead of going directly on to New York, I am branching off and going down for a few days to my home around Claremore, Oklahoma. That is the home of the radium water, a curative liquid that will cure you of everything, even a presidential ambition. I think the time will come when everybody will be made to stop off at Claremore on their way to any place they may be going. If Fred Harvey can stop you for 40 minutes to make you buy a Navajo blanket, I should be allowed to stop you at least long enough to give you a bath, especially after traveling through there by train. We don't want your money. Los Angeles and Albuquerque will clean you financially. But we will cleanse you physically, free of charge.

I am mighty happy I am going home to my own people, who know me as "Willie, Uncle Clem Rogers' boy, who wouldn't go to school but just kept running around the country throwing a rope, till I think he finally got in one of them shows."

One of the Lyceum managers had me booked for three or four dates to lecture at Seattle, Spokane and Portland, where I was to deliver a lecture like a regular ex-senator. But I passed it up just to go home, not to do any talking, but to listen, and see all my old friends, and hear 'em call me Willie, and they will give me some political opinions that will beat all your senators, and maybe I will tell 'em a little about Hollywood, and the night life, for I want to keep on the good side of them. They don't know how I make a living. They just know me as Uncle Clem's boy. They are my real friends and when no one else will want to hear my measly old jokes, I want to go home. It won't make no difference to them.

The above was penned as I was speeding across Kansas on my way to Kansas City, where I mailed it. I planned to leave the train there and go to Claremore on the fast Frisco train which did not stop at Chelsea, Oklahoma, where I was to stop off and see my sisters. So the conductor told me to wire to the Frisco passenger agent at Kansas City, and ask him to please stop and let us off. I wired him but I didn't think he would do it. But at Kansas City the conductor handed me a wire, telling me that all had been arranged.

I was awful tickled. Then I happened to think that in my last weekly letter, which I had just finished and mailed, there was a joke which told about our town of Claremore, Oklahoma, having the greatest baths in the world, and that everybody passing through there should stop off and take one, for even if they had already had one that week, they could use another on account of being on the Frisco train.

Well, after I received this nice wire from their agent, I happened to think of what I had said in my article, and I felt plum ashamed. Here, after this man being so nice to me, why, I am saying his railroad was unclean. I had already mailed it, and I didn't know what to do, and then they met us in Kansas and were so nice to us. That rubbed it in more than ever. So I happened to think I will wire in to have that gag about the untidiness of the Frisco Railroad cut out and put on the Missouri Pacific, instead.

That was certainly smart of me, thinking of that. Why, I wouldn't have had that come out in an article for anything. I would be a fine fellow, wouldn't I, after officials doing me such favors, to go and tell things on their railroad. I realized afterwards that I should have included the Missouri Pacific with them in the first place. I was absolutely wrong in discriminating. It certainly learned me a lesson. Never knock anybody as long as they do favors for you. Even if I was right in the first place, I shouldn't have put that in, until I had at least heard from them to see if they were going to stop the train.

The reason I am telling you all this is, just to show you how near I came to being very ungrateful. Why, I wouldn't have that get out for anything in the world.

Come to think of it, it was not me that thought of sending the wire; it was Ed Wynn, the comedian. And when I say comedian, I mean comedian. He of the Perfect Fool fame, he and his wife were on the train with us. Ed and I spent three days on that train trying out jokes on our wives, jokes that we were going to use in New York this year. I just looked at Mrs. Wynn who is a lovely woman, and perfectly sane, and Mrs. Rogers, who, if I do say it myself, after sixteen years of forced laughter, is bearing up remarkably, and under happier surroundings might retain her faculties for years. In a kind of abstract moment I just looked at both of them and thought what have these women done in their lifetime that they should be subjected to this brand of jokes, not only for three days, but for life? Truly providence acts in a strange manner, and justice is sometimes long delayed.

When the Women's Hall of Fame is laid out, along with Joan of Arc,

Nellie Revell, Florence Nightingale, and Mrs. Chapman Catt, I will be much disappointed if I don't find a tablet which reads about as follows: "To the loving memory of those unselfish, and long suffering women who have married comedians (and remained so)."

Well, when we got into Kansas City, in the wonderful big depot, it reminded me of the times I had spent in that old station, which was really just a valise, or grip, exchange. I popped through there one time, jumping to Seattle, Washington, to do my little act in vaudeville on the Orpheum Circuit. Well, do you remember, in those days every man that traveled any further than from the house to the barn, thought he had to have an alligator bag, with big warts on the side of it, that would rub bunions on the side of your legs if you carried it over a block. That, and a diamond ring, were the first things you were supposed to buy, especially if you were a traveling man, or in the theatrical business.

So, I had just worked long enough to have both. One toothbrush, a couple of shirts, and five ropes, were nestling in this crocodile-bound enclosure, with not only warts but horns on the side of it. I had to buy a ticket, and in those days it took an agent longer to make out a ticket to Seattle, than it did to get there. It sold by the footage, one foot to the mile. The excess baggage on your ticket cost you more than your fare. He handed it to you so neatly folded, in yard lengths, and all you had to do was to sign it for each town you went through.

Well, the afternoon I spent buying my ticket, I forgot to keep one foot solidly implanted on my deceased crocodile. Some lover of animals kindly annexed my prosperous trademark, and when I turned around, the one year's savings I had invested in hides was just passing over the Kaw River. I went to relate my unhappy ending to a policeman, and found a line longer than Congressional Investigating Committee witnesses, all trying to find out where their grips had gone to. I didn't even get a chance to tell him about mine.

And by the way, coming back I played Butte, and lost the diamond ring. So it took two thieves to at least try and give me the appearance of a gentleman. Now when I see a man wearing either a diamond ring, or an alligator valise, I offer up thanks to the two men who robbed me.

Anyhow, we boarded the train at the hands of their agent who was so nice and thoughtful of our welfare, and who said he always went to see my pictures (but couldn't think of the name of any he had seen). Why, he and the conductor showed us one of the newest model sleeping cars. They raved over it, and it was beautiful. The porter went to make down the berth in our room and a pillow was caught in that chain that lets down the top. This poor porter, assisted by everybody on the train, including the engineer, held a clinic. I was getting sleepy and tired, and was sorry I had wired to have that joke taken out, and was just about to wire them to put it back in again, when I happened to think this was Pullman's fault, and not the Frisco's.

Along about daylight they gave it up, and moved us into another car. I guess they had to send that berth back to the factory to have that pillow amputated.

Now I ask you, who but a comedian could a fool thing like that happen to? As I say, it's just another one of the bad breaks for any woman who marries one.

Congress Is Funniest When It's Serious

I just got back from Washington, D.C. (Department of Comedy). I had heard that the Congressional Show was to close on June 7th. I don't see why they are closing then. They could bring that same show, with the original cast they have, to New York, and it would run for years.

I am going into Ziegfeld's new Follies, and I have no act. So I thought I will run down to Washington and get some material. Most people and actors appearing on the stage have some writer to write their material, but I don't do that. Congress is good enough for me. They have been writing my material for years, and I am not ashamed of the material I have had. I am going to stick with them. Why should I go and pay for some famous author, or even myself, to sit down all day trying to dope out something funny to say on the stage? No sir, I have found that there is nothing as funny as things that have happened, and that people know that they have happened. So I just have them mail me every day the Congressional Record. It is to me what the Police Gazette used to be to the fellow who was waiting for a haircut. In other words, it is a lifesaver.

Besides, nothing is as funny as something done in all seriousness. The material on which the Congressional Record is founded is done there every day in all seriousness. Each state elects the most serious man it has in the district, and he is impressed with the fact that he is to rescue his district from certain destruction, and to see that it received its just amount of rivers and harbors, post offices, and pumpkin seeds. Naturally you have put a pretty big load on the man. I realize that it is no joking matter to be grabbed up bodily from the leading lawyer's office of Main Street, and to have the entire population tell you what is depending on you when you get to Washington. The fellow may be all right personally, and a good fellow, but that Big League Idea of Politics scares him.

Now, they wouldn't be so serious and particular if they only had to vote on what they thought was good for the majority of the people of the U.S. That would be a cinch. But what makes it hard for them is every time a bill comes up, they have a million things to decide that have nothing to do with the merit of the bill. They first must consider whether the bill was introduced by a member of the opposition political party. If it was, why then something is wrong with it from the start, for everything the opposition party does has a catch in it.

Then the principal thing is of course: "what will this do for me personally back home?" If it is something that he thinks the folks back home may never read, or hear of, why, then he can vote any way he wants to, but politics and self-preservation must come first, never mind the majority of the people of the U.S. If lawmakers were elected for life, I believe, they would do better. A man's thoughts are naturally on his next term, more than on his country.

From the House of Representatives I went to the Senate. You see, they have two of these bodies—Senate and House. That is for the convenience of visitors. If there is nothing funny happening in one, there is sure to be in the other, and in case one body passes a good bill, why, the other can see it in time, and kill it.

Outside the Congress I met all my old friends, Representatives from Oklahoma, Los Angeles, Texas, Kansas, Arizona, and from all over, and I want to tell you, they are as fine a bunch of men as anyone ever met in his life. They were all full of humor and regular fellows. That is, as I say, when you catch them when they haven't got politics on their minds, but the minute they get in that immense hall, they begin to get serious, and it's then that they do such amusing things. If we could just send the same bunch of men to Washington for the good of the nation, and not for political reasons, we could have the most perfect government in the world.

Wilson Could Laugh at a Joke on Himself

Some of the most glowing and deserving tributes ever paid to the memory of an American, have been paid in the last few days to our past President, Woodrow Wilson. They have been paid by learned men of this, and all nations, who knew what to say, and how to express their feelings. They spoke of their close association and personal contact with him. Now I want to add my little mite, even though it be of no importance.

I want to tell of him as I knew him, for he was my friend. We of the stage know that our audiences are our best friends, and he was the greatest audience of any public man we ever had. I want to tell of him as I knew him across the footlights. A great many actors and professional people have appeared before him, on various occasions in wonderful high-class endeavors, but I don't think that any person met him across the footlights in exactly the personal way that I did on five different occasions.

Every other performer, or actor, did before him exactly what they had done before other audiences on the night previous. But I gave a great deal of time and thought to an act for him, most of which would never be used again, and had never been used before. Owing to the style of act I used, my stuff depended a great deal on what had happened that particular day, or week. It just seemed by an odd chance for me, every time I played before President Wilson, that on that particular day there had been something of great importance that he had just been dealing with, for you must remember that each day was a day of great stress with him. He had no easy days. So when I could go into a theater and get laughs out of our president, by poking fun at some turn in our national affairs, I don't mind telling you, it was the happiest moments of my entire career on the stage.

The first time I shall never forget, for it was the most impressive, and for me the most nervous one of them all. The Friars Club of New York, one of the biggest theatrical social clubs in New York, had decided to make a whirlwind tour of the principal cities of the East, all in one week. We played a different city every night. We made a one-night stand out of Chicago and New York. We were billed for Baltimore, but not for Washington. President Wilson came over from Washington to see the performance. It was the first time in theatrical history that the president of the United States came over to Baltimore, just to see a comedy show.

It was just at the time that we were having our little set-to with Mexico, and when we were at the height of our note exchanging career with Germany and Austria.

The house was packed with the elite of Baltimore. The show was going great. It was a collection of clever skits, written mostly by our stage's greatest man, George M. Cohan, and even down to the minor bits, was played by stars with big reputations. I was the least known member of the entire aggregation, doing my little specialty with a rope, and telling jokes on national affairs, just a very ordinary little vaudeville act, by chance sandwiched in among this great array.

I was on late, and as the show went along, I would walk out of the stage door, and out on the street, and try to kill time and nervousness until it was time to dress and go on. I had never told jokes even to a president, much less about one, especially to his face. Well, I am not kidding you when I tell you that I was scared to death. I am always nervous. I never saw an audience that I ever faced with any confidence, for no man can ever tell how a given audience will take anything.

But here I was, nothing but a very ordinary cowpuncher, who had learned to spin a rope a little, and who had learned to read the daily papers, going out before the aristocracy of Baltimore, and the president of the United States, and kid about some of the policies with which he was shaping the destinies of nations.

How was I to know but what the audience would rise up in mass and resent it? I had never heard, and I don't think any one else had ever heard of a president being joked personally in a public theatre about the policies of his administration.

The nearer the time come, the worse scared I got. George M. Cohan, and Willie Collier, and Frank Tinney and other performers, knowing how I felt, would pat me on the back and tell me, "Why, he is just a human being; go on out and do your stuff." Well, if somebody had come through that dressing room and hollered "Train for Claremore, Oklahoma, leaving at once!" I would have been on it. This all may sound strange, but any who have had the experience know that a presidential appearance in a theatre, especially outside Washington, D.C., is a very rare and unique feeling, even to the audience. They are keyed up almost as much as the actors.

At the time of his entrance into the house, everybody stood up and there were plain clothes men all over the place, back stage and behind his box. How was I to know but what one of them might not take a shot at me if I said anything about him personally?

Finally a warden knocked at my dressing room door, and said, "You die in 5 minutes for kidding your country." They just literally shoved me out on the stage.

Now, by a stroke of what I call good fortune, (for I will keep them always) I have a copy of the entire act that I did for President Wilson on the five times I worked for him. My first remark in Baltimore was, "I am kinder nervous here tonight." Now that is not an especially bright remark, and I don't hope to go down in history on the strength of it, but it was so apparent to the audience that I was speaking the truth, that they laughed heartily at it. After all, we all love honesty.

Then I said "I shouldn't be nervous, for this is really my second presidential appearance. The first time was when William Jennings Bryan spoke in our town once, and I was to follow his speech and do my little roping act." Well you all know that Bryan never made the White House, even though he was the Democratic candidate three times, but I heard them laughing, so I took a sly glance at the President's box, and sure enough he was laughing just as big as any one. So I went on, "As I say, I was to follow him, but he spoke so long that it was so dark when he finished, they couldn't see my roping." That went over great, so I said "I wonder what ever become of him?" That was all right, it got over, but still I had made no direct reference to the president.

Now General Pershing was in Mexico at the time, and there was a lot in the papers for and against the invasion into Mexican territory to capture Pancho Villa, after he had raided an American town.

I said, "I see where they have captured Villa. Yes, they got him in the morning editions and then the afternoon ones let him get away." Now everybody in the house before they would laugh looked at the president, to see how he was going to take it. Well, he started laughing, and they all followed suit.

"Villa raided Columbus, New Mexico. We had a man on guard that night at the post. But to show you how crooked this Villa is, he sneaked up on the opposite side. We chased him over the line 5 miles, but run into a lot of government red tape, and had to come back. There is some talk of getting a machine gun, if we can borrow one. The one we have now they are using to train our army with in Plattsburg. If we go to war, we will just about have to go to the trouble of getting another gun."

Now mind you, the president was being criticized on all sides for lack of preparations, yet he sat there and led that entire audience in laughing at the gags on himself.

At that time there was talk of forming an army of 2 hundred thousand men. So I said, "We are going to have an army of 2 hundred thousand men. Henry Ford makes 3 hundred thousand cars every year. I think, Mr. President, we ought to at least have a man to every car. I see where they got Villa hemmed in between the Atlantic and Pacific. Now all we got to do is to stop up both ends. Pershing located him at a town called Los Quas Ka Jasbo. Now all we got to do is to locate Los Quas Ka Jasbo. I see by a headline that Villa escaped net and flees. We will never catch him then. Any Mexican that can escape fleas, is beyond catching."

After various other ones on Mexico, I started in on European affairs which at that time was long before we entered the war. "We are facing another crisis tonight, but our president here has had so many of them lately, that he can just lay right down and sleep beside one of those things." Then I pulled the one which he afterwards repeated to various friends as the best one told on him: "President Wilson is getting along fine now to what he was a few months ago. Do you realize, people, that at one time in our negotiations with Germany he was 5 notes behind?"

How he did laugh at that! Well, due to him being a good fellow and setting a real example, I had the proudest and most successful night I ever had on the stage. I had lots of gags on other subjects, but the ones on him were the heartiest laughs with him; and so it was on all other occasions I played for him. He come back stage at intermission, and chatted and shook hands with all.

What he stood for and died for will be strived after for years. It will take time, for with all our boasted advancement and civilization, it's hard to stamp out selfishness and greed. For after all, nations are nothing but individuals, and you can't even stop brothers from fighting sometimes. But he helped it along a lot, and what a wonderful cause to have laid down your life for! The world lost a friend. The theatre lost its greatest supporter. And I lost the most distinguished person who ever laughed at my little nonsensical jokes. I looked forward to playing for him every year.

Now I have only to look on it as my greatest memory.

Dollar-a-Year Men

When President Wilson formed the War Industries Board, the famous Dollar-a-year men, he told Bernard Baruch, the great American businessman and multi-millionaire, to go out and get all the prominent business men in every line together, and see if they couldn't form some kind of association to speed up supplies for the war. The president thought, of course, that Baruch would come in with members of both political parties. But when they are all rounded up, why, they are all Republicans!

So President Wilson asked him why he was so partial to one political party. And Mr. Baruch told him: "You told me to get prominent men from every industry, and I did. Now I can go and get you some Democrats, but they won't be very prominent, and won't have any industries with them. Besides, Mr. President, I doubt if you can get a Democrat to work for $1.00 a year. They are used to getting at least a $1.00 a day."

Well, President Wilson decided to use these Republicans, and let the Democrats do the fighting. He knew they could do that.

What Women Need

I read in the papers where Ma Ferguson was elected governor of Texas. When they nominate a Democrat in Texas, they stay nominated. You don't catch them wasting any nominations. They won't even let a Republican pass through there on a train, if they know it. Men have been set free for every crime on the calendar—murder, robbery, and parking near a fire plug. But if a prosecuting attorney can show where the defendant ever voted the Republican ticket, the jury don't even retire to deliberate.

But I was certainly glad to see a long-haired woman get somewhere, and the reason Ma was elected, was that she didn't stop to powder her nose. That's what is holding women back nowadays. I tell you, when you take time out for powdering, the day is just about gone. It's getting so this country has two main occupations now. One is women pawing at their nose with a powder puff, and the other is the men talking about their golf scores. I don't know what started all this color scheme in women's noses. In the old days, there didn't seem to be any particular reason why the nose couldn't go along bearing some slight resemblance in shade to the rest of the face. If it happened to be red, why it at least was pale in comparison to the men's noses of that time.

In those days, the nose was a thing considered just for blowing purposes, and it was never thought it would some day be used as a background for 50 million amateur female scenic artists. The blowing of the nose was done in those colorless days, just before arriving in a crowd, and not after you were in the midst of it. In fact, I think that custom still prevails. You are supposed to blow your nose in private, and paint it in public. Why the blowing, which is an absolute necessity, should be relegated to privacy, while the tinting, which is an absolute luxury, should be performed on exhibition, is beyond my understanding.

Everybody is talking about what this country needs. What this country needs is less powder puffs, and more babies' rattles. The ratio of sales of the two objects is now about 20 to 1, in favor of the puffs. And why should a mirror always accompany the kalsomining operation? With all the practice they get, any woman that can't find her nose without a mirror should not be allowed to have a nose. Suppose the man of the species, (who usually is more dumb than the female) had to take out a mirror to find his nose every time he wanted to blow it! Suppose he had lost his mirror! His nose would go blowless.

If this thing keeps on and women keep hammering at their noses even with such a frail thing as a powder puff, in two generations you will have your nose hammered right down into your face, because, as Lloyd George so aptly said: "Even the dripping of water will wear away at a stone."

Why you want your nose, which has a natural tendency to be red, to be changed to white, while your cheeks, which are naturally white, to red, I also don't know. You take a freshly powdered nose against a red background of the rest of your face, and there is nothing that you so much resemble as a white face Hereford cow.

Mind you, I am not criticizing, because I am working on a scheme whereby I will benefit financially far beyond my expectations. I am going to arrange like the hairdressers do with the permanent wave, some kind of preparation that will give your nose a permanent shade.

Just think of the joy of a woman going out in the morning, knowing that she can be gone all day and never have to worry about her nose being shiny! Look at the advantage of a permanent shade about the nose! Another benefit of this permanent coloring is this: did you ever notice that every time a woman powders her nose, she draws her mouth down out of shape? I don't know why she does it, but she does. Now, in the course of a couple of generations that will begin to tell on the race, and you will all have drooped mouths.

My permanent nose paint will even allow you to go in bathing, and still retain the original blend. Noses are receiving entirely too much attention, anyway. You can hardly pick up a paper nowadays, without the story of some prominent person having the contour of his, or her, nose re-assembled. In the old days, you used to be born with an appendix and a nose, and you went through life practically ignorant of the shape of either. Now the appendix in a bottle has replaced the Family Bible as an exhibit in the home, and a nose that hasn't been overhauled, don't count in society.

There are today in New York City, more doctors removing superfluous nose structures, than there are dentists removing teeth. Every nose has a doctor all its own. They are landscaping noses just like flower gardens. If an architect has not yet drawn up a blue print of your nose, you are as old-fashioned as red flannel underwear. I haven't had mine charted yet, as the face gardener said it would take more than a re-adjusted nose to do me any good. In fact, he said, my nose was about the only thing about my face that seemed to be properly laid out.

From Nuts to Soup

A couple of weeks ago I wrote the following: "If Mrs. John William Davis, wife of the Democratic presidential candidate, ever gets into the White House, we will have a mistress whom no titled European visitor can embarrass by doing the right thing first. She will never tip her soup plate, even if she can't get it all."

Now comes along an old friend of mine, Percy Hammond, a theatrical critic on the Chicago Tribune and the New York Tribune (pardon me, Percy, for having to tell them who you are, but my readers are mostly provincial). He takes up a couple of columns, part of which follows:

> For years I have been tipping my soup plate, but never until Mr. Rogers instructed me, did I know that I was performing a social error. Consultation with the polished and urbane head waiters of the Middle West, where I spent my boyhood, taught me, I believed, to eat soup. One wonders if Mr. Rogers has given as much thought to soup as he has to the lariat. Perhaps he does not know, being recently from Oklahoma, that in many prominent Eastern dining rooms one may tip one's soup plate, without losing his social standing. I regard Mr. Rogers' interference as prairie, impudent and unofficial. The stewards of the Dutch Treat Club assure me that it is proper to tip one's plate, provided (and here is the subtlety that escapes Mr. Rogers), provided that one tips one's soup plate from, and not toward.
>
> Mr. Rogers might well observe the modesty in such matters that adorns Mr. Tom Mix, his fellow ex-cowman. Mr. Mix, telling of a dinner given in his honor at the Hotel Astor, said: I et for two hours and didn't recognize a thing I et, except an olive.

Them are Percy's words (you notice I call you Percy, because if I keep saying "Mr. Hammond, Mr. Hammond," all through my article, it might possibly appear too formal). Percy, I thought you were a theatrical critic. Now I find you are only a soup critic. Instead of going, as is customary, from soup to nuts, you have gone from nuts to soup. Now, Percy, I have just read your article on "My Ignorance of Etiquette" (I don't know if that etiquette thing is spelled right, or not; if it is not, it will give you a chance for another article on my bad spelling). Now you do not have to write articles on my lack of etiquette, my ignorance, my bad English, or a thousand and one other defects. All the people that I ever met, or any one who ever read one of my articles, know that. It's too well known to comment on. Besides, I admit it.

Percy, I am just an old country boy in a big town trying to get along. I have been eating pretty regular, and the reason I have been, is because I have stayed an old country boy. Now I wrote that article, and technically I admit I may have been wrong, but the newspapers paid me a lot of money for it, and I never had a complaint. And, by the way, I will get the same this week for writing about you as I got for writing about soup. Now both articles may be wrong. But if you can show me how I can get any more money by writing them right, why, I will split with you.

Now you took my soup article apart to see what made it float. I will see if we can't find some small technicalities in your literary masterpiece. You say I came recently from Oklahoma, while you came from the Middle West and "by consultation with the head waiters have learned the proper way to eat soup." I thought Oklahoma was in the Middle West. Your knowledge of geography is worse than my etiquette. You say you learned to eat soup from a head waiter in the Middle West. Well, I admit my ignorance again: I never saw a head waiter eat soup.

Down in Oklahoma, where I come from, we won't let a head waiter eat at our table, even if we had a head waiter, which we haven't. If I remember right, I think it was my mother who taught me what little she knew of how I should eat, because if we had had to wait until we sent and got a head waiter to show us, we would have all starved to death. If a head waiter taught you to eat soup, Percy, I suppose you were sent to Borden's to learn how to drink milk.

Then you state: "The stewards of the Dutch Treat Club assured me that it is proper to tip one's plate." Now if you had learned properly from the great social head waiters of the urbane Middle West, why did you have to consult the stewards of the Dutch Treat Club? Could it be that after arriving in N.Y. you couldn't rely on the information of the polished head waiters of your phantom Middle West? Now I was in the Dutch Treat Club once, but just as a guest of honor at a luncheon, and of course had no chance to get into any intimate conversation with the stewards. At the time, the place did not impress me as being one where you might learn the last word in etiquette.

And as for your saying that "anything of subtlety would escape me," that I also admit. I attribute it to my dumbness. But as for me being too dumb to get the idea of "the soup plate being tipped away and not toward one," that's not etiquette; that's just self-protection. As bad as you plate tippers want all you can get, you don't want it in your lap. Custom makes manners, and while I know that it is permissible to tip plates, I still say that it is not a universal custom.

Manners are nothing more than common sense, and a person has no more rights to try and get every drop of soup out of his plate than he has to take a piece of bread and try and harvest all the gravy in his plate. If you are that hungry, they ought to feed you out of a nose bag. So, "prairie impudence," or no "prairie impudence," I claim there are lots of them that don't do it, even if it is permissible, head waiters and Dutch stewards to the contrary. It's permissible to get drunk, but we still have a few that don't.

Now, Percy, suppose they all did as permitted. Picture a big dinner with everybody with their soup plates all balanced up on edge, rounding up what little soup was left. If that was the universal custom, I would invent a triangle that could be pushed under the plate, so it would permit you to have one hand free, if by chance you might want to use a napkin.

So don't ask head waiters and stewards what to do, Percy, look around yourself. You will find hundreds of them that are satisfied with just what soup they can get on the level. Why, I bet you are a fellow, Percy, if you took castor oil, you would want to lick the spoon.

You know, Percy, I might know more about etiquette than you think I do. I wrote a review on Emily Post's Book on Etiquette, and it was recopied in the Literary Digest. Now have you or any of your Mid-Western head waiters or retinue of stewards, ever been asked to write a criticism on such an authoritative work as that? So you see, I am somewhat of a critic myself. I am the Hammond of the Etiquette book business.

Another thing, Percy, I spoke of a particular case; I mentioned Mrs. Davis. Well, I happened to see the lady in question eat soup, and she did not try and corral the whole output. She perhaps knew it was permissible, still she did not seem eager to take advantage of it.

Now you speak of my friend Tom Mix, where he says, "He et two hours and did not recognize anything he et but an olive." Now that is bad grammar, even I will admit, but it's mighty good eating. Don't you kinder envy him that he can eat two hours? I bet you that you would trade your knowledge of the English language, for his constitution. Tipping that soup plate at all your meals for years, is what put that front on you, Percy. Leave some! And the fact that Tom has done something to be given a dinner for, should make him immune from attacks from the press table.

Personally, I don't think his word "et" on Mix's part will seriously affect the drawing power of his films. You see, Percy, Tom said "et" but you know better than him what to say. Still, if a western picture was to be made to amuse the entire world, I would trust Tom's judgement to yours. Percy, everybody is ignorant, only on different subjects.

So Percy, you string with the high brows, I am going to stick to the low brows, because I know I am at home with them. For remember, if it was not for us low brows, you high brows would have no one to discuss. But God love you, Percy, and if you ever want to leave them and come back to us where you started, we will all be glad to welcome you, even if you do feel like you are slumming. You must remember, Percy, that the question of the world today is not how to eat soup, but how to get soup to eat.

Will Basks in Reflected Sunshine

My daughter was graduated at a girls preparatory school. They read off what course each girl had taken. When they said "Mary Rogers, Diploma in English," I had to laugh at that. One of my children studying English? Why, it's just inherited, you don't have to study that in our family!

Douglas Fairbanks had a niece graduating, Wallace Beery had a relation, Frank Lloyd, the great director, a daughter, and all four of us sat there, and purred like four old tomcats, basking in a little reflected sunshine, and secretly congratulating ourselves on choosing a profession where education played no part.

1925

At the Locarno conference Germany agrees to a demilitarized Rhineland and "guarantees" Belgo-German and Franco-German borders. Despite this written "guarantee," France begins construction of the Maginot line, a deeply dug fortification along the entire French-German frontier. Events will prove that the German guarantee and the French Maginot line are equally unreliable.

Sun Yat-sen, Chinese revolutionary leader and first elected president of a Chinese republic, dies. His chief aide, Gen. Chiang Kai-shek, is appointed commander in chief.

With everyone else discussing disarmament, the Soviet Union introduces conscription, decreeing universal military service for two years, and an additional three years on reserve.

In America, as the new year begins, Herbert Hoover predicts that 1925 will be the best year since the war. Of course he is only secretary of commerce, while Calvin Coolidge, the president, is sound asleep—so *The Times* reports—having gone to bed even before his accustomed early hour.

In Topeka, Kansas, a sixty-three-year-old country doctor named Charles F. Menninger begins group practice. Assisted by his two sons, he treats the mentally ill in a farmhouse—the beginning of the Menninger Clinic.

In the middle of winter, a virulent diphtheria epidemic breaks out in the area of Nome, Alaska, threatening some ten thousand.

Antitoxin must be brought in by the only possible means—dog sled. In a heroic effort, through blizzards with wind gusts up to seventy-five miles per hour and temperatures hovering around fifty degrees below zero, veteran mushers reach Nome in time—averaging 120 miles per day, a record achievement.

Charles Arthur ("Pretty Boy") Floyd begins his life of crime in the Middle West by robbing a Saint Louis post office of $350—all in pennies. In the next twelve years he will rob some three dozen banks and kill ten people.

Al Capone becomes undisputed head of Chicago's underworld when Johnny Torrio retires after being shot. Capone, not satisfied with controlling bootlegging, diversifies by extending his dominance to prostitution and gambling.

After spending an estimated $50 million to build and furnish his castle at San Simeon, California, William Randolph Hearst moves in. The estate—a quarter million acres overlooking the Pacific Ocean—is also a working ranch.

In sports, the year opens with an upset victory by Knute Rockne's Notre Dame football team and its "Four Horsemen" over Stanford in the Rose Bowl game. The New York Giants, a professional football team, is founded by Timothy J. Mara.

Henry Louis ("Lou") Gehrig comes to the New York Yankees as their first baseman, and on June 1 begins a fourteen-year streak of 2,130 consecutive games played; it will end May 2, 1939.

The New Yorker begins publication, as does *Parent's Magazine,* started by a bachelor.

John T. Scopes, a schoolteacher in Dayton, Tennessee, stands trial for violating a state law against the teaching of any theory denying the divine creation of man as taught in the Bible. His defense counsels: Clarence Darrow, Dudley Field Malone, and Arthur Garfield Hays. Former secretary of state and three-time Democratic candidate for president William Jennings Bryan comes to assist the local prosecutor. On July 21, the verdict is rendered: guilty, $100 fine, plus costs. Five days later William Jennings Bryan dies. The verdict is appealed, and in 1927 Scopes is cleared on a technicality.

Among the most read fiction of the day: *An American Tragedy,* by Theodore Dreiser; *The Great Gatsby,* by F. Scott Fitzgerald; *Arrowsmith,* by Sinclair Lewis; and *Gentlemen Prefer Blondes,* by Anita Loos.

Among the still silent films: *Phantom at the Opera,* with Lon Chaney; *The Big Parade,* with John Gilbert; *Ben Hur,* with Ramon Navarro and Francis X. Bushman; *The Gold Rush,* with and by Charlie Chaplin.

"Grand Old Opry" from Nashville, Tennessee, is first broadcast; it is called "Barn Dance," and in 1927 it will change its name, but not its format.

Broadway offers a variety of favorites, among them: *No, No, Nanette,* with songs "Tea for Two" and "I Want to Be Happy." *The Vagabond King,* by Rudolf Friml; *The Cocoanuts,* with the four Marx Brothers; and *Tip-Toes,* by George Gershwin, with Queenie Smith and Jeanette MacDonald.

Favorite songs are: "Yes, Sir, That's My Baby!" "Sleepy Time Gal," "Sweet Georgia Brown," "Dinah," "Always," "Jealousy," "Five Feet Two, Eyes of Blue," and a most surprising entry during Prohibition, "Show Me the Way to Go Home."

Brig. Gen. Billy Mitchell is America's foremost combat air commander, who during the Great War had innovated the use of up to two hundred planes in mass bombing raids on German targets. Appointed assistant chief of the air service, Mitchell advocated a strong, independent U.S. Air Force. In demonstrations for the general staff in 1921 and 1923, Mitchell's bombers sank the former German dreadnought *Ostfrieseland* and two obsolete U.S. ships. The U.S. Navy began an immediate vigorous rebuilding program around a new ship, the aircraft carrier.

But the army did not wish to be taught a lesson and banished Mitchell to an obscure post in Texas. Steadfastly, the army refused to listen to Mitchell, who finally publicly accused the high command of "incompetence, criminal negligence, and almost treasonable administration of the national defense." The army had to respond.

In December 1925, Billy Mitchell is court-martialed and convicted of insubordination. Will Rogers is in the courtroom. Mitchell is sentenced to suspension from rank and duty for five years, but he resigns from the army as of February 1, 1926.

Billy Mitchell dies February 19, 1936, and therefore never witnesses the unfortunate accuracy of his predictions, including his warning about Hawaii's openness to sneak air attacks "early some Sunday morning."

January 1925 finds Will Rogers appearing in the *Ziegfeld Follies* in New York City. It will be the last *Follies* for Will, much to Ziegfeld's regret. Will continues as a most popular speaker at various groups, conventions, and charity affairs. Will is asked to appear on a broadcast with Franklin D. Roosevelt (former assistant secretary of the navy, and Democratic nominee for vice-president in 1920), Al Smith (governor of New York), Chauncey Mitchell Depew (former U.S. senator, and chairman of the board of directors of the New York Central Railroad), Bishop William Thomas Manning (Episcopal bishop of New York), and Father Francis Patrick Duffy (chaplain of New York's "Fighting Sixty-ninth" regiment, also called the "Fighting Irish").

Will agrees to address the radio industry's banquet, scheduled for September 16. Naturally his speech is to be broadcast and the event is well advertised. Then some confusion arises. Will has signed a contract with Charles L. Wagner to go on a lecture tour, and that contract specifically prohibits his appearing in any way that could possibly conflict with his tour. The Wagner office feels that the broadcast, reaching a wide audience outside the city, could seriously affect attendance in other communities. They insist that Will cancel his appearance.

The newspapers allude to the fact that "Rogers had backed out on a firm commitment," and Will is upset, despite his innocence. When members of the entertainment committee come to see him once more, he promises to speak on the appointed day.

On September 16, having been introduced, Will strides to the microphone and for the next fifteen minutes has his listeners roaring with laughter while he explains why he would not possibly be able to broadcast this evening.

Will has also begun a new syndicated daily column called "The Worst Story I've Heard Today." He will write more than five hundred of these before the series is stopped.

This is the year that the town of Dewey, Oklahoma, starts a boom for Will Rogers for governor of Oklahoma. Not to be outdone, Arkansas too starts to promote Will for governor. Will is pleased that Betty's native state wants him for governor, but in his inimitable style he gratefully refuses both honors.

On October 1, Will—accompanied by a male quartet, the De Reszke Singers—starts on his "lecture tour." Until the end of July 1928, with some time out, Will is scheduled to appear on more than four hundred lecture platforms—on some of them more than once.

Regrets That Washington Monument Has No Handles

All I know is what I don't read in the papers. For the last couple of weeks it seemed like war time, with Von Hindenburg on the front page again. When the war ended, I thought the only way he would ever make the front page again would be to die. But he fooled me. Here he pops up as President of Germany, whatever that title may imply.

A great many papers editorially have viewed with alarm this election of the Von, but Ye Olde Reliable Illiterate Digest, is able to point to it with pride, seeing as we always do, the bright side of everything. In the first place, there should be no reason for surprise at the Von running a good race, for as good a candidate as Pershing and his American constituents were never able to overtake the Von in a race. A great many seem to think that this election really meant the election of the Kaiser, but I don't think so. When the Allies broke the Hindenburg Line, and Von and Wilhelm started their memorable detour across Germany, Kaiser Wilhelm was going so fast, he was in Holland before he could check himself; but when Von pulled up, he was still on German soil, so that is why he was elected, instead of Wilhelm. They wanted to pay honor to one of their countrymen for not going to Holland.

After all, elections are a good deal like marriages, there is no accounting for any one's taste. Every time we see a bridegroom, we wonder why she ever picked him, and it's the same with public officials. So Germany is the bride! She picked him. So let her live with him. He may make her a good man. If any man had a chance to profit from his experience in the war, the Von is the one that should.

But this election proves one thing. Germany is the only nation that remembers the war. For losing the war, seven years later Von Hindenburg is made President; while Pershing, for winning the war, seven years later is let out of the army, and half of his pay is taken away from him. For winning it, he was reduced to half pay and half rations. He was retired on account of old age at sixty-six, yet Hindenburg is elected president at seventy-seven. According to that, Pershing is too young to be of any real service to his country.

But the people certainly haven't forgotten him. Two weeks ago tonight, at the Metropolitan Opera House in New York City, at the Lamb's Club Gambol, a very distinguished audience was gathered. At the finish of my little turn, when I came off the stage, General Pershing was standing in the wings, having just returned from some other affair given in his honor. He had dropped in to see the rest of the show. I immediately seized onto him and dragged him out on the stage, where the entire audience arose and not only applauded, but cheered him.

He is a very modest, bashful fellow (when he is not talking to a soldier); but I held him there and made him make a short speech. He thanked the audience for their reception, and then told them that he had come into the theatre at the finish of my act purposely, as he had heard my jokes at the Gridiron Dinner in Washington a few nights ago, and that he certainly didn't want to have to listen to them again, which showed that his mind was working pretty keen, even if he had been retired for old age.

I interrupted him and made him stand at attention (I suppose I am the only civilian that ever did that) while I told the audience how they had received him at this dinner in Washington. Out of all the prominent men there, his was the biggest reception.

Speaking of this dinner in Washington, Mr. Andrew Mellon, secretary of the Treasury, and General Billy Mitchell of the ex-Air Service, also received tremendous applause. After the dinner, I met General Mitchell for the first time, and he asked me if I wouldn't like to go and see Washington with him the next morning, and that he would call at the hotel for me. So I foolishly told him—yes!

Well, next morning he came and got me, and we drove across the river to an aviation field. I thought naturally that he was going to show me the field, but instead of pointing out any places of interest, an assistant handed me a straight jacket, a kind of one-piece suicide suit, and a kind of a derby hat with the brim turned down over your eyes. It slowly began to dawn on me that at last there was going to be some flying done in the Army, and that I was supposed to be one of the participants.

There is an old legend that says, "Nine-tenths of all the brave things done, are performed through fear." I don't know whether Lincoln said it, as they lay all the smart things onto him, but whoever concocted this aforementioned legend certainly had this air voyage of mine in mind. I did not want to see Washington by air. In fact, I never had any desire to see anything from the air. Besides, Congress was not in session, and I didn't know whether there would be enough air to keep us up, or not.

Well, there was so many standing around, that there was no way to back out. Right at that moment I thought the fellows who were trying to get this Mitchell out of the Air Service, were right, and I wished they had got him out sooner. He says, "Do you use cotton in your ears?" He seemed to think that I was an old experienced aviator.

I says, "No, I only use cotton in my ears when I visit the Senate gallery." I couldn't imagine what the cotton was for, unless it was to keep the dirt out of your ears in case of a fall.

Photographers were there to get our picture. I could just see the picture with the label under it: "Last Photograph Taken of Deceased."

But General Mitchell asked them if they would wait until we came back. Well, that didn't make me feel any too good. It looked like there might be a doubt in his mind as to whether we would come back. There was a superstition connected with it some way, that didn't make me feel any better. But I never let on. I remembered how nice the papers always speak of the man who goes to the gallows with a smile on his face, and how they laud his nerve.

A man buckles you in so you won't change your mind after you leave the ground. General Mitchell says, "I will point out the places of interest to you." I didn't see him point, nor I didn't see what he pointed at. I have always heard when you are up on anything high, don't look down—look up! So all I saw was the sky. The trip from a sightseeing point of view, was a total loss to me, outside of seeing the sky at short range.

Washington's home at Mount Vernon might have been William Jennings Bryan's in Miami, for all I know. We flew around Washington's Monument, and if the thing had had handles on it, Mitchell would have lost a passenger.

Here I was thousands of feet up in the air, when you can't even get me to ride a tall horse. I had always figured that if the Lord had intended man to do any flying, he would have sprouted something out of his back beside just shoulder blades. He asked if I saw the Mayflower, the President's private tug. How was I going to see it, unless it was flying over us? I didn't come any nearer seeing it, than I'll ever come riding on it. When we landed and got out and walked away, I was tickled to death. I thought the drama was all over. But it wasn't.

The most impressive part of the whole thing was in the next few words. General Mitchell said, "You have been with me on the last flight I will ever make as Brigadier General. Tonight at 12 o'clock I am to be demoted to a Colonel, and sent far away where, instead of having the entire Air Force at my command, there will be seven planes."

Well, I got a real thrill out of that. To think that I had accompanied such a man on such a memorable flight. I had a long talk with Mitchell. He never squealed, and he never whined. He knows some day America will have a tremendous Air Force, but he can't understand why we are not training it now. But it does seem a strange way to repay a man who fought for us through a war, and who has fought harder for us in peace, to be reprimanded for telling the truth.

And wasn't it a coincidence that we had just flown over Washington's home, the Father of our Country, whose first claim to fame was telling the truth about a cherry tree? But George wasn't in the Army then, and the cherry tree had nothing to do with National Defense.

Automatic Pistol Is Standard Equipment Today

The biggest question that is agitating the public is the following: Are all escaped lunatics to be furnished with guns and ammunition?

This gun thing is getting pretty serious here around New York. Everybody that hasn't got a gun is being shot by somebody. A flask and a gun are now considered standard equipment, and are supposed to accompany every tough kid when he steps into long pants. They pinch a thousand people a day here for parking 5 minutes too long, or for not putting their hand out when they are going to make a turn, but I have yet to ever read where a policeman searched a bunch of tough guys hanging around a place, to see if any of them carried concealed weapons. In fact I don't know if it is against the law, or not. They could start searching everybody, and in one day here they would get enough pistols and stilettos to dam up the Hudson River.

I was born in the Indian Territory, at Claremore to be exact. (A town that has cured more people than Florida has swindled.) Well, that country, along about the time I was a yearling, was supposed to have some pretty tough men. Of course, as I grew up and began to be able to uphold law and righteousness, why, these men gradually began to thin out and drift on down to politics, a big part of them becoming governors. Well, even in those days out there, it was against the law to carry guns, and every once in a while the sheriff would search a fellow to see if he was overdressed—and if they was, they fined 'em heavy. Mind you, those were men carrying guns that knew what they were; knew the danger of them, and knew how to use them.

A bad man in those days consisted of a careful, deliberate, cool-headed, steel-nerved individual who was really a protector of women and children, or innocent people. But nowadays, the so-called bad man is either a lunatic or a thick-headed drug fiend, or somebody full of terrible liquor. He shoots people just to get his picture in the papers. Some of our newspapers, if you take the murders out of them, would have nothing left but the title of the paper. To compare one of the numbskull killers nowadays with a Jesse James or a Bob Dalton would almost be sacreligious. Still these addle brains can go and buy a gun any place they want to.

Do you know what has been the cause of the big increase in murders? It's been the manufacture of the automatic pistol. It's all right to have invented it, but it should never have been allowed outside the Army, and then only in war times. The automatic pistol is as much more dangerous and destructive than the old six-shooter, as poison gas is over perfume. In the first place there is no skill or nerve required in using it. You just touch the trigger and aim the thing around like you would a sprinkling can, or a hose. It is shooting all the time, and the more unsteady the nerve of the holder, why, the better the shooting he can do, because he takes in a bigger radius.

There has never been a case where the attempted killer missed everybody with an automatic pistol; but on the other hand, there has been very few cases where only the one originally shot at, has been hit. But they always got somebody because they didn't have presence of mind enough to even stop the thing from shooting. They should advertise those guns: "Killing Made Easy!" You don't have to have a steady nerve; you don't have to have good eyesight, no practice needed. Just hold the trigger down, and we will guarantee you somebody.

When a man used to have to know something about a gun, and had the nerve to take aim at the party being used as a target, there was at least some skill and dignity connected with the profession. A bad man at least carried the admiration for his cool nerve, if not the respect of other people. But with these city killers, you know they are either over-educated or undernourished. If your boy is over-bright, and starts reading a lot of books by some old guy called Nitsky (or some Bolshevik name like that) why, look out for your boy. He is just one jump from an automatic pistol emporium.

If killers had to learn to shoot before shooting somebody, we absolutely know there wouldn't be as much killing, because you can look at them and tell they would never have had sense and patience enough to have learned to shoot. You let the government confiscate and forbid the entire sale of automatics, even to police officers, and everybody, because officers kill ten innocent people to one guilty one with those sprinkling cans, and prohibit guns of even the older variety to any but officers, and then, when you catch a guy with a gun, send him to jail, not just fine him.

But I see where a lot of men are advocating letting everybody carry guns, with the idea that they will be able to protect themselves. In other words, just make Civil War out of this crime wave. When you see a man coming and he looks like he hasn't got as much as you, and might want to rob you, why, just open up on him with your miniature

Gatling gun. Wave it around in his general direction (your eyes can be shut if you prefer) and you will get him, or somebody else. He may start shooting at you, thinking you are trying to murder him, or rob him. So let every man protect himself—no policeman necessary—that is the slogan of these people.

Look at the women murderers today, that in the days of the six-shooter were afraid to take a chance on missing their husbands. But with this cute little automatic, which just fits into their handbag—why, you can't miss him. In the old days a woman had to go out and practice shooting for weeks, perhaps months, before she would dare open up on the better half. But with this marvelous invention, the automatic, the more hysterical she gets, and the more he dodges about, the more direct hits will be scored. Then comes the pictures in the papers, and a wonderful trial, and the acquittal, with her parting remark to the newspapers: "The dear men on the jury were just lovely to me."

If she had been compelled to use the old-time weapon, the crime would never have happened, because the present-day woman don't wear enough clothes to conceal a real six-gun. Women used to be the alleged "weaker sex," but the automatic and the sentimental jury have been the equalizers. Why divorce him when you can shoot him easier and cheaper?

And here is another thing. If it's a small crime, say robbery, we fine them; and if it's confessed murder, why, it's "Insanity!" Psychiatrists are busier, and get more than policemen. We go on the theory that if you confess, you must be insane. In the old days a man would go to any extremes to keep from getting into any shooting affray when he was under the influence of liquor, because he knew he was at a disadvantage. But now a guy must be drunk, or drugged, or he wouldn't think of such terrible crimes; and the more drunk, or drugged he is, the more people he will hit.

And if you think that being armed protects you, why, how about the number of policemen that are shot down? They are all armed. Yet these hop heads shoot 'em, and all with automatics, because they wouldn't have the nerve to do it with anything else. But if you are going to do away with capital punishment, and sell guns to everybody, the surest way out of the whole thing would be to punish them, but, of course, that is out of the question—that's barbarous, and takes us back—as the hysterics say—to the days before civilization.

Slogans, Slogans Everywhere

Everything nowadays is a saying, or slogan. You can't go to bed, you can't get up, you can't brush your teeth, without doing it to some advertising slogan. We are even born nowadays by a slogan: "Better Parents Have Better Babies." Our children are raised by a slogan: "Feed your Baby Cowlick's Malted Milk, and he will be another Dempsey."

Everything has a slogan, and of all the bunk in America, the slogan is the champ. There never was one that lived up to its claim. You can't manufacture a new article until you have a slogan to go with it. You can't form a club unless it has a catchy slogan. The merits of the thing has nothing to do with it. It is, just how good is the slogan?

Even the government is in on it. The Navy has a slogan: "Join the Navy and see the World!" You join, and all you see for the first 4 years is a bucket of soap suds and a mop, and some brass polish. You spend the first 5 years in Newport News. The sixth year you are allowed to go on a cruise to Old Point Comfort—10 miles away. So there is a slogan gone wrong.

Congress even has slogans: "Why sleep at home, when you can sleep in Congress?"

"Be a Politician—no training necessary!"

"It's easier to fool 'em in Washington than at home—so why not be a Senator."

"Come to Washington and vote to raise your own Pay."

"Get in the Cabinet: you won't have to stay long."

"Work for Uncle Sam, it's just like a Pension."

"Be a Republican and sooner or later you will be a Postmaster."

"Join the Senate and investigate something."

"If you are a lawyer and have never worked for a Trust, we can get you into the Cabinet."

All such slogans are held up to the youth of this country. You can't sit down in a street car after a hard day's work without having a slogan staring you in the face: "Let the Bohunk Twins do your work." "Chew Wiggley's Gum: The Flavor Lasts." Now they know it don't last when they tell you that. In two minutes after you start anybody's gum, you might as well have an old rubber boot to chew on as far as any flavor is concerned. I know, because that's all I have done for 20 years, is to throw old gum where somebody will step on it. I have to talk a great deal to the public, and I use gum just to keep my jaws in good shape. If it wasn't for gum, my jaws couldn't go through a rigorous season of truth telling. So gum has its place, but the slogans are all wet.

Even if you want to get married, a sign will stare you in the face: "You get the Girl, we will furnish the Ring." That has led more saps astray than any misinformation ever published, outside the prize one of all, which is: "Two can live as cheap as one." That, next to "Law Enforcement," is the biggest bunk slogan ever invented. Yes, two can live as cheap as one, if you don't want to eat or wear anything during its lifetime. Two can't even live as cheap as two, much less one!

Then the preacher says: "Let no man put asunder," and two-thirds of the married world is asunder in less than three months. Then comes the furniture slogan: "A Dollar down and a Dollar a Week." It's few wives that last with the same husband until the cook stove is paid for.

"It's cheaper to buy than pay rent." That's the next bunk slogan that attracts the love-sick boobs. Half the people in the United States are living on interest paid by people who will never get the last mortgage payment out.

Even political campaigns are run, and won, on slogans. Years ago some fellow run on "The Full Dinner Pail," and after he was elected and they opened it, there was nothing in it. Another slogan went wrong. The William Jennings Bryan run on a slogan: "16 to 1." He was defeated, of course, because he didn't explain what the 16 meant. It meant 16 defeats to 1 victory.

We even got into the war on a slogan that was supposed to keep us out. After we got in we were going to "Make the World safe for Democracy." And maybe we did—you can't tell, because there is no nation ever tried Democracy since. Our boys went over singing: "Over There," and came back singing: "I am always chasing Rainbows."

The next president was elected on a slogan: "Back to Normalcy!" Back to normalcy consisted of the most cuckoo years of spending and carousing and graft we ever had. Another slogan knocked crosswise.

Last election, out came the slogan makers again. Some fool that didn't know American politics had J. W. Davis run on "Honesty." Well, that had no more place in politics than I have on the Harvard faculty. It was one of the poorest selections of a slogan that was ever invented. Coolidge ran on "Economy," and "Common Sense," which is always good for the boobs. It's like getting up at a dinner, and saying: "I am proud to be here." It's an old gag, but it always goes over. Now you know "Common Sense" is not an issue in politics, it's an affliction. And as for "Honesty," neither is that an issue, it's a miracle. And the returns showed that there was 8 million more people in the United States who had the "Common Sense" not to believe that there was "Honesty" in politics. And as soon as the "Economy" boys got in, they raised Congress' and the Senate's salary and redecorated the White House. So away goes another slogan!

P.T. Barnum came nearer having a true slogan than anybody: "There is a Sucker born every minute." And the car manufacturers are right there to take care of him the minute he becomes of age. General Pershing said: "Lafayette, we are here," and France sent him a bill for the use of the grounds.

Kaiser Wilhelm's slogan was "Germany Uber Alles." I don't know what that Uber means, but whatever it means he was wrong, and it's too late to look it up now.

You see, a fool slogan can get you into anything. But you never heard of a slogan getting you out of anything. It takes either bullets, hard work or money to get you out of anything. Nobody has ever invented a slogan to use instead of paying your taxes.

But they will fall for 'em. You shake a slogan at an American, and it's just like showing a hungry dog a bone. We even die by slogans. I saw an undertaker's sign the other day, which read: "There is a satisfaction in dying, if you know the Woodlawn Brothers are to bury you."

Life in New York

We had quite a panic here the other day in New York; in the subway several people were trampled and crushed. The cause of the trouble was that someone hollered out: "Here is a vacant seat!"

Then yesterday, another New York catastrophe happened in one of the hourly shooting affrays which are held on the public streets. An innocent bystander was shot. You stand around in New York long enough, and be innocent, and someone will shoot you.

One day there was four innocent people shot here in New York. That was the best shooting ever done in this town. Hard to find four innocent people in New York, even if you don't shoot them.

You shoot a man nowadays, and they hand you a ticket telling you to please appear in Court Monday at 10 o'clock. If you can't come, send your chauffeur. There are more of those tickets that never come back, than there are I.O.U.'s that are never taken up.

There is an awful lot of other news. That's why I am not using it, it's awful. We sure are living in a fast age—if we can live.

The Diplomatic Note

Have you been reading in the papers about the note that Secretary of State Kellogg sent to Mexico, and the one he received in reply? Now Mr. Kellogg has just been appointed Secretary of State; he was, before that, Ambassador to England. Well, he had been sitting around Washington, and there wasn't much to do, so one hot day he says to one of the underlings, or secretaries: "Have we sent any notes since I have been in?"

"No, Mr. Secretary, our only correspondence so far in Washington has been relative to gas, water, light and rent."

"Well, most of the Secretaries of State I ever heard of gained fame be sending diplomatic notes to some other nation. Who can we send one to?"

"Well, we could write to almost any of them, but I doubt very much they would answer. To attract any notice, it's not the note you send but the answer. France, and Italy and Belgium and a bunch of other countries have not paid us on what they owe us from the war, or even acted like they were going to pay. We might send them a note, or just a bill as a suggestion."

"No, we can't do that," says Mr. Kellogg, "that would interfere with diplomatic relations. We have to be very careful with them as each of them has a Navy and Army, and their feelings are very sensitive. By the way, what about Mexico? I have always heard that when the U.S. couldn't find anybody else to pick on, that they picked on Mexico."

"I know, Mr. Secretary, but Mexico has not done anything; in fact, they have been behaving themselves almost beyond recognition. They are so peaceful you would hardly think they were a Republic."

"Well, we will send 'em a note anyway. I will show Washington I can write just as good as any of these other Secretaries of State. Get out a tablet and take down the following. By the way, do they owe us anything?"

"Yes, Mr. Secretary. They do; not as a nation, but we have claims against them for damages for individuals. But they don't owe us near as much as these other nations."

"Well, you send them the following: 'America is getting very tired of your nation down there not paying us what you owe us for land we claim was taken by the Revolutionists from some of our respectful citizens. It's funny to me you can't control the revolutions. Now, we want Americans protected. Remember, MEXICO IS ON TRIAL BEFORE THE EYES OF THE WORLD. Remember, this is a friendly note,' Put a Special Delivery stamp on that, boy, and send it down at once. Where is my golf clubs?"

"Mr. Secretary Kellogg, why don't you send a note demanding the protection of our American tourists in France? They have been skinned alive there for years."

"Yes, I know they have, but France has an air force, and a navy. You have to be diplomatic in these things, that's why I am able to be Secretary of State. Don't ask any more questions, please."

Now all the above is just what took place, and we were very much excited when Mexico replied and told us that they were paying the taxes in Mexico, and that naturally they felt they should have some saying as to how their country should be run, and that as for the EYE OF THE WORLD being on them, the world was cock-eyed nowadays anyway.

Now what this Olde Reliable Illiterate Digest wants to know is what the devil business is it of ours how some other country runs their business? How does our Secretary of State and our President know what the eyes of the world are on? As a matter of fact, the eyes of the world are on a dollar bill, and especially if somebody else has it. Outside of the oil interests and Americans who want to make money out of Mexico, the rest of the world's eyes don't even know Mexico exists.

America has a great habit of always talking about protecting American interests in some foreign country. Protect them here at home! There is more American interests right here than anywhere. If an American goes to Mexico and his horse dies, we send 'em a note wanting American interests preserved and the horse paid for.

We don't guarantee investments here at home. Why should we make Mexico guarantee them? Our papers are always harping on us developing Mexico. Suppose Mexico don't want developing. Maybe they want it kept as it was years ago. How much do Americans spend in the summer to get some place where there is no development—no street cars, elevators, Fords, telephones, radios, and a million and one other things that you just like to get away from once in a while. Well suppose they don't want them at all down there. Why don't you let every nation do and act as they please? What business is it how Mexico acts and lives? Every village and community in Mexico has a church (and they go to it, too) where up here, if we have a filling station we think we are up to date.

75

If America is not good enough for you to live in and make money in, why, then you are privileged to go to some other country. But don't ask protection from a country that was not good enough for you. If you want to make money out of a country, why, take out their citizenship papers and join them. Don't use one country for making money, and another for convenience. The difference in our exchange of people with Mexico is: they send workmen here to work, while we send Americans there to *work* Mexico.

I left home as a kid and traveled and worked my way all through the Argentine, South Africa, Australia and New Zealand and was three years getting enough money to get home on. But I never found it necessary to have my American rights protected. Nobody invited me into those countries, and I always acted as their guest, not as their advisor.

America and England, especially, are regular old busybodies when it comes to telling somebody else what to do. But you notice they (England and America) never tell each other what to do. You bet your life they don't. If Mexico, or the Boers, or the Philippines, or India, was as strong as either one of them was, you bet you our Secretary of State would consult somebody else besides our President or the head of the Senate Foreign Relations Committee, before he commented on where the eyes of the world was located.

For instance, if an American is killed in Mexico, we send them a note saying: "The murderer must be punished within 24 hours, and $100,000 must be paid at once to his relatives." Now maybe this guy wasn't worth alive over 10 cents, and couldn't return to America without being hung, but "we must protect American rights." Now suppose, on the other hand, a Californian is killed in New York City. Why, they will never in 100 years find out even who killed him, much less punishing him. And do his people get any bounty on him? No, Sir, not a cent. They even have to bury him. But if he was killed in Mexico, oh how his value would rise! Getting killed in Mexico is better than having an insurance. We discover one murder in a hundred, yet we ask them to catch him and punish him in 24 hours.

Big nations are always talking about "honor." Yet, here is England promising to protect France against Germany, IF FRANCE WOULD PAY THEM WHAT THEY OWED THEM. In other words, they would act as a police force for pay.

What is the consequence? As soon as Germany gets strong enough so she thinks she can lick both of them, there will be another war. There is only one way in the world to prevent war, and that is for every nation to tend to its own business. Trace any war that ever was, and you will find some nation was trying to tell some other nation how to run their business.

Look at Switzerland! There is an example of a country minding its own business. No wars, no notes. Just tending to its own business.

1926

King Husein is expelled from Hejaz and Ibn Saud takes over the throne. The new ruler's first official act: to change the name of his country to Saudi Arabia.

In Berlin, a treaty of friendship and neutrality is signed between Germany and the Soviet Union. On July 31, the USSR signs a nonaggression pact with Afghanistan.

May 1 marks the beginning of the British coal miners' strike, and two days later a general strike is called. The general strike is settled on May 12; the coal strike will last until November, when miners give up.

In the Soviet Union, Joseph Stalin begins to eliminate all opposition, as the Politbureau expels Leon Trotsky and Grigori Zinoviev.

On December 25, Emperor Yoshihito of Japan dies. He is succeeded by his son, who solemnly pledges Japan to a policy of peace; his name: Hirohito. In less than fifteen years, after a drawn-out war of expansion on the Chinese mainland, he will condone the attack on Pearl Harbor.

Early in May, U.S. troops land in Nicaragua to preserve and protect American interests. President Emiliano Chamorro faces a revolt and will be forced to resign. Despite criticism in Congress and in the liberal press, five thousand marines stay in Nicaragua. In 1927, twenty marines are killed and some fifty wounded in guerrilla warfare waged by rebel forces led by Augusto Sandino. Still there in 1928, marines will supervise the Nicaraguan election.

In America, midway through the "Noble Experiment" called Prohibition, it is evident to all but the most zealous that it has failed. Illegal liquor traffic is conservatively estimated to total $3.6 billion per year, which averages to $31.30 for each man, woman, and child in the United States. One bright spot: Machine-made ice production reaches an astronomical 56 million tons—of course, most is used to chill illegal beer.

The federal Treasury expects a budget surplus of almost half a billion dollars. An improved, waterproof cellophane developed by E. I. du Pont will revolutionize packaging. The first motion picture with sound is demonstrated, but found too expensive. David Sarnoff combines several independent radio stations and forms NBC, the National Broadcasting Company.

In aviation, Richard Evelyn Byrd and pilot Floyd Bennett take off from Spitsbergen, Norway, fly seven hundred miles to the North Pole, circle several times, and return. On April 15, a young flyer takes off from Saint Louis on the first regular scheduled mail flight to Chicago; his name: Charles Augustus Lindbergh.

These are among the best-selling books: Ernest Hemingway's *The Sun Also Rises*, Edna Ferber's *Show Boat*. And A. A. Milne gives the children of the world a present with his *Winnie-the-Pooh*.

The Pierce Arrow, a luxury car, uses an entirely new advertising approach by stressing economic gas consumption. The ads say: "The famous Series 80 gets 14 to 17 miles per gallon gasoline!"

On September 5, Ford Motor Company plants introduce the eight-hour workday and the five-day workweek. Prestone, the first ethylene glycol antifreeze, is introduced. It sells for $5 per gallon.

The latest five-tube Atwater Kent radio set, in "exquisite" cabinet, sells for $114.95, installed free, with terms as low as $2 per week.

In sports, America's Gertrude Ederle becomes the first woman to swim the English Channel. Gene Tunney wins the heavyweight boxing championship from Jack Dempsey. A new, cork-centered baseball is introduced, and the St. Louis Cardinals win the World Series by beating the New York Yankees, 4 games to 3.

On Broadway, show business is booming. Ziegfeld has two hits: *Sunny*, starring Marilyn Miller, and *Betsy*, starring Belle Baker, but no new edition of the *Follies*. Mae West draws crowds in something called *Sex*. Others on Broadway are Eva Le Gallienne, Ethel Barrymore, Walter Hampden, Fred Stone and daughter Dorothy, Beatrice Lillie, Otis Skinner, Pauline Frederick, Alison Skipworth, Gertrude Lawrence, Victor Moore, and Fay Bainter. George White's *Scandals* stars Ann Pennington, who introduces a new dance that will rival the Charleston; it is called the Black Bottom.

In silent movies, you can choose from: *The Scarlet Letter,* with Lillian Gish; *Don Juan,* with John Barrymore; *Beau Geste,* with Ronald Colman; *KIKI,* with Norma Talmadge; *What Price Glory,* with Victor McLaglen; and the Russian film *Potemkin.*

The most popular songs are: "Muskrat Ramble," "Baby Face," "Charmaine," "Gimme a Little Kiss, Will Ya' Huh?" "Bye, Bye, Blackbird," "In a Little Spanish Town," and "When the Red, Red Robin Comes Bob, Bob, Bobbing Along."

To the sorrow of millions of devoted fans, Rudolph Valentino dies of peritonitis; so does the great Houdini, two months later.

In England, Elizabeth Alexandra Mary is born, and before her twenty-sixth birthday, she will become Elizabeth II, queen of Great Britain and Northern Ireland.

On a farm near Auburn, Massachusetts, Dr. Robert H. Goddard demonstrates the first rocket using liquid fuel. The flight lasts 2.5 seconds, and the height reached is only 184 feet, but a new age has arrived.

For Will Rogers, 1926 is one of his most productive years. He resumes his lecture tour late in January. By April 30, he is aboard the luxury liner *Leviathan,* headed for England with his oldest son, Will, Jr. Betty and the other children, Mary and Jim, are to follow later. Arriving in England, father and son are confronted by the paralyzing general strike.

In addition to his already taxing writing commitments—the daily column, "The Worst Story I've Heard Today," and his weekly column—Will now embarks on still another writing assignment.

Will visits American-born Lady Astor, the wife of Lord Waldorf Astor, and the first woman to sit in the House of Commons. On July 29, he sends a cable to Adolph S. Ochs, publisher of *The New York Times,* praising Nancy Astor's loyalty to her native land. Ochs promptly prints the cable the following day on page 19. This is the beginning of a new feature, called the "Daily Telegram," which will give Rogers more national and international exposure than any other contemporary columnist.

While in Europe, Will and Carl Sterns Clancy film twelve travelogues in a number of countries. With titles written by Will Rogers, these films will be released by Pathé Exchange, Inc., in 1927.

Will also applies for a visa to fly to Moscow. His observations on that trip appear in ten installments in the *Saturday Evening Post,* and later as two books: *Letters of a Self-Made Diplomat to His President* and *There's Not a Bathing Suit in Russia & Other Bare Facts.*

Back in England, Will makes a motion picture, *Tip Toes,* with

Dorothy Gish and Nelson ("Bunch") Keyes. When approached by his friend Charles Cochran, often called Britain's Ziegfeld, Rogers agrees to help save his faltering show. Will is billed as "The Famous American Humorist." Featured with Will are Hermione Baddeley, Annie Kroft, and Ernest Thesinger.

Though he is warned that the British sense of humor is quite unlike America's, Will decides to present an act similar to his performances in the *Follies;* he will simply comment on the events of the day.

Will Rogers opens on Monday, July 19. As usual before any appearance, he is nervous. Writes *The Times* of London on Wednesday, July 21, 1926:

> Mr. Will Rogers, the American comedian and film actor, appeared on Monday night in Cochran's Revue at the London Pavilion. He is presenting each night for a season of at least six weeks, the "turn" that has earned him such popularity in America. He walks on to the stage in an ordinary, shabby suit—and just talks. At the first performance on Monday night, he talked a little too much, but that mistake can be rectified. At the beginning, Mr. Rogers seemed a little timid. He need not have been. Humour of the kind in which he delights, is international, and in a very few days he will be attracting all London to the Pavilion.

And James Agate, the dean of London's critics, writes in *The Times* of Sunday, July 25, 1926: "Mr. Rogers frankly and generously accepted our recognition of him as an exceptional person, belonging to an exceptional race. . . . A superior power has seen fit to fling into the world, for once a truly fine specimen, fine in body, fine in soul, fine in intellect. . . . America's Prime Minister of Mirth enchanted in both matter and manner."

No salary had been agreed between Rogers and Cochran, no contract had been signed. At the end of the limited engagement—the show is now sold out nightly—Cochran offers a blank check and suggests that Will fill in the amount. Will tears up the check.

Will also finds time to appear at a number of benefits, including one in Dublin, for the victims of a disastrous theater fire in Dromcolliher. Eamon de Valera is in the audience.

Will Rogers has been in Europe less than five months. During that time, he has written daily and weekly columns; he has made a feature film and twelve travelogues; he has appeared in benefit performances, and for six weeks in a West End show; he has traveled around Europe and flown to Moscow; he has started the "Daily Telegram," and gathered enough material for ten feature articles—and two books. It is time to return to America, and go back to work.

On September 22, the Rogers family is on the *Leviathan* headed for New York City. While aboard, news is received of a devastating Florida hurricane. Will immediately arranges for special benefit performances, and corrals fellow passenger Charles Evans Hughes, the former secretary of state, as his partner in a comedy act. Together the two men raise almost $40,000 in two nights. On October 4, Will Rogers is back on the lecture circuit.

Returning home to Beverly Hills, California, on December 21, Will is greeted by a celebrating crowd. In his absence he has been chosen honorary mayor of Beverly Hills.

Watching the Action of a Paris Taxi Meter

Well, I felt I had a right to go to Europe because I believe that I am one of the few Americans that have seen America first. I haven't seen near all of it, and when I get back I am going to look over some more. Now I had been over to Europe two or three times, years ago, but I thought: Well, I will go and see if the Boys have scared up anything new. They hadn't anything new, but the prices.

Well, we was in London, little Bill and I, he's 14. We were over there prowling around, waiting for school to be out and the rest of the troup to come on over. Well, after doing London, of course in the natural course of the tourist route, why, Paris comes next. We had read and heard a lot about all this "Flying to Paris." Bill was pretty strong for it. He had been up in a plane before, out in Los Angeles and flew around over our house and waved to us. So he was sure that this would be just like that. Well, I wasn't so sure about that, but it's pretty tough to have a little kid kinder make a sucker out of the old man, in a way daring him to do something, and I didn't want to let him know that I was getting old that fast. So I finally said: Bring on your Airship! Trot out your old English Channel, here is an old country boy that will either fly the Channel, swim it, or jump it!

No son was going to feel ashamed of the old man, especially away from home. Now they fly over there every day, rain or shine. I had always sorter thought that they couldn't do much airshipping in the rain. But, my goodness, if that was the case over in that country, they never could fly at all.

Well, there is two big lines that go over, the English and the French. I got to thinking and I said, "I think we better go over on the French. I think they had more Aces in the war, and then, when they get across the Channel, they ought to know the country better." In other words, I picked them because they would be flying toward home, and I figured it was better to be with a fellow that was trying to get home, than one that was trying to get away from home. He will use a little more effort. Now in coming back this way, why, of course, I would choose the British. But it wasn't the coming back, it was the getting over that was worrying me right then.

We drove out to the edge of London, and when you drive out to the edge of London, why, you have drove out to the edge of something. It begin to look from the taxi meter, like London didn't have any edges. Between the constant clicking of the taxi meter, and the thought of that airship over the Channel, why, I was what you might call a mildly nervous man.

It was a frizzling rain and a high wind. I thought, well, if it takes wind to keep an airship up, we certainly ought to be able to stay up, for we sure got us some wind.

We started right in not being able to understand anybody, for everybody around the joint was a Frenchman. The rate over to Paris, in our money, was about $32.50. Flying in Europe is really about as cheap as railways, when you take into consideration sleeper fares and meals and all the extra time it takes. They have a line from Berlin to Moscow. In one day they fly over all those countries, and think nothing of it. And the funny part is, that Americans go over to Europe and fly, that at home if you wanted one to get up on a ladder and hang a picture, they would say, "Oh, I just can't stand to be up in the air!"

There was eight or ten big planes out there, and some smaller ones. Finally a man that spoke what he thought was English, said to me: "Do you want to go in a small plane, or a big one?"

Bill said a small one. I said a big one. I asked how many would be in the small plane and he said three. Bill asked if the small plane wasn't faster. The man said, "Oh, yes."

Well, that didn't particularly appeal to me. I got to thinking and I couldn't think of a single thing that I was in a hurry to get to Paris for. So then I got Bill off to one side, and I explained to him what a wonderful thing it would be to go home, and tell about this big plane, this giant airplane that he flew across the Channel in. That if he told that just three of us flew over, that would be no novelty, but if he could tell them a whole gang flew over, why, that would be different. I was sparring to get some company, in fact as much company as possible on that plane with me. I had read somewhere that there is supposed to be safety in numbers.

I saw a plane a-loading up and on it we got. The wind pretty near

83

blowed us off the steps, climbing up into it. I thought maybe on account of the wind and rain, they will declare, "No flight today!" And that would give me another day to think up some new excuse for going on the boat. I thought maybe they give out "wind checks." But no sir, they just started packing us in there. There was room for 10 passengers, and there were 10 passengers, and the pilot, and another fellow that stood by the pilot. It looked like he was there in case of the thing falling, he could advise the pilot just where would be the best place to fall.

It's all closed in. The people are in the middle, and the engines are out to the side, one on each side of you, all right out in the open. When that big thing commenced leaving the ground, and getting up in the air, no Britisher ever craved London any more than I did. Then I started to think, maybe Bill was right, the little plane would have been better. This one is so heavy, I doubt if the air will hold it up.

If you ever saw a beautiful country in the world to look at, it's England from the air. You would just start to try and enjoy a wonderful old castle and fields down below, when somebody would take what air there was under us away, and the plane would settle straight down, like an elevator. Your stomach would try to change places with your head. Then we would find some nice, concreted air road and we'd be sailing along fine. Then it would just remind you of surfaced roads back home. You would come to a place where somebody didn't vote road bonds, and you would hit a bunch of ruts. The old stomach would commence to sorter want to get through your throat again. I looked back in the seat behind me, and poor little William had located a kind of lunch basket effect, that seems to be standard equipment on one of those Cross-Channel planes. He wasn't just examining it, he was seeing if it was practical.

A Japanese across the twelve inch passageway, looked like he would like to commit hari-kari. After making my examination of adjoining companions, I happened to glance out the window. Somebody had taken the land out from under us. We had no air just a minute ago; now we had no land! And what scares you is that you know the ship is not made to land on water. It only has wheels, and no one has ever been able to coast very far on any kind of wheel on the water.

I commenced wanting France. I said, "Lafayette, here I come! Bring your land to meet me!"

By this time all the sick had totally passed out. Little Bill was asleep, and I begin to envy him then. We hit France finally, and somebody hadn't paid their poll tax, and we hit more air pockets, or chug holes.

It reminded me of motoring in Virginia. By continuous gulping, and main force, it looked like I would land with my original cargo, when all at once I looked out, and there was an airport below us, and the plane didn't coast down to it. He just dropped right down into it. Well, he broke my clear record with the last 500 feet that he dropped.

Bill claims that he didn't get a fair chance at it, and wants another crack at some other trip. Well, airplanes are great, but take it from me, it's the last 500 feet that's the hardest.

That's how Bill, Jr., and I blowed into what is familiarly called, the Gay City. I only had a couple of days to spend there, as I was on my way to Geneva, to see what a delegation of good Americans were doing in the way of disarming at an annual argument they were holding there.

Anyhow, we step off our airplane, kinder pale and staggering, but we make it to a taxicab. The taxicabs in France have the lowest start in the way of money, of any taxicab in the world. That is, they start in at one Franc. Now a Franc on the Tuesday afternoon, at four-thirty, when we were in this cab, was worth in our money less than three cents, and there is, Lord knows, how many Centimes in a Franc. Well, at each turn of the front wheel of the cab, the meter jumped 10 Centimes. Well, you have just settled back, figuring here is something in Paris that I will get for nothing, for this thing is only one Franc and that is just about half a nickle. You have gone about a couple of blocks, and you are looking out, watching what they call Peasants, pushing their wine carts by. In our country, with the same load, they would be called Plutocrats. You have just missed some dozen odd people by less than a quarter of an inch, driven on every side of the street there is, over the edges of the sidewalks, down a couple of what we would call Alleys, where you would say, "Well, we are safe here; it's a one-way street because there is no one that could pass us in here." All at once, here comes a truck, loaded with fresh wine, labeled 1888. You say we can't pass that in this narrow place, and you can't, but you do. Then, when your blood pressure is approaching normal again, you just casually glance at the taxi meter. It registers in Francs and in Centimes, but the figures are rolling by your eyes so fast, you would have to stop them to see what they did say. No human mind can read 'em as fast as they click by. You say, my goodness, I have only gone a couple of blocks, but the number of Francs is caught up with the Centimes, and now they are both chasing each other around the clock.

Traffic halts you, but it don't halt that thing. They have a way when they are standing still, that it don't interfere with the movement of the meter. You arrive at your destination, some ten American blocks away, and you hand them a hand full of Francs, and then he comes back with "For Me! You no pay For Me!" Of course, I tipped him, but I give him another little bale. And if you stop to count up, it has just cost you $3.80 to ride what you could have made the same trip in New York, for 45 cents, and no argument about "For Me!" One always tips the driver, but that "For Me!" that's an extra tip for giving them the first tip.

So your last chance of getting anything cheap in Paris has gone a-glimmering. They certainly started right with the meter when you got in, but from then on, brother, it showed you some speed. You think, on account of these Francs changing so fast in the rate of exchange, that you should be getting the best of it. Yes, that's another pet illusion. But those French, they are up in the morning setting those prices, and no jump that Franc will make during the day will ever catch up with them. It could drop to one cent a piece in American money, and they would still be ahead of you. You know, the American gets the idea that when he sees in the last paper that the Franc has reached a certain low price, he just can't hardly keep from going out and buying. He gets the idea that he is putting something over on his foreign hosts. I don't know why he thinks the Frenchman can't read those same reports. So I couldn't spend any particular time worrying about the poor, downtrodden Frenchman with the low cost of the Franc, especially if he comes in contact with Americans in any way. It may be tough on them to deal with each other, but if you will just give one of them 10 minutes with an American, you can save your pity for something that needs it.

Then there is another great gag they have over there. You know people in all these countries speak different languages, but they are supposed to write figures in the same language. For instance, when you get your bill in a cafe, all you should have to do, is read the figures on it. A hand writing expert can't read the figures. Now every American always warns every other one, "Do add up your bill! You really are supposed to. It's not considered cheap, like it is in America, when you do it. Always add up!" Well, here is what you will find. The 3's are all made to add up, and look like 8's; 7's like 9's. So you take to figuring a system where there is no such thing as three and seven, and jump them up a few notches to 8's and 9's and you have a pretty good percentage system working for you. The men running Monte Carlo are just apprentices in the percentage figuring game, compared to these.

You see, there is another thing over here that we are slow getting accustomed to. Over home, if you go into a place and order ham and eggs, and coffee, why, when the bill comes, it would have those two objects on it. Ham and eggs so much, and coffee so much. There would be two items, that's all. But in France, and other places, there would be a long slip. So many Centimes or Francs for waiter taking order, so much for rent, so much for bread, so much for butter, and if by any chance you had a glass of water with it, that would be harder to get and costs more than the ham and eggs. Now the ham and eggs would be split in the addition. They don't pair any two things in billing over there. Bread and butter may eventually get together in the hands of an expert American, but they will be priced separately.

Then there is luxury tax; then a cover charge, even if you are eating on the sidewalk with no cover over you. Pepper and salt are only served on demand. So generally, what started out to be only a light breakfast, will add up to be a dinner. Just try to find out what these 12 items are on the bill. They all speak English when selling you something, but if asked to explain a bill, their English gets back to native again.

So from what I have been able to learn about these people in a kind of an offhand way, I'd say that they don't take bad care of themselves in any financial arrangement. Europe is supposed to be artistic, but if I had to judge, I should place their financial ability ahead of their artistic one.

So in offering prayers for downtrodden races, I would advise you not to overlook the downtrodden tourist.

What to Look Out for—and at—in Italy

I wish you could see Rome. It's the oldest uncivilized town in the world. New York is just as uncivilized, but it's not as old. Rome has more churches and less preaching in them than any city. Everybody wants to see where Saint Peter was buried, but nobody wants to try to live like him.

Rome wasn't built in a day. It's not a Miami Beach by any means. All tourist agencies advise you to spend at least 10 days seeing it. The hotels advise you to take four months. Now what I wanted to do, was to cover Rome from a human-interest point of view. In other words, I wanted to see something that was alive. I am, I bet you, the only one that ever visited the city that didn't run myself ragged dragging from one old church to another, and from one old oil painting to the next.

87

In the first place, I don't care anything about oil paintings. Ever since I struck a dry hole near the old home ranch in Oklahoma, I have hated oil, in the raw, and all its subsidiaries. I just don't want to see a lot of old pictures. If I wanted to see old pictures, I would get D. W. Griffith to revive the Birth of a Nation. That's the best old picture there is.

You know, about 9-10th of the stuff going under the guise of art, is bunk. They call it art to get to take off the clothes. When you ain't nothing else, you can claim to be an artist—and nobody can prove you ain't. No matter how you built anything and how you painted anything, if it accidentally, through lack of wars or rain happened to live a few hundreds of years, why, it is art now. Maybe when the guy painted it at the time he never got another contract.

Now we call Rome the Seat of Culture, but somebody stole the chair. Today it has no more culture than Minneapolis or Long Beach, California. They live there in Rome amongst what used to be called Culture, but that don't mean a thing. We have men in Washington, who live where Washington and Jefferson and Hamilton lived, but as far as the good it does them, they might just as well have the capitol down in Claremore, Oklahoma. You see, association has nothing to do with culture.

I know Englishmen that have had the same well-bred butler all their lives, and they are just as rude as they ever were. Why, do you know, one of the most cultured men I ever saw came from Texas, and where he learned it, the Lord only knows.

Then another thing you got to take into consideration. If a town had any culture, and tourists commenced hitting it, your culture is gone. Tourists will rub it out of any town. Now you take tourists. There is one of the hardest working business that you could possibly adopt— the business of trying to see something. They will leave a nice, comfortable home with all conveniences, and they will get them a ticket to Europe, and from then on they stop being human; they just turn sheep. The guide is the sheep herder. After a bunch of tourists have been out a couple of weeks and get broke in good, the guide don't have to do much; they know about when to bunch up and start listening. They kinder pull in together like a covey of quail and form a sort of half circle while the guide tells them what he has read in the guide books. They listen and mark it off and move on over to another picture. They come dragging into the hotel at night, and you would think they had walked here from America. If you asked them to do that hard a day's work in their own towns, they would think you was cuckoo.

But I want to tell you they are taking this sight-seeing serious. It's no pleasure; it's a business. They get up early in the morning to start out to see more old churches. Now a church is all right, and they are the greatest things we have in our lives, but not for a steady diet. They figure the earlier they can get out, the more churches you can see that day.

Then they go in great for old ruins. A ruin don't just exactly spellbind me; I don't care how long it has been in the process of ruination. I kept trying to get 'em to show me something that hadn't started to ruin yet.

They got a lot of things called Forums. They are where the senators used to meet and debate—on disarmament, I suppose. They say there were some bloody mob scenes in there. Well, that's one thing they got us licked on. Calling each other a liar, and heaving an inkstand, is about the extent of our senatorial gladiators' warlike accomplishments. I didn't know before I got there, and they told me all this—that Rome had senators. Now I know why it declined. There is quite an argument over the exact spot of Caesar's death. Some say that he was not slain in the senate; they seem to think that he had gone over to a senatorial investigation meeting at some committee room, and that that is where Brutus gigged him. The moral of the whole thing seems to be to stay away from investigations.

Then they show where Mark Anthony delivered his oration, which, as it wasn't written till 500 years after he was supposed to say it, there was some chance there of misinterpretation. I have heard some of our public men's speeches garbled in next morning's paper.

Then they speak of Vergil, he must have been quite a fellow, but he didn't know enough to put his stuff in English, like Shakespeare did, so you don't hear much of him, only in high school and colleges, where he is studied more and remembered less than any single person. I bet you, yourself, right now, don't know over three of Vergil's words. E Pluribus Unum, will just about let you out. I never got to him in school, and I remember that much.

There is quite a few of those old Forums besides the senate one. Evidently Rome was afflicted with a House of Representatives, a Supreme Court, and a Foreign Relations Committee. Course it's just a lot of broken-down marble now. Most of the old pieces are big enough so the tourists can't carry them away. That's the only reason they are there.

Just between you and me, there is one trait that I don't believe any other people in the world have developed to the extent that our folks have. It's impossible to show the American folks something, that if you turn your head, they won't try to carry it home. There is absolutely nothing the American tourist won't carry off. The Grand Canyon is the only thing they haven't carried away yet, and that's only because it's a hole in the ground.

Did you know they used to have a wall around Rome? But the people got to climbing over it so much, they sorter neglected it and let it run down. The wall wouldn't keep the people from getting out. You can't keep people in a place with a wall. If they don't like a town, they will leave it. That wall system is a failure, and always was.

The whole of Rome seems to have been built, painted and decorated by one man; that was Michelangelo. If you took everything out of Rome that was supposed to have been done by Michelangelo, Rome would be as bare of art, as Los Angeles. He was a picture painter, sculptor, a house painter, both inside and out—for in those days they painted the ceilings. He was an architect, a landscape gardener, interior decorator, and I wouldn't doubt if he didn't strum a mean guitar. It's hard to tell you what all that fellow was. We have over home today no single person that compares with him, not even in California.

There was another sort of artistic breed, called the gladiators. A fellow was a gladiator as long as he remained alive. Saturday night was always a rather ticklish time in the life of a gladiator, for that was when they generally announced the entries for the bulldogging contest with the lions the following day. If you defeated your lion, you were allowed to be a gladiator for another week.

These Romans loved blood. What money is to an American, blood was to a Roman. A Roman was never so happy as when he saw somebody bleeding. That was his sense of humor. If we see a fellow slip and fall and maybe break his leg, that's a yell to us; or if his hat blows off and he can't get it. Well, that's the way the Romans were. Where we like to see you lose your hat, they loved to see you leave a right arm and a left leg in the possession of a tiger and then try to make the fence unaided.

The emperor set in his box and would announce with his thumb whether the man was to go to his death or let him live. If the thumb was down, you passed out poco pronto; but if the thumb was up, why you left your phone number and address, where you could be reached the following Sunday afternoon. There was no heavyweight boxing stuff of four years between combats, no dickering over terms. The gate receipts went to the emperor, and you went to the cemetery.

No, sir, Americans are standing guard over not only the best little patch of ground in all the various hemispheres, but we got it on 'em even when it comes to things to see, if we could just make these locoed tourists believe it. Why, say, if the Mississippi ever flowed through, for instance, Switzerland, why, there wouldn't be enough dry ground left to yodle in. If they had Niagara Falls, they would have had 85 wars over it at various times, to see who would be allowed to charge admission to see it. And the Grand Canyon—well, I just don't want to hurt their feelings talking about it. No, sir, Europe has old age to recommend it, and the Petrified Forest in Arizona makes a sucker out of it for old age. Why, that forest was there and doing business before Nero took his first violin lesson.

They do rave over Venice; but there's nothing there but water. Why, Louisiana has more water in their cellars than the whole Adriatic Sea. But I must tell you about Venice. I stepped out of the wrong side of a Venice taxicab, and they were three minutes fishing me out. They have taxi meters on those gondolas, so many knots to the Lira. The greatest drivers in the world are these skippers on these Venice Hansom cabs. They can take two of these crafts and make 'em pass in a bath tub, and never touch either. There is no such thing as a bent fender on one of those hulls. The chauffeur can row so quiet that you can't hear a sound, till you start to pay him and don't tip enough, and then you would think it was a drunk seal in an Aquarium.

I got seasick crossing an alley. These gondoliers that row the boats, hate the motor boats, and when no one is looking, they just casually and accidentally slip an oar into the propellers as they pass. If you love to have someone row you in a boat, you will love Venice. But don't try to go for a walk, or they will be searching for you with grappling hooks.

Monte Carlo is next, then Nice. That's pronounced neece, not nice. They have no word for nice in French.

A Visit to Monte Carlo

I had heard all my life of this pleasant and accommodating little place, called Monte Carlo. We had heard about "The Man that broke the Bank at Monte Carlo." Well, I was down in Italy and got caught in a tourist drive drifting north, and was swept right along with them. No man in the world is strong enough to buck a tourist tide when it gets in full swing. They had visited all the old churches, and they were looking for new churches to conquer. They were just a-raring to see some more old ruins. So while they was headed for some old cathedral that they were keeping standing just for the American trade, why, I branched off over toward this Monte Carlo layout. Not that I was in any way raring to speculate, but I wanted to see it so I could warn you readers just what numbers to play when you get there.

Well, Monte Carlo is not only a game, but it's a country. It's the only country in the world that has practically no rural population. You either live in the city of Monte Carlo, or you don't live in Monaco. If you are out of town, you are in France or Italy; or, if you get too far out in the country, you are in Spain or Switzerland. There is some pretty good ideas about the place. For instance, you don't have any taxes to pay. The casino takes care of everything. I thought maybe it was going to be hard to get in there, but there is only one requirement and that one is not so hard for an American to live up to. That is to answer: Do you live in Monaco? You see, they won't let a fellow from the old home town go in and wager. He has to go to France to bet his excess tax money. Now that struck me as being a very fine trait in the government of Monaco. They practically say to their own flesh and blood: Stand back till we trim these suckers. If we ever need any extra money for yachts or palaces, we will let you home folks know, but we don't want to call on you until we absolutely have to.

I didn't think there was room for anyone else to live in Monaco, unless they went out and annexed some more territory. You show your passport. Well, you do that anywhere over in Europe. Also, if you have never written an autobiography of your life, you haven't signed a foreign hotel register. All an American newspaper will have to do when you pass out, and leave no record of yourself, they can get a continental register and add the date of your death, and it will give everything you ever did, and the great part of it is that it was written by yourself. Oh, yes, at Monte Carlo they also collect a fee on entrance. If I live a thousand years I will never know why they do that. It seems so unnecessary. Unless that entrance money goes to a different corporation.

The casino is a very large building; that is, it is large for such a small country. They been wanting to put another wing on it, but France won't lease them the ground. As you go in, you will see a beautiful big yacht floating majestically by the dock. It does not, as you might think belong to someone who is playing there. It belongs to the Prince of Monaco. His uncle, whom this prince succeeded, died a year or so ago, in what you wouldn't hardly call destitute circumstances. So this young prince moved into the palace and the family yacht. Due to the good feeling of all the world, the old fortune has not been allowed to dwindle away to any great extent.

The old uncle was a great fisherman that was always touring all over the world, searching for strange fish. He had an aquarium there, showing them, but most of them are dead and stuffed. He didn't seem to be able to capture many alive, like he does in that casino.

I wanted to shoot a little craps and take a hand at stud poker, but they just had a lot of women's games like baccarat and roulette. The roulette wheel only had one "0" on it, it didn't have a double "0" that fooled me to the idea that it was pretty near on the level.

Well, to make a fair bankroll short, it don't take me long to learn about the game. If ever in your life you saw queer people, I bet you they couldn't touch the ones there. Some of them, they say, have been there for years. Mostly old ones, they would be sitting there for hours, keeping track of what number come up, and marking it down. They might not make a bet an hour. They seemed to have it timed perfectly, just when to lose. A fellow there told me they were playing a system, and they only bet at certain times. When I bet without a system, why, they looked at me like I was crazy. I don't know why, because I was losing just as good as they were.

There is one or two rooms where the bigger bettors go. You pay extra to get in there. I tried it too. It was much better than those common rooms, you could lose faster.

This Monaco is the only place I have been where everything is running fine. There is no government, there is nothing to interfere with anything, or anybody, just that little old wheel running for them all the time.

Monte Carlo has the right idea; fix a game where you are going to get people's money, but the people don't mind you getting it. A fellow can always get over losing money in a game of chance, but he seems so constituted that he can never get over money thrown away to a government in taxes.

Yes, that prince has a great business; it works while he sleeps.

A Lecture on Russia

This is about Russia. It has always been a source of wonder to me how some congressmen can go to Paris to investigate the cafes, have four cocktails and a Russian caviar sandwich—which they didn't like—and then go back home and tell of the conditions as they exist today in Russia.

There has been more said and written about Russia than there has been about honesty in politics, and there has been just as little done about it. Now there is Russia, the biggest country in the world, and men and women will write authoritative opinions on it that couldn't give you a bird's eye view of the Principality of Monaco. I am the only person that ever wrote on Russia that admits he don't know a thing about it. And on the other hand, I know just as much about Russia as anybody that ever wrote about it. You see, nobody knows anything about Russia. If you are looking for me to solve the Russian problem, you are not going to get it done. Now a congressman could do it in twenty minutes, and a senator in ten, but I am just going to tell you everything I saw in Russia.

I left London one morning about 9:30, and flew over some of the prettiest country before striking out across the Channel. Flying over Holland in an airship is the only real way to see it, 'cause if you are down on the level—and if you are in Holland you will be standing on the level—Holland's highest point is eight feet six and a third inches above sea level. That is called the mountain region of Holland and that's where they do their skiing and winter sports. Mind you, it's the prettiest and cleanest little country you ever saw in your life.

Amsterdam was the next stop—changed planes for Berlin. Everybody got out and had a few sandwiches and a couple of steins of Holland gin. Into a German plane and out over Germany. We saw forests, the most beautiful forests, all out in rows. Every time they cut down a tree, it looks like they plant two in its place. Every time we cut one down, the fellow that cuts it down sets down to have a smoke and celebrate. He throws his cigarette away and burns up the rest of the forest.

We hit Berlin at 5:30 that afternoon, and at two o'clock in the morning, or night, I left for Russia. This plane was a big German Junker—not only had two engines, and two propellers, but three. One big one in front, and two others as assistants. Well, when a German outfit says they are going to leave at two o'clock, don't you get there at one minute past two. If you do, you will just hear the propeller buzzing around up in the air.

We had about twelve aboard. They had a wireless, or radio, on there, getting weather conditions ahead of them. We got into Koenigsberg about eight o'clock, went in and had breakfast and come out, and there was a German Fokker plane waiting.

It didn't do my nerves any good when they pointed our plane out to me, for it had only one engine. You know, there is some confidence attached when you know there is a sort of bevy of engines, and if one goes wrong, why, some of the others will keep percolating. But I looked at this one and thought, Sister, if you stop on us, we are just smeared over the landscape of Western Russia.

I said that was the plane WE were going to Russia in. I was mistaken—that was the plane *I* was going to Russia in, for I constituted Russia's sole aerial immigration that day. Well, in one way I am generous. If I am going to drop, I don't want the pleasure all to myself; I want to share it with somebody. The plane really could seat five passengers. There was just room for the pilot out in front; the mechanic was sort of in the compartment with me. I didn't know a word of Russian, and this lad in the compartment with me, or the pilot either, didn't know a word of American—not even English.

Now this is 8:30 in the morning, and barring accidents, this same old wash-boiler is scheduled to breeze into Moscow at 6:30 that same afternoon with only one stop, and that was to be Smolensk. I didn't know where this Smolensk was, or what time we were supposed to get there. You know, I think what worried me more than anything else was being somewhere and not being able to talk to anybody. I wouldn't have minded having a wreck, if I could just have asked him on the way down: How fast are we falling? Or any little casual remark, just so he would have understood. It wasn't the height that bothered me, it was keeping my mouth shut a whole day.

Well, we are flying along, and all at once I feel the old Overland stage kinder doing like she was circling. Then I felt her nose heading down like a bronc when he starts to swallow his head. I looked out to see what he was dodging, and below was a little town along a river.

This bird could have lit on an egg, and never broke it. We piled out and I noticed these old hombres getting their passports out and I started reaching for mine. That's one thing you want to carry in your hand anywhere in Europe. They just seem to get a pleasure out of having you dig for it. Well, the officer that took it, started in yapping about something and I told him that he was fooling away his time, and wasting some kind of mighty good language on me; that I didn't even know what language it was, much less the words; that I spoke only English, and that up to only two syllable words.

He went off and dug up another one that knew a little English. There was a lot of soldiers and a lot of activity there. This new one said to me: "You have no veesay!" I showed him my passport and the damage the Russians had done to it in London for quite a few dollars.

"Yes, Russia; but no Lithuania!"

Lithuania? Why, I never even heard of it, much less getting a veesay to it. Where are we anyway? I thought I was going to Russia. Well, they soon made it known to me that they had them a country all right, from the looks of all the officers running around there. At first, when I saw them, I thought they was making a moving picture—it looked just like Hollywood. I soon found it was on the level.

"You should have veesay!" I had to tell them that I didn't even know I was flying over their country, much less landing in it. They called a general war conference. Then they decided to telephone down to the capital, to deal with such an unusual case. So instead of phoning back, they sent a soldier on a bicycle, that I was to pay $3.50. I gave them a Russian ten ruble piece. They wasn't any too anxious to take it, but they did and went off for change, when I told them just to keep the change and let the army have a drink on me.

If I had just thought and told them I was a friend of President Wilson's, I would have got by, because he is the one that laid out all these countries. It was one of those self-determination of small nations. No man ever lived that had more noble ideas than Mr. Wilson, and any time a committee would come to him with ten names signed on an application, and tell him that they wanted a country, why, he would give them one.

Anyhow, I gathered up my two Russians, and we was off. Now in going into Russia, I think I am just like a majority of people—we don't know what it is like. My one impression of Russia was a sleigh going through the forest, with deep snow on the ground, pulled by a horse with a big high yoke up over its neck, and the wolves jumping up, biting at the horse's throat. So after thinking of that picture and the wolves, I believe that is why I took the airplane in there. We were flying nice and low and you could see all the people out in the fields working—well, not exactly *all* the people, but the ones that were women. Then every time we would pass over a little town or village, you would see a kind of market place, and all the men would be gathered there. If the wives raise anything, why, the husbands are perfectly willing to take it to town and sell it.

The only mysterious occurrence of the trip happened just before we got into this Smolensk. This mechanic in there with me pulled the curtains tight over the windows on both sides and I couldn't see out. Then I felt the plane turning and knew we were landing. There was nothing to see after I got on the ground. There was some kind of military operations going on around there, as they are always arguing with Poland, and this is near the border. Every nation in Europe goes to bed with a gun under its pillow.

Whatever they were trying to keep from me—they kept it. The plane was loaded with gas. It's along in the afternoon by now, and this old Russian Casey Jones grabbed his throttle and this other one kept his blinds pulled till we were away out of town. I tell you, we were breezing along and we went into Moscow right on the dot—not a minute late. The field was full of airplanes. These guys over in Europe, they have left the ground and they are up in the air. Nobody is walking, but us; everybody else is flying. So in a few years, when somebody starts dropping something on us, don't say I didn't tell you!

You see, if America don't look out, they will be caught in the next war with nothing but a niblick and a putter. If you think there ain't going to be any next war, you better see some of these nations drilling and preparing, and they are not the people that will go to work and learn a trade that they are not going to work at. Of course, I am like the old rooster when he brought out the ostrich egg and showed it to all the hens, and said: "I am not criticizing, but I just want you to know what others are doing!" Now that's an old gag, but it has to be an old gag to get over. So I want you all to know what even Russia is doing. Everybody is using their air for something besides speeches, but us.

Now everybody had said to me about going into Russia: "Now don't take anything with you. They examine everything." So I took in only one suit and four extra shirts, as I was told that if I took in too much, I would be suspected of capitalistic tendencies. I debated with myself for a long time in the hotel in Berlin the night before I left, whether two extra pair of socks, instead of one, would constitute capitalistic affluence.

Anyhow, I went into a little customs office. Talk about bringing in anything, why, I could have had a grand piano in there and he would never have seen it.

Now the next thing I want to dispel is one popular illusion that everybody has to watch his conduct while in there. Everybody said: "Be very careful what you say or do while in there; they have spies and secret police all over the place. Every waiter or servant in the hotel, they let on they don't speak English, but they do, and they report everything. It's that G.P.U., the famous secret police organization of Russia."

Well, they had me so scared, if anybody said to me: "It's a nice day today," I would be afraid even to agree with them. I would just nod my head both ways, kind of half yes, and a 50 per cent no. I was as agreeable to everybody as an insurance agent before he lands you. I had seen pictures of long trains wending their way along the Trans-Siberian Railway, hauling heavy loads of human freight, when nobody had a return ticket but the conductor, all perhaps for getting funny with Russia. So if I thought of an alleged wise crack, it was immediately stifled before reaching even the thorax. I looked, I absorbed, but I didn't utter.

I talked to various government officials connected with the Foreign Department and they would explain anything that I would ask them about the government, or the country. One thing that a Communist can do, is explain. You ask him any question in the world, and if you give him long enough, he will explain their angle, and it will sound plausible then. Communism to me is one-third practice, and two-thirds explanation.

I wanted, of course, to see Trotsky. I wanted to tell you how he stacked up. Well, I went to see a man about seeing Trotsky, a little fellow named Rothstein, who spoke English and used to work on a paper in England; he has now to do with censoring all that goes out to the press. I told him that the nature of the visit to Trotsky was to find out just what kind of a guy he was personally; that I didn't want any of his state secrets. I just wanted to see did he drink, eat, sleep, laugh and act human, or was his whole life taken up for the betterment of mankind.

Mr. Rothstein informed me: "We are a very serious people; we do not go in for fun and laughter. We have a great work to perform for the betterment of mankind. We are sober."

Well, I explained to him that I didn't hardly expect Trotsky to make any faces for me, or to turn a few somersaults, or tell funny stories. I told him that on account of being in America at one time, Trotsky had always been of special interest to us. I wanted to tell them that what they needed in their government was more of a sense of humor, and less of a sense of revenge.

I saw that this old boy wasn't so strong for me x-raying Trotsky, but I bet you, if I had met him and had a chat with him, I would have found him a very interesting and human fellow, for I have never yet met a man I didn't like. When you meet people, no matter what opinion you might have formed about them beforehand, why, after you meet them, and see their angle and their personality, why, you can see a lot of good in all of them.

Anyhow, the real fellow that is running the whole thing in there is a bird named Stalin, a great two-fisted egg from away down in the Caucasian mountains. He is the stage manager of Bolshevism right now. He don't hold any great high position himself, but he tells the others what ones they will hold.

I met a big, nice jovial fellow from Chicago—forgot his name. He was feeling pretty good about the whole way things were running in Russia, and he was very enthusiastic about it all; he was strong for them—but he had a passport back! I bet you, if you had stolen that passport away from that old boy, you would have just had 284 pounds' worth of suicide on your hands. And Americans you meet over there visiting, they are so enthusiastic about it, and believe in it away above our form of government—but they all go back home. It just looks to me like Communism is such a happy family affair, but not a Communist wants to stay where it is practiced. It's the only thing they want you to have, but they keep none themselves.

I read so many of that fellow Marx's books that I don't even want to see the Marx Brothers, as clever as they are. I have come to the conclusion that the reason there is so many books on Socialism is because it's the only thing in the world you can't explain easy. It's absolutely impossible for any Socialist to say anything in a few words. You say: "Is it light, or dark?" and it takes him two volumes to answer yes, or no, and then I know there is a catch in it somewhere. If Socialists worked as much as they talked, they would be the most prosperous style of government in the world. But there is not two of them with the same idea of what it is.

Liberty don't work as good in practice, as it does in speech. That bunch of fellows in Russia are playing with the biggest toy in the world. Now you have to have some kind of training to handle something big, or else you have to do a lot of practicing on it after you get in, which is generally pretty expensive. So you see, they are practicing, but unfortunately they are practicing on all those millions of people that have to remain the horrible example, till these guys in charge find out just what it is all about. It's no disgrace not to be able to run a country, but it is a disgrace to keep on trying when you know you can't do it.

You see, the Communism that they started out with—the idea that everybody would get the same and have the same—Lord, that has all been changed. The idea that the fellow that was managing the bank was to get no more than the man that swept it out, why, that talked well to a crowd, but they got no more of that than we have. They get what they can, and where they can get it. When the government runs anything, as they do practically everything over there, there is always about twice or three times as many working in the place, as would be found in private enterprise. It takes about two to watch one, and then four to watch those two.

Of course, anyone going into Russia will ask: Is everybody happy? Well, they are not. Over 90 per cent of the population are farmers, and live out in the country, or villages. The revolution was to get the peasant the land. They took the land that the rich had away from them, and it's now owned by the government. They give it to the peasant, but the government tells the farmer what he shall get for his products! Well, the farmer, when he sells his grain, he can't take the money and go buy what he needs. That costs him more than his grain brought him; and if he did happen to have enough money, then the things he needs are not to be found to buy. So what does the farmer do? Well, the Russian farmer may be illiterate, but he is not what you might call dumb. He just raises enough for his own use, and he is living on what he raises. He has got the whole Communist Party about cuckoo at this minute. One thing I do know: The Russians think they figured out everything in their Communist system, except how to get enough to eat.

It seems to me the whole idea of Communism, or whatever they want to call it, is based on propaganda and blood. Their whole life and thought is to convince somebody else. It looks to me like if a thing is so good, and if it is working so fine for you, you would kind of want to keep it to yourself. But they start their propaganda at the cradle in Russia. They have a great many schools which seem intent not so much to eliminate illiteracy, as they are to teach propaganda. Political propaganda starts with their A B C. Everything is of the revolutionary type. If it is a painting, the main character has one foot on a capitalist's neck, and he is punching another capitalist in the jaw. Talk about some of our states controlling what their schoolbooks contain, why, these children never get a chance to read anything, only how horrible everything is but Communism. You can't go to a book store and buy any book you want. Every book that is sold in Russia has to be O.K.'d by the Soviet Party. So you have to learn their angle, or you don't learn anything; there is nothing else to form an opinion about.

But the people are no more Communists than you are. The country is run by the Communist Party, which has less than 600,000 members, and they run all those millions. Siberia is still working. It's just as cold on you to be sent there under the Soviets, as it was under the Czar. The only way you can tell a member of the party from an ordinary Russian, is that the Soviet man will be in a car. They are all supposed to receive $112 a month, which is supposed to be the salary of all Communists that do work for the government. Well, some of them must be pretty good managers to get along as well as they do on that.

There is as much class distinction in Russia today, as there is in Charleston, South Carolina. Why, I went to the races there, and the grandstand had all the members of the party, and over in the center field stood the mob in the sun. Well, there was Bourgeois and Proletariat distinction for you.

You see, here is what makes it look kinder bad: these fellows took over a country that was already a going concern; they didn't have a cent of debt—they repudiated all of the old Russia's debt. Now the biggest expense of any country is its interests on its national debt. The Communists confiscated everything, paid nobody for anything, and had everything that the entire country possessed. They claimed they didn't want any salary for doing it, so that should have eliminated another big expense. Now if you can't take a country that's handed to you like that, what chance have you got with it when there is a big indebtedness? So it don't look like they have manipulated their affairs any too good. They have been messing with Russia and it's a good thing that those millions are not organized, or there would be a change in government.

And the funny thing is that they have changed their scheme around a dozen times since they been in, and they are liable to change it a dozen more times, because none of them ain't what you would exactly call a-hitting right. Communism will never get anywhere till they get that basic idea of propaganda out of their head, and replace it with some work. If they had plowed as much as they propagandered, they would be richer than the Principality of Monaco. The trouble is they got their theories out of a book. Why, that guy Marx was like one of those efficiency experts; he could explain to you how you could save a million, and he couldn't save enough himself to eat on. He wrote for the dissatisfied, and the dissatisfied is the fellow who wants to figure out where he and his friends can get something for nothing.

The Communists have some good ideas, of course, but they got a lot that sound better than they work. They say Russia is supposed to be run by everybody—well, it looks it.

Some days in there, it would really look to me like they were trying to do something, and were going to get somewhere; and the next day you would see stuff that would make you think: What have all these millions of innocent, peace-loving people done, that through no fault of their own they should be thrown into a mess like this, with no immediate prospect of relief?

And now we are going to get down to religion. The Russians, from what little I have read, were about the most wholehearted, God-fearing people. Practically all of them were devout members of the Russian Orthodox Church. Some of the most wonderful churches in the world are in Russia. Now the basic foundation of the Communist

Party is to be an atheist. You can't belong to the Party and belong to a church—no matter what church.

They will tell you that the worship of Lenin is their religion. Lenin preached revolution, blood and murder in everything I have read of his. Now they may dig themselves up a religion out of that, but I don't think anyone that just made a business out of proposing revolutions for a steady diet would be the one to pray to, and try to live like. I can't understand by what reckoning they think that everybody connected with running the country should be a non-believer. If the Communists say that religion was holding the people back from progress, let it hold them back! Progress ain't selling that high. If it is, it ain't worth it.

Anyhow, think of everybody in a country going to work! I mean to produce something, to be of some benefit to the whole community. Just look at the millions of us here that today haven't done a thing that helps the country, or that helps anybody. We have just gone along and lived off the country, and we are just lousy with satisfaction in ourselves. We prospered for years on nothing but our natural resources. Well, Russia got twice as much of anything we ever had before we used it up.

Those rascals, along with all their kooky stuff have some good ideas. If just part of 'em work out, it's liable to have us winging on our foreign trade, and they are going to be hard to get along with. But that's for the president, and our secretary of war to worry about.

Good Crops Can Do a Lot for a President

Well, all I know is just what I read in the papers, and it's so long before we get a paper over here in England. I been wanting to get a line on some home politics, but by the time the paper gets here, my candidate has been beaten in the primary and is hollering for a recount, before I even know he has run.

Just how is things breaking at home anyway? Some papers we get over here say Coolidge is sorter skidding on the turns and they look for him to throw a tire in the home stretch. Other papers of the opposition form of public insanity claim that it is just a little natural reaction setting in, that a man can't go on high every minute; that he has to sorter slow up and look back every once in a while to see if anybody is getting close to him. Course, there has been a lot of races lost by looking back at the wrong time.

They claim that the farmers are kinder losing confidence in the president helping them out. Well, he is pretty wise; he knows there ain't many farmers. There is an awful lot of people farming, but if it's only the farmers that are against him, why, he hasn't lost much strength. You got to do more than just live in the country, to be a farmer.

Then you got to figure that it's a long time till the next election. A couple of good crops and any fair luck working along the line of an epidemic of appendicitis among the Boll Weevil, or fallen arches in the Chinch Bugs, all play just as big a part in the national career of a man, as his executive ability does.

You give me a few showers, just when I need them most, and let me have the privilege of awarding them around among the doubtful states as I see best; let a certain demand for steel crop up which I didn't even know was going to crop, let the Argentine and Russia have a wheat failure, let the foot and mouth disease hit every country, but west of the Mississippi; let, as I say, all these things happen over which I have no control, but let them happen anyway, and have even me in there as president, and I will be re-elected by such a large majority that I won't even take the pains to talk to you over the radio.

Give me all those things for 8 years in succession, with me as president, and I will give Lincoln a run for his laurels, even if I can't spell "cat," eat with my knife, and don't know a tariff bill from a T-bone steak.

Being great as president is not a matter of knowledge, or farsightedness. It's just a question of the weather—not only in your own country, but in a dozen others. It's the elements that make you great, or break you. If the Lord wants to curse about a dozen other nations that produce the same thing we do, why, then you are in for renomination. If we are picked out as the goat that year, and are reprimanded, why, you might be Solomon himself occupying the White House, and on inauguration day you would be asked to "call in a public conveyance and remove any personal belongings that you might have accumulated." So it's sorter like the World Series—you got to have the breaks.

Everybody figures politics according to what they have accumulated during the last couple of years. Maybe you haven't earned as much as you did a few years ago, because you haven't worked near as hard as you used to, but all you look at is the old balance sheet and if it's in the red, why, his honor, the president, is out in the alley as far as you are concerned. It takes about 20 or 30 years to really tell whether any president really had anything with him, besides sunshine and showers. We have to look over your achievements in view of what they have to do with the future. Course, bad advice will ruin you just about as a total earthquake all over the land would do. If you are trying to be elected, and then listen to a typical politician, or a bunch of them (for there is nothing as shortsighted as a politician, unless it is a delegation of them), why, that's more unlucky than an earthquake.

Well, if you are going to pay any attention to politicians during your administration, you can just right away imagine yourself being referred to as "Ex-President Jasbo." They, I think, can ruin you quicker than unseasonable weather.

Now your personal habits, your looks, your dress, whether you are a good fellow, or not with the boys, the old assumed Rotary or Kiwanis spirit, why that don't mean a thing. You can shut up and never say a word for the entire four years; you can go out and talk everybody deaf, dumb and blind, so it's only when you are asleep that you are quiet; you can be a teetotaler; you can have a drink whenever you like, in all these things and a million others, you can be either on one side or the other, and it won't make the least bit of difference in the world—that is, it won't if the country has enjoyed prosperity, over 90 per cent of which you had no personal control.

Every guy just looks in his pocket and then votes. And the funny part of it is, it's the last year that is the one that counts. You can have three bad ones, and then wind up with everybody having money, and you will win so far, you needn't even stay up to hear the returns. You can go to bed at 10:30. On the other hand, you can get a great first three years of your incumbency, and then the last, or election year, flop on account of drought, and you will be beat so far they will think you was running as a populist.

Who will be president after the next election hasn't got a thing to do with any candidate, or what they do from now to then. Each one of their cards is in the pack, and "Conditions" will be the one to draw out the winner. They say you must have the tide with you to swim the English Channel. Well, you certainly must have the weather with you for four years to keep on being president.

Let's Live Slower and Longer

There is something that we all read in the papers every morning, no matter what paper it is we pick up. It's in there every morning, just like a Florida and California paper has the same headline all winter: Big Blizzard Hits East! New York Freezing! Tremendous Suffering! That stays on the front page from November to March, even if New York has had a heat wave. But that's only during the winter. The item I am speaking of stares you in the face so constantly that you don't even read the names any more: "Four killed and three wounded by Automobile!"

Maybe it's more; maybe it's less, but it's the same every day. As I sit here, writing this, it's Monday and I have the Chicago Tribune in front of me, and here is yesterday's toll just in Chicago: "12 killed, 13 hurt by Autos in City Sunday. Cook County death toll goes to 169 in 1926, an increase over this time last year of 44 deaths, or 34 per cent."

Right over in the adjoining column of the same edition of the paper, is the following: "Annual Auto Bill of U.S. is 14 Billion Dollars per Year."

That's billions, not millions, and it takes a smarter fellow than I am to even tell how many millions there is in one billion. I know our entire debt from the war that foreign nations owed us, even if they had paid it, was only 11 billions. In another part of the paper it tells that 22 thousand met their death last year by auto, and that we are well on the way to beat that record. Fourteen billion dollars we paid to kill 22 thousand. About $635,000 a piece with no charge at all for the wounded. They will run at least two or three times as many as the killed, and FOR WHAT? Why, just to get somewhere a little quicker, that is if you get there at all. Why don't they get on an airship? We can get there three or four times as quick as an automobile. No detours, no kick about bad roads. But no, we won't do that.

Statistics show that of those 22 thousand killed, 70 per cent were pedestrians. So you see the fellow in the auto knows that even in case of an accident, his chances of being hurt is only 30 per cent, while the one walking, is 70 per cent. It don't take any nerve to step into a fast car and go burning 'em up down the road, and maybe have a man step out from behind, or in front of his car, and you bowl him over; or a child maybe, darting across the road and not seeing you.

Now they call all these accidents PROGRESS. Well, maybe it is progress. But I tell you it certainly comes high priced. Suppose around 25 years ago, when automobiles were first invented, that a man—we will say it was Thomas A. Edison—had gone to our government and he had put this proposition up to them: "I can in 25 years time have every person in America riding quickly from here to there. You will save all this slow travel of horse and buggy. Shall I go ahead with it?"

"Why, sure Mr. Edison, if you can accomplish that wonderful thing why we, the government are heartily in accord and sympathy with you."

"But," says Mr. Edison, "I want you to understand it fully, in order to accomplish it, and when it is in operation it will kill 15 to 20 thousand a year of your women and children and men."

"What? You want us to endorse some fiendish invention that will be the means of taking human life? Why, you insult us by asking us to listen to such a plan! Why, if it wasn't for our previous regard for you, we would have you thrown into an asylum! How dare you talk of manufacturing something that will kill more people than a war? Why, we would rather walk from one place to another the rest of our lives, than be the means of taking one single child's life."

Now that is what would have happened, if we had known it. But now, why, it don't mean anything. It's just a matter of fact. Too bad.

Well, we should have been watching. Maybe we was deaf, maybe blind or nearsighted. If Cholera or Smallpox, or some disease killed and left affected that many, why, congress and every agency of the government would be working and appropriating money and doing every mortal thing necessary, to do something about it. But as it is, we go right on, building 'em faster and getting better roads, so we can go even faster and knock over more of them. This is the age of progress; live fast and die quick. That's the slogan. Let's get a gun for our 14 billion bucks per year!

We are always talking about putting something to a vote of the people. We seldom do. Our legislature makes up our minds for us. But suppose you left it to a vote of everybody: Do you want to keep on killing 22 thousand and maiming 50 thousand more every year and pay for the privilege of doing it 14 billions, besides your tremendous road taxes? Now how do you think they would vote on that? It's a pretty tough thing to vote to take human life. Of course it will never come up. The human side of anything can't compare with so-called PROGRESS.

Imagine taking that 14 billion dollars, you know, making them pay it in just the same, and in a couple of years our National Debt would be paid and that would do away with 70 per cent of our taxes; because there is where 70 per cent goes, in interest on our own debt. It would be pretty near worth driving a buggy and team again, if you knew you wasn't killing anybody and that you lived in a country that didn't owe a single dime. Then we would also get the taxes of those 22 thousand. Sounds almost like a promised land, don't it? Well, don't get too enthusiastic about it, because nothing will be done about it. It would pass a national vote, but it ain't going to get there.

1927

About one thousand U.S. Marines are landed in China to protect American property in the raging civil war. Despite precautions, both the U.S. and British consulates are looted.

In France, American dancer Isadora Duncan is strangled to death when one end of her long scarf becomes entangled in the rear wheel of her moving sports car.

On May 20, just minutes before eight o'clock on a rainy morning, Charles A. Lindbergh takes off from Roosevelt Field, Long Island. His plane, the *Spirit of St. Louis,* is powered by a single 220-horsepower engine and carries 450 gallons of gasoline. Thirty-three hours, 29 minutes, and 30 seconds later, on May 21, Lindbergh lands at Le Bourget airfield in Paris. He wins the prize of $25,000 offered in 1919 by Raymond B. Orteig for the first nonstop New York to Paris flight.

In White Plains, New York, real-estate tycoon Edward W. ("Daddy") Browning, aged fifty-one, is sued for divorce by his sixteen-year-old bride of less than a year, Frances Heenan ("Peaches") Browning. During the litigation, which lasts several weeks, the disclosures by Daddy and Peaches on the witness stand receive nationwide coverage.

Nicola Sacco and Bartolomeo Vanzetti die in the electric chair in Massachusetts, despite years of efforts to have the charges against them dropped. Accused of participation in a robbery in which two men are killed, they are tried as "revolutionary Bolsheviks" when anti-United States propaganda leaflets are found in their possession. In 1977, Massachusetts governor Michael Dukakis will issue a proclamation stating that Sacco and Vanzetti had been improperly tried for murder.

For almost twenty years Ford's Model T has been the basic, most reliable automobile, but it has recently been losing ground to the competing Chevrolet. Ford now unveils the Model T's successor—the Model A. There are now more than 20 million cars on U.S. roads. It is not surprising that at least one state, Massachusetts, passes the first compulsory state automobile insurance law. And with increasing automobile traffic come improvements in the highway system. The Buffalo Peace Bridge, joining Canada and the United States, opens in August; in November the Holland Tunnel is dedicated, linking New York City with Jersey City under the Hudson River. The sole prior link between the two neighboring cities were ferry boats.

Transatlantic telephone service is established. The cost is seventy-five dollars for three minutes.

Al Capone, the nation's most notorious gangster, is said to have an annual income of more than $100 million—never equaled by a "private" U.S. citizen. Perhaps with that in mind, the U.S. Supreme Court rules that illegally received income is taxable, too. Armed with this new law, the federal government begins prosecution against the underworld.

In literature, these are the most-remembered books: *Elmer Gantry,* by Sinclair Lewis; *The Treasure of the Sierra Madre,* written first in German by Ben Traven, and then translated; *The Unpleasantness at the Bellona Club,* by Dorothy Sayers.

In Hollywood, where Syd Grauman's Chinese Theatre opens, these films make news: *Flesh and the Devil,* starring Greta Garbo and John Gilbert; *The Unknown,* with Lon Chaney and Joan Crawford; Cecil B. DeMille's *King of Kings,* with H. B. Warner; *The Way of All Flesh,* with Emil Jannings; *Seventh Heaven,* with Janet Gaynor and Charles Farrell; *Wings,* directed by William A. Wellman and starring Clara Bow, Charles ("Buddy") Rogers, Richard Arlen, and Gary Cooper; *The General,* with Buster Keaton.

In May, the Academy of Motion Picture Arts and Sciences is founded, with Douglas Fairbanks, Sr., as its first president. The first awards, nicknamed Oscars, are presented to William A. Wellman for best director, Janet Gaynor for best actress, and Emil Jannings as best actor.

In October, *The Jazz Singer,* starring Al Jolson, opens. It features a combination of written titles, spoken dialogue, and Jolson's songs. Though not the first to demonstrate a film with sound, it creates a demand for more "sound" films and causes havoc in the industry.

Many established stars see their careers end because of regional or foreign accents or voices that do not match their public images.

On Broadway, these were the hits of the season: *Saturday's Children* by Maxwell Anderson, with Ruth Gordon and Roger Pryor; *Burlesque* by George Manker Wattes and Arthur Hopkins, with Barbara Stanwyck and Oscar Levant; *Porgy* by DuBose Heyward, and his wife Dorothy; this play will be the basis for George Gershwin's *Porgy and Bess;* and *The Royal Family* by George S. Kaufman and Moss Hart.

The most popular songs of the year: "I'm Looking Over a Four Leaf Clover" by Harry MacGregor Woods; "Me and My Shadow" by Al Jolson and Dave Dreyer, lyrics by Billy Rose; "Chloe" by Neil Moret; "My Blue Heaven" by Walter Donaldson; "Let a Smile Be Your Umbrella" by Sammy Fain; "Ain't She Sweet" by Milton Ager; and "Strike Up the Band" by George Gershwin.

At Chicago's Soldier Field, Gene Tunney retains his world heavyweight boxing championship against Jack Dempsey, with the fullest cooperation of the referee. Having knocked Tunney down in the seventh round Dempsey does not go immediately to a neutral corner, as a new rule requires. Valuable seconds tick by before the referee begins "the long count." Tunney, who has been out for fifteen seconds, finally gets to his feet and wins by a decision.

George Herman ("Babe") Ruth hits a record sixty home runs during the season, and in the World Series his New York Yankees overpower the Pittsburgh Pirates 4 games to 0.

Spring floods in the lower Mississippi Valley cause great suffering. More than four million acres are covered by water, causing $300 million in property losses.

Will Rogers leaves his home immediately after New Year's to continue his lecture series. By this time his newest writing venture, the "Daily Telegram," is so well established that on January 14 he writes the last "The Worst Story I've Heard Today."

Greatly disturbed by the suffering of the Mississippi flood victims, Will arranges and plays benefits wherever he can. Florenz Ziegfeld offers his brand-new theater in New York City, and the world famous singer John McCormack agrees to appear with Will. On April 30, the two men raise $18,000, which is turned over to the Red Cross. On June 1, in New Orleans, Will raises $40,000, which he also gives to the Red Cross. For his services Will is made a life member by the American Red Cross.

Because of his firsthand knowledge of the disaster, Will Rogers is called before a congressional investigating committee to help them formulate plans and legislation. Will testifies to the annual plight of the white and black tenant farmers, but he comes away from the hearings writing: "You hear a good deal about what Congress is going to do for the Mississippi Valley. I don't want to discourage the valley, but I would advise them to put more confidence in a boat builder. I got more faith in high ground than any senator I ever saw."

Will, who has enjoyed vigorous health, suddenly has several severe abdominal attacks. He arrives back in California gravely ill and must undergo surgery. Will Rogers, Jr., sixteen years old at the time, remembers how their mother assembled the three children in the master bedroom, and how for the first time they knelt and prayed as a family.

While Will is in the hospital, frequent bulletins are released to an eager press and an even more eager public. Wishes for a speedy recovery flood the hospital, including telegrams from President Coolidge, Alice Roosevelt Longworth, Ring Lardner, Theodore Roosevelt, Jr., Florenz Ziegfeld, Samuel Goldwyn, J. J. McGraw, W. C. Fields, Will Hays, Herbert Bayard Swope, Louise Dresser, George H. Lorimer, Tom Mix, and Ty Cobb.

Recovering, Will makes a full-length motion picture, *A Texas Steer*, with Louise Fazenda, Lilyan Tashman, Sam Hardy, and Douglas Fairbanks, Jr. Since the plot centers around a congressman, the company goes on location to Washington, D.C. Because of his recent operation, a stuntman doubles for Will in—of all scenes—riding a horse.

While in the capital, the National Press Association honors Will with a dinner and names him "congressman-at-large."

In late December, Will has been invited to Mexico City with Charles Lindbergh, as guests of Ambassador and Mrs. Dwight D. Morrow. Rogers and Lindbergh spend days with Mexico's President Plutarco Elías Calles. It is unanimously agreed that the presence of Lindbergh and Rogers, two unofficial ambassadors of goodwill, helps substantially in improving relations between Mexico and the United States.

On Preparedness

I am just back from California and in my official capacity as mayor, I naturally had a chance to look into all our resources in and around Beverly Hills. Now the government has adjoining the outskirts of my municipality what they refer to as an "aviation field." It is a field. It's a good field. It's called "Clover Aviation Field." There is no clover on it, neither is there any aviation. But there is plenty of room for both. If the army is not going to put any aviation on it, I personally will furnish some clover for it. For I don't want it to be misnamed any more than it has to be. It's situated near Santa Monica. It's where back in 1924 four U.S. army planes took off from on their 'round-the-world flight. But we don't want to limit it to that exclusively. We would welcome some local flying, somebody that maybe wasn't going any further off than Hollywood. We just want enough activity there so we won't be called a liar when we refer to it as an "aviation field."

Now in the government "fiction" records, this is what this field is supposed to house. "The 322 Pursuit Group, consisting of the following units, 476th, 477th, 478th and 479th Pursuit Squadron, the 385th Service Squadron, and a Headquarters Detachment." Now in a presidential message, that would be the statistics of the preparedness of this particular field. Now here is the funny part about it that will fool you. This whole thing, all these numbers and different detachments, are officered and manned up to their real strength. There is between 500 and 600 men all in the Air Corps Reserve that are there to get training at this field. More than in any other area in America. Conditions are more suited to such training. These officers are all from the war, and cost the government $15,000 a man to train, up to the time they got their commissions, and they received as much since then, so you see, they represent an investment to the government of at least $10,000,000.

Well, I had heard about the field, and I had heard about the men, so, as it was right across the canyon from me and I had never seen any of them flying from where I was, I just saddled up an old plug the other afternoon, and rode over. I thought maybe they was doing some invisible flying that I couldn't see from over my way. I saw some old hangars and I thought well, they got them full of airplanes. I rode up and peeped in. I couldn't see even an old broken propeller. Here was a beautiful field, 600 trained men, and if you think this is comedy that I am going to tell you, you are cuckoo. It was so sad, it wasn't even funny. Six old-time army planes, 6 mind you, of the type we trained the boys in before we went into the war in 1917. Here was 600 men offering to give their time and risk their lives—(without pay, mind you)—and here is what they have to do it in. Made in 1917, ten years old! Talk about flying them, why, there wasn't enough of them for some of the boys to even see. It figures out that if each of these 600 men in the Reserve Flying Corps wanted to kinder keep his hand in, it would come around to each one flying 15 minutes every month. That is if none of the planes were ever out of order, and they changed flyers in the air; when your 15 minutes was up, why, you jumped out and another man jumped up in the air and took the wheel. Of course, if say, three of these old planes was to die of old age, and leave you a flying strength of only 50%, why, then you would only get 7 and ½ minutes, or about an hour and a half a year, that is in case all three planes keep going night and day, 365 days in the year.

Now an hour and a half is not what you would designate as intensive training. Of course it gives these men a chance to do something else on the side, their mind is not exactly taken up entirely with aviation.

But don't go and sit down and start to reconcile yourself with the fact that you are being protected on our west coast by these 600 men, all trying to get into three planes at once. I don't want to be an alarmist, but you haven't got near that much protection. Father Gloom is knocking on your door with the following greeting: there is a little minor thing you hadn't given any thought to after you felt so safe, knowing that we had those six planes and we had the men. I bet you couldn't think of what it was in a year's guesses. It's the fuel! The government lays out so much fuel for each area for these Reserve Officers training, regardless of the number of men there. In one area there is only nine men, yet they give them just as much fuel as they give these 600. It looks like they are kinder sore at this area because so many of them got back alive. So now there is only fuel enough to operate for one third of the time, even if they only flew one third of the time. So during the month, when it comes your time to fly your seven minutes, why, you get out there and you will find everybody waiting till they get in a tank load of gas from Washington. So the gas shortage cuts your flying time down to 2 and ¾ minutes per month. So you are not getting very far on the $30,000 that was invested in the man when we originally started into the aviation business.

Mr. Coolidge, on account of his economy plan, has suggested that they fly as high as they can on what little gas they have, and then coast down. In that way they get twice the amount of distance out of the same amount of gas. Now of course, this old "economy" is a good slogan. It's a great horse to ride. But look out you don't ride it in the wrong direction. If something happened to us right now, and it comes to a showdown, the shape we are in with our Army, Navy and Aviation, there would be such a howl, Coolidge would have a tough time not being impeached.

Never mind appropriating all this money for River and Harbor Bills, to get the rivers to meet the oceans. Say, the rivers will meet the oceans without any appropriations from Congress. The Almighty saw to that. If you got anything to sell, throw it in a flat boat and start it down the river; it will get to the sea without any locks and channels. We don't want things coming up the river. Raise what you want up there, so you won't have to ship anything up. We better start doing something about our defenses. We are not going to be lucky enough to fight some Central American country forever. Build all we can, and then take care of nothing but our own business, and we will never have to use it. Our world heavyweight champion hasn't been insulted since he won the title.

If you think preparedness don't give you prestige, look at Japan. We are afraid to look at them cross-eyed now for fear we will hurt their "honor." Before they got a navy, neither them nor us knew they had any honor. It ain't your honor that is respected among nations, it's your strength. Japan, or England either, would have just as much honor without any navy at all, but the navy helps to remind you of it.

Holland, Belgium, Switzerland, and half a dozen other countries got just as much honor as England, France, or Japan, but you don't see them with a permanent seat on the League of Nations. The difference is the navy.

All we got to go by is History, and History don't record that Economy ever won a war.

Relax—Lay Perfectly Still

This is the day of specializing, especially with doctors. Say, for instance, there is something the matter with your right eye. You go to a doctor and he tells you, "I am sorry, but I am a left-eye doctor; I make a specialty of left eyes." Take the throat business. A doctor that doctors on the upper part of your throat he doesn't even know where the lower part goes to. And the highest priced one of them all is another bird that just tells you which doctor to go to. He can't cure even corns or open a boil himself. He is a diagnostician, but he is nothing but a traffic cop for ailing people.

The old-fashioned doctor didn't pick out a big toe, or a left ear, to make a life's living on. He picked the whole human frame. No matter what end of you was wrong, he had to try and cure you single-handed. Personally, I have always felt that the best doctor in the world is the veterinarian. He can't ask his patient what is the matter—he's got to just know.

Anyhow, mine really wasn't a disease, or anything at all. The plot first appeared when my stomach was at a tender and growing age. It would generally appear after too many green apples, too many helpings of navy beans, of which said stomach has always been particularly fond, and right after hog killing time. With all the backbones and cracklins and chitlins, why, the old plot would bob up again.

As I think back on it, we were a primitive people in those days. There was only a mighty few known diseases. Gunshot wounds, broken legs, toothache, fits, and anything that hurt you from the lower end of you neck on down as far as your hips, was known as bellyache. Appendicitis would have been considered as the name of a new dance, or some game with horseshoes. Gallstones would have struck us as something the old-time Gauls would heave at the Philistines or the Medes and the Persians.

I don't remember when I first had this pain in my stomach, but I sure do remember one of my dear old mother's remedies for it. They just built a fire in the old kitchen stove and heated one of the round flat kitchen stove lids—the thing you take off if you want your cooking to burn. Well, they would heat it up—not exactly red hot, but it would be a bright bay. Then they took it off, wrapped it up in something and delivered it to your center. I don't care which extremity that was in pain—that was the cure. You get that thing hot enough and I have known it to cure a broken arm. I have seen it cure corns and headaches—in the same treatment.

We didn't know what a hot-water bottle was, and the only thing made out of rubber then, was boots and the top of lead pencils, oh, yes, gents' wearing collars.

Well, the heat from one of those stove lids burned you so you soon forgot where else you were hurting. It not only cured you, it branded you. You would walk stooped over for a week to keep your shirt from knocking the scab off the parched place. Anybody that would look at you who was not familiar with a stove cap would think that an elephant had stepped on you. All it needed was the little scalloping around the edges to make it look like where his toes had sunk in.

After a little spell of this the plot maybe wouldn't show up for a year, or maybe two years. Well, a little thing like that didn't compose much sickness for a strong-bodied and weak-minded boy to have. Having a cramp colic every two years didn't hardly bring me under the heading of what you would call an invalid. I could get out and do a fair kid's day's work.

Oh, yes, I did have some chills, too, one summer, from what we afterwards learned was malaria. I used to have one chill every other day. Some people have them every day, but you can't expect in this world to have everything. Well, I finally shook the chills, and in years to come I was never bothered with them any more. But the old plot of this piece, the stomachache, she would play a return date about every couple of years.

It hadn't shown up in some time, when on this tour of national annoyances, I hit a town called Bluefield, West Virginia. I hadn't been there long when the old plot showed up. Now ordinarily when a pain hits you in the stomach in Bluefield, West Virginia, you would take it for gunshot wounds. But the old town has quieted down now and the sharpshooters have all joined the Kiwanis and Rotary clubs. So I knew it wasn't wounds. Then the pain struck me before the lecture and I knew no one would shoot me before the lecture, unless by chance he had heard it over in another town.

The next time it hit me was just a few weeks later, out at my old ranch where I was born, and where I had previously balanced those flat irons on my stomach years before. My niece, who was living there now gave me some asafetida. The only thing it tastes like is spoiled onions and overripe garlic. I tell you, the longer after you have taken it, the worse it gets. If I was a baby and I found out that somebody had given me that, even if it took forty years, I would get them at the finish.

Just a few nights after that, on my last night on the train coming home to check up on the moral conditions of Beverly Hills and Hollywood, the Sodom and Gomorrah of the West, the old pain hit me again. You see, the plot is slowly thickening. Instead of quitting me after a few hours, as it generally had, it kept hanging on. If it did go away, it would be right back.

When I got home they called in a doctor. He gave me some powders and the pain just thrived on those powders. I never saw a pain pick up so quickly as it did when the powder hit it. Finally my wife called in Doctor White, a famous physician. You see, we got this doctor, as our children are growing up and they are getting to be pretty good-sized little old children, and they wanted to go around to parties and they couldn't go to any decent parties because they still had their adenoids and tonsils. So my wife got this doctor and she had their tonsils taken out. That's not really a medical precaution, it's a social one.

Well, this doctor come over to the house and he had these old tubes where you stick one end in your ear, and hold the other end against the patient's chest, and see what you can get. He just pulled it away and shook his head. I thought maybe he had found that I wasn't breathing and didn't know it. Then he would lay his hand on my stomach and thump the back part of his own hand with his other one.

"What part of your stomach hurts?" he asked.

"Practically all of it, Doc."

He got to thumping and feeling around down low on the right hand side, where I had always been led to believe the appendix was. I could tell from the way he was messing around that he was looking for an appendicitis operation—scouting out in the southwest 40. I didn't know what I had but I had heard enough about appendicitis to know I didn't have it. It gave me great glee, even in all my pain, to see this guy who was just looking to operate and I said: "It's a good joke on you, it ain't down there at all."

He felt rather discouraged. It seemed to kinder lick him. An appendicitis operation within his grasp, and here it was slipping through his hands. But he was a resourceful fellow. He never, like a lot of these other doctors, hung all his clothes on one line. I could see his mind was enumerating other diseases that I could have. "Just where is the pain," he asked.

I said, "Right up there, right in the middle."

Well, he moved up there and found gallstones—a much more expensive operation than an appendectomy. I would have saved $1,500 if I had just left him where he was in the beginning. When I told him that it hurt in the middle, I never had any idea that I was announcing a lead for pay dirt. His face began to brighten, he turned and exclaimed with a practiced and well-subdued enthusiasm, "It's the gallbladder—just what I was afraid of."

Now you all know what the words "afraid of," when spoken by a doctor, lead to. They lead to more calls.

Now I had heard of the gallbladder in a kind of indirect way, but I never had given much thought about where it was, and what it was doing. Anyhow, he then said, "Look up!" And as I looked up, he examined the lower parts of my eyes. Then he says, "Yes, it's gallstones."

Then I says, "Doc, are they backed up as far as my eyes?" And I asked him, "What do you do for them?"

He didn't answer me direct, but he casually inquired if I had had a good season. I told him that outside of Waxahatchie, Texas, Hershey, Pennsylvania, and Concord, New Hampshire, and Newton, Kansas, I had got by in paying quantities.

He then says, "Will, you've got to have an operation."

My wife says, "Operate?" And as soon as I come to enough, I says, "Operate?"

And my wife says, "Is there no easier way out?" Then I showed that the pain had not entirely dulled my intellect, "Yes, is there no cheaper way out?"

"No," he says, "you will always be bothered."

I said, "Wait a minute. I've heard that lots of times you fellows are too quick with these operations. I've read in the papers a lot of times where they would operate on a man and the first thing you know, he dies, and he don't even die from the thing you are operating on."

"Oh," he said, "that'll not be the case with me. If I operate on you for gallstones, you will die of gallstones!"

So I says, "Is it a very dangerous operation?"

"Many people have it," he says, "women have it all the time. It's a woman's disease—eight women have it to every two men."

Well, that didn't make me feel any too good. Here I was, a great big rough-neck lummox, laying there with an effeminate disease. "Can't they feed me something heavy to wear out the stones?"

"No," he says, "you will always be bothered. The best way is to go down and have them taken out. Where is the phone?"

I didn't know whether he was going to phone for knives, the hearse, the ambulance, or what. The wife pointed to the phone kind of dumbfounded. Why didn't I think of telling him the phone wasn't working? That would have stalled the thing off a little longer.

Well, he phoned for what seemed like a friend, but who afterwards turned out to be an accomplice. These doctors, nowadays, run in bunches. Very few of these robberies are pulled off single-handed. They don't need each other medically, but when they send the bill, it lends moral support.

This new doctor come, and there was a kind of knowing look between them, and the first one said, "I'm glad you come; it looks like business."

The new one was a Doctor Moore, the operating end of the firm. He is the most famous machete wielder on the western coast. He come over to where I was laying, and he says, "Well, how are you, Will? Ha - ha- ha- ha - kind of sick? - ha - ha - ha - ha- that's good - ha - ha - ha - ha- you've had a pretty tough season? Haven't you worked pretty hard? You've done well?"

And me, like a fool, said, "Yes." Leave it to an actor to be so conceited that they hurt their own business.

Doctor Moore then asked the same line of questions, but before I could get a chance to answer them myself, why, Doctor White answered them for me the way they should be answered to show that I had a very severe case of gallstones.

The first doctor said, "What do you think?" The second one says, "I think gallstones." The first one says, "That's what I think."

I says, "I'm glad you boys are guessing together."

"What do you advise?" the first doctor asked. "I advise an operation," said the second. "That's what I advised," said the first one. Imagine asking a surgeon what he advises! It would be like asking Coolidge, "Do you advise economy?"

My wife said, "When?" The whole thing seemed to have gone out of my hands. I was just lying there, marked exhibit A.

One doctor was for doing it that night, but the other one was more of a humanitarian; he suggested they take me down that evening, and operate in the morning. Well, when my wife heard this—my poor Betty, we have been married these twenty years, the same husband—she left the room. I knew she must be all broke up. I thought to myself, "Poor Betty, she can't stand this; it's too much for her; she's gone so I can't see her." I got up and went in to console her. She was digging in an old musty leather case, marked "Insurance Papers."

The number one doctor rushed to the telephone and made a call. I couldn't think who they would be calling now; they already had the doctor and the surgeon. I says, "The only other man he can possibly work with, is the undertaker." But I was relieved to hear that it was only the hospital he was calling, asking for a nice room.

Finally the two doctors are reaching for their hats, and they are all smiling, and you would have thought we had all made a date to have some fun. Now after the doctors had left, that gave my wife and I a chance to do a little thinking. What they had talked about had scared the pains clear away. We got to wondering what had brought on this severe attack at this time. We laid it to everything we could think of, including the Republican Party.

This going to the hospital was a new thing to me. I had never been in one in all my life, only to see somebody else. Outside of those stove-lid episodes, and the malaria, I had never been sick a day in my life. I had been appearing on the stage for some twenty-odd years, and had never missed a show.

But I was going to make up for it now. They had a pretty cozy room for me. The whole thing was like a big hotel—everything was jolly and laughter. The stomach had quit hurting—of course. Did you ever have a tooth hurt after you got to the dentist? I couldn't see any use being in bed at ten o'clock in the morning when I hadn't been out the night before.

A young girl came in, she was not a nurse, she had on a short skirt, and looked like a manicurist, and she said, "Give me your hand." I didn't know what she was going to do with it—kiss it, wash it, read it or hold it. But she took blood for a blood test. And they kept taking blood—they took so much blood, I was sure they was keeping a friend who was anemic.

That night before the operation, Mrs. Rogers got to studying: "Now these two doctors just came in here and they say there should be an operation. Of course I know they are fine, capable men, the best doctors to be secured on the western coast, but I just wish I could get some more advice. Poor, old Will, maybe I give him up too quick. While he hasn't been a good husband, he's done about the best he could, and knew how. While he's been funny to some people he has, at times, been very sad to me. But as ornery as he is, I'm not going to give him up without a struggle."

So Betty calls up Mary Pickford, who lives on the expensive end of the same hill. Betty thinks Mary is very smart, and she is a very good friend of ours. Mary is a Christian Scientist, but she has a doctor who has been able to keep Douglas Fairbanks jumping all these years. So Mary sent her doctor.

Then our old friend William S. Hart called up. He had a fine doctor that he wanted her to talk to, and have see me. So Betty asked our two doctors if they minded having these other two look me over and then all confer.

Of course our two didn't mind and they knew it would make her feel better to have more opinions on it, and they felt their case would stand up before any witnesses. She made them promise that they wouldn't operate the next morning until they had held this foursome over my fairway.

The next morning, after what should have been breakfast—but I didn't get any—in filed the battalion of doctors. Oh say, I like to forgot to tell you that during this time I was turning yellow. One of the symptoms of gallbladder trouble is jaundice.

Well, the doctors were remarking, "He's getting yellow—very yellow." Ha - ha! They didn't know it, but I wanted to tell them that this yellow was from my heart, not from the liver, or gallbladder.

One of the new doctors would ask a question, and before I had a chance to answer, why, one of my original cast would explain in so many fewer words than I could. And not only that, but their answers were in such a way that it shows if I am not operated on within a half hour, I will perhaps die, although I have had this disease for 44 years.

Those four listened, they thumped the same as the first one did. They discussed it all between themselves. I, the defendant, wasn't put on the stand at all. Finally they filed out. The clinic was over. The nurse and I were alone, Betty had gone out too.

I asked the nurse, "How long do you think the jury will be out, and do you think there is any chance of a disagreement?" A hung jury was the best I could hope for. I knew a verdict in my favor was out of the question. I could see by the way they acted that the doctoring profession was a kind of closed corporation, and while they might be professional rivals, they wouldn't purposely do each other out of anything.

I asked the nurse again how she thought things would turn out. She said, "Oh, they have the operating room engaged; they will have to go through with it now."

"Well," I said, "I had better go ahead then, for I certainly don't want to cancel an operating room. Those people up there are going to be all broke up if I don't come up and be all cut up. But I just wonder if there is not someone that would like a nice operation, and I could send them up in my place."

There was a knock on the door and the jury came in. They was for hanging. It stood four for operation—in fact five, for poor Betty had been won over with tales of the advantages of a nice, neat operation. I knew the moment they opened the door that I had lost, for they all came in smiling and said, "You are going to feel much better after this is over."

I thought, "Yes, it depends on how I have lived, where I will finish up when this is over."

It is customary, I have heard, for the defendant to shake hands with the jury, but that's only in case he's acquitted. They all went out but forgot to shut the door, and I heard my two bidding the other two goodbye, saying, "We'll do as much for you sometime, boys."

My surgeon stepped back into the room, with his gown on. That shows you the verdict was framed beforehand, for he must have had this one on under his other suit. Oh, they were tickled to death. The main carver said he had a lot of operations on that day, but that mine would be first. I asked him if he couldn't take somebody else first—that there might be someone in pain, and that I had never felt better in my life. Then I also thought that his hand might be a little shaky early in the morning.

They got me ready for the operation. All I had on was alcohol. I could have licked my arm and got soused. Then they put on me what looked like flannel boots that come pretty nearly up to my knee. They looked like those galoshes that girls wear in the winter and don't fasten, and when they come down the street, they sound like a mule that's running loose with chain harness on. Anyhow, I never did find out what those boots were on me for, unless it was to catch the blood in case I got up and run out during the operation, or to keep me from biting my toe nails in case I got nervous.

I had a sheet kind of draped over me. They tied a white thing around my head, then all I needed was a Ku Klux Klan card. The doctor had a thing over his mouth, so he wouldn't catch the same disease I had.

I was on the wagon and all ready. We were waiting for signals from the operating room. Betty, God bless her, came over to hold my hand. I told her to go over and hold the surgeon's hand for the next thirty minutes, and we would all be safe.

Then we got the signal that we were next. You never saw such hustling around. They seemed to think, "Do you realize there's not a soul in this place being whittled on at this minute?" I bid goodbye to my Betty, and the parade started down the hall to the elevator. Just as they were rolling me into the operating room, they were rolling another guy out. That will make you shudder, I don't care how tough a guy you are. I wondered if he would live or die, and what he had been operated on for. Then I heard him cussing. Well, of all the cussing I ever heard, that man was doing the best job I ever heard. I never heard such beautiful cussing; it really had a rhythm to it. He was under the effects of ether, but his timing was perfect. I thought, "Well, even if you don't know what happens to you, you've had the pleasure of telling them what you thought of them, anyhow."

Well, they rolled me in there with my retinue of nurses and doctors as outriders. You know they have a little balcony in there where you can go and see operations. That must be where people with a wonderfully well developed sense of humor go. Imagine meeting somebody on the street. "Hello, Marjorie, what are you doing this morning?" "Oh, nothing." "Come on, I have got two seats for an operation."

Well, I looked up, and there was nobody up there. That kind of hurt my pride. I thought, "Here I am, maybe playing the last act of my life, and this is the poorest business I ever did."

Now the night before I went in there, naturally I didn't know what might happen to me, so I said, "Well, I've got a lot of laughs in my lifetime, and I want to pass out with one." So I thought all night of a good joke; I was going to have a good joke, and just before they operated I thought I'd pull this joke, and they would all laugh hilariously, and say, "Well, old Will wasn't so bad at that."

So I got ready to pull that joke, but there is a fellow standing behind me—he's the fellow you can't see. He is the fellow that is going to knock you out. He has a kind of hose with a big nozzle on the end of it.

I was all ready to set the world laughing uproariously, and I thought when this old guy reaches over, I'll just reach up and pull it off and tell my joke, and then let him go ahead. That was my little idea—it was entirely my own.

Well, I reached up—I started to reach up—I just opened my mouth to utter my comical wheeze, when this old hose boy just gently slipped that nozzle right over my mouth and nose, both. I wanted to tell him, "Just a minute!" but a couple of interns, who are really wrestlers on vacation, had me by each hand. I certainly was sore. Here I had this last aspiring wise crack, and it had been snuffed out before I could give vent to it.

Out I went, and from that day to this I have never been able to remember that joke. I would give a thousand dollars, if I could just think of that joke. It was the best joke I ever had.

I don't know what else they operated on me for, but they certainly took out that joke.

Just what caused the stones to form? Well, there are various reasons. Republicans staying in power too long, will increase the epidemic; seeing the same endings to moving pictures is a prime cause; a wife driving from the rear seat will cause gastric juices to form an acid, and that slowly jells into a stone as she keeps hollering.

Of course, I will always believe that mine was caused by no sanitary drinking cups in the old Indian Territory, where I was born. We used a gourd, raised from a gourd vine. Not only did we all drink out of the same gourd, but the one gourd lasted for years, till Prohibition weaned some of them away from water.

You see, in the old days, when we wasn't sanitary, why, we were strong enough to withstand germs. But nowadays we have to be careful of the microbes, for if they get a hold on us, we are goners.

I tell you, the old-fashioned gourd that the whole family drank out of, from birth till death, would today kill more of the modern population than a war.

But while laying in the hospital recuperating, I just accidently stumbled on what I really think caused the operation. For years I had carried a very big—that is too big for my circumstances—Accident and Disability Insurance. Well, I would notice that my wife would get a little irritable every year when it would come time to pay the premiums on these various sickness and accident policies, and say, "Well, that's pretty large to carry, isn't it, when you never got a cent out of it?" And I would admit it did seem like a bad investment.

It was getting terribly discouraging to keep paying year after year and not being able to get sick, and with no prospects of ever getting sick. Here I was betting a lot of insurance companies that I would get sick or hurt, and they were betting me I wouldn't. Now if you think you are not a sucker in a case like that, all you have to do is to look at the financial standing of the company, in comparison to the financial standing of the people who bet on the other side. It's just a case of somebody knowing more about you than you know about yourself.

Why, they have the highest priced doctors to look you over. If you look like nothing but lightning can kill you, why, he sends in a report to the company to go ahead and bet you that you won't get sick. But if you look the least bit like you are going to get sick, they don't bet you. Any time they approve of you, that should show you right there that there is nothing going to happen to you. But you, like a fool, go ahead and bet them in the face of all this professional knowledge that you know more than they do.

I argued with my wife, saying, "Well, I may get sick."

"Yes, you might get sick, but you never do."

Well, you see, she had me licked. I then said, "I may get hurt in a polo game by falling off my horse."

She said, "No, you have fallen off so much, you've got used to it, so I have no more hopes along that line."

So last summer, when paying time came, and as she's my banker, my insurance man—he really shouldn't be one, he is so different from the others—he advised her to reduce the policies. They decided to cut down on the accident and disability, but they allowed the straight life insurance to remain. They figured I would die, but that I would die without illness. Well, I didn't know the thing had been cut down.

One day, I was a-laying in the hospital and I just happened to have the only bright thought that had come to me in weeks. "Say, this thing I'm doubled up here with comes under the heading of "sickness"; it even comes under the heading of "accident," for wasn't I getting well from an operation?"

So I thought of those policies I had been paying on for years. This sickness was going to turn out all right, at that. I began to think of how I could stretch it out into what might be termed a slow convalescence. So I was grinning like a moving picture producer who had just thought of a suggestive title for his new picture. So when my wife called again, I broke the good news to her.

I says, "If we can get a bona fide doctor to say that I have been sick and couldn't spin a rope and talk about Coolidge, we are in for some disability."

Well, I noticed the wife didn't seem so boisterous about this idea. Then I got to thinking: "Maybe I haven't been sick enough, or maybe I haven't got a bona fide doctor."

Then the truth came out slowly; she told me the sad story of the cutting down of the insurance. It read like a sentence to me. She said my physical condition had misled them. Of course, she said, there would be some salvage out of our shortsightedness, but that the operation would be by no means money-making. Whereas, if the original policies had prevailed, I would have reaped a neat profit.

So, if you want to stay well, just bet a lot of rich companies that you will get sick; then, if you can't have any luck getting sick, have the policy cut down, and before six months you'll be saying: "Doctor, the pain is right there!"

1928

In the Soviet Union, Joseph Stalin launches the first five-year plan, which begins by eliminating—via death, Siberian camps, or exile—all landowners who oppose collectivization. In widespread protests, peasants burn their crops and slaughter their livestock.

Mussolini's Italy signs a twenty-year treaty of friendship with Ethiopia. But within seven years, Italian forces will be slaughtering their "friends."

In the war in China, Peking falls to Chiang Kai-shek and the Nationalists. Chiang is elected president of China—at least of that part that is under his control.

In August, the Kellogg-Briand Peace Pact—also called The Pact of Paris—is initialed. It condemns the use of war as an instrument of national policy, and signers agree not to seek settlement of any dispute except by peaceful means. This treaty is subsequently ratified by sixty-three nations.

The Olympic Games are held at Amsterdam, with forty-six nations participating. Johnny Weismuller retires from active swim competition, having won three Olympic gold medals, and having set almost seventy world records. In 1930 he will make the first of nineteen films portraying Tarzan.

In June Amelia Earhart flies from Newfoundland to Wales, becoming the first woman to fly across the Atlantic. The German dirigible *Graf Zeppelin* crosses the Atlantic in the opposite direction, from

Friedrichshafen to Lakewood, New Jersey, taking five days and one hour. It is the beginning of regular transatlantic service.

Natural disasters claim 1,836 lives when a killer hurricane causes Lake Okeechobee to overflow; 450 are killed when the three-year-old Saint Francis Dam just north of Los Angeles breaks. Among man-made disasters: More than two thousand Americans die from drinking illegal, homemade liquor; uncounted hundreds are blinded.

Freeman Gosden and Charles Correll met in 1919 and formed a blackface vaudeville act called "Sam 'n' Henry." In 1926, they brought the act to Chicago radio, with moderate local success. On March 19, 1928, they change the name to "Amos 'n' Andy," and a legend is born. The following year, the two proprietors of the "Fresh-Air Taxi Company" will go on national radio, and their daily fifteen-minute show will be tuned in by two-thirds of all radio sets. Motion picture houses will advertise that their feature film ends before 7 P.M., will not resume until after 7:15 P.M., and that during intermission the "Amos 'n' Andy" show is piped into the auditorium. Department stores that stay open late broadcast the show onto the sales floors, lest customers stay home to hear the latest episodes in the lives of the Kingfish, Madame Queen, lawyer Calhoon, Lightnin', Sapphire, and Brother Crawford. When television becomes popular, a new team portrays Amos and Andy. Finally, in 1958 the radio show is discontinued; the television show survives until 1965.

Scottish bacteriologist Alexander Fleming discovers penicillin, launching the age of antibiotic medications.

In Britain, women at last gain the right to vote on exactly the same terms as men. In Mussolini's Italy, however, women's suffrage is abolished, and through a new law, seven million men are disenfranchised as well, leaving an electorate of barely three million.

Chrysler Motors introduces a newcomer to its line to compete with Fords and Chevrolets—the Plymouth.

This being an election year, the two major parties hold presidential nominating conventions. The battle lines are clearly marked and well defined. The Republicans have Herbert Hoover, Protestant, Puritan, and for Prohibition; Al Smith, the Democrat, is Roman Catholic, eastern, and for "fundamental changes in the present provisions for national Prohibition."

Hoover is elected with 444 votes to Smith's 87. Almost as an aftermath to the election, the National Conference of Christians and Jews is founded to oppose bigotry wherever it is discovered.

Among the remembered books of the year: *The Bridge of San Luis Rey,* by Thornton Wilder; *Lady Chatterley's Lover,* by D. H. Lawrence; and *Point Counter Point,* by Aldous Huxley.

In the theater, among the plays of the season are: *Strange Interlude,* a Pulitzer Prize winner by Eugene O'Neill; *The Front Page,* by Ben Hecht and Charles MacArthur; and *Elmer the Great,* by George M. Cohan and Ring Lardner.

In films, the first all-talking movie, *Lights of New York,* opens at the Strand; and Walter Elias Disney, in the first animated cartoon with sound track—called *Steamboat Willie*—introduces a new star: Mickey Mouse.

The songs most often heard: "Makin' Whoopee," "I Can't Give You Anything But Love, Baby," "The Breeze and I," "I'll Get By," and "Carolina Moon."

On January 4, 1928, Will Rogers is master of ceremonies for the "Dodge Victory Hour," a new concept in radio programs, as different stars are in major cities around the country. Thus Paul Whiteman is in New York City, Fred Stone and his daughter Dorothy are in Chicago, Al Jolson is in New Orleans, while Will Rogers is in his own home in Beverly Hills. It is on this national hookup, with millions listening, that Will introduces the president of the United States, Mr. Calvin Coolidge. Will, who is an excellent mimic, does not bother to inform his listeners that the humorous monologue that follows is his own, not Coolidge's. The New England accent is perfect, and few listeners are familiar with their president's voice—but could their dour Calvin utter lines like: "Everyone I come in contact with is doing well. They have to be doing well, or they don't come in contact with me!"

When Will concludes his mock "State of the Union" address, he feels sure that everyone knows that he had imitated the president's voice; any explanation would have been an insult to the listeners' intelligence. But there are editorial repercussions around the country. Apparently quite a few listeners had been taken in by the parody. Will writes President Coolidge: "It would give me great pain if I annoyed you in the least. . . ." President Coolidge sends back a two-page letter, written in his own hand: "Will, I know that anything you did, you did for good-natured amusement. Don't give a moment's thought to it. . . ."

Early in the year, Will attends the opening of the Sixth Pan-American Conference, held in Havana, Cuba, but by mid-February he is back on the lecture tour. In June Will covers the Republican National Convention in Kansas City, and from there he goes to Houston to watch the Democrats fight among themselves.

Will's best friend, musical comedy star Fred Stone, is seriously injured in a plane crash in Connecticut. The doctors hold out little hope for his recovery; at best, they say, he will be permanently crippled. Will rushes to his friend's hospital bed in New London. Fred was about to begin rehearsals, with his daughter Dorothy, for a new musical comedy, *Three Cheers*. Will makes a decision that, though made in selfless friendship, earns him additional respect and admiration. At great financial sacrifice, he cancels all his commitments and offers to take his friend's place in the new show. Producer Charles Dillingham is delighted with this unexpected solution to what had loomed as a serious problem.

Although Will goes through the motions of consulting a script, the tryouts in Springfield, Massachusetts, starting September 30, clearly show that this will be one of the most unusual shows Broadway has seen. Performances in New Haven, starting the week of October 7, are no improvement.

Opening night in New York City, October 15, is a joyous celebration, but hardly the show Anne Callwell had written—probably to her distress. But the show is a success, even though no two performances are ever the same.

Will stays with the show until it closes in Pittsburgh, the end of May 1929.

A Jackson Day Dinner

Well, all I know is just what I see in the papers, or what I hear as I sit behind the free lunch table and listen to the boys bark for their meals. Did I tell you that I broke bread with the Democrats in Washington? I passed myself off as a Democrat one night just to get a free meal.

I had watched the Republicans eat, but I had never seen them feed the Democrats, so I crawled in under the tent and watched 'em throw the good old raw Jeffersonian oratory right into the cages with them. When a Democrat is hungry and can't manage to get anything to eat, he can always satisfy his hunger by dreaming and harking back to the "Old Jeffersonian Principles." Nobody knows what they were, but they have furnished a topic for the poor Democrats to rave about for a couple of generations. He always wants a return to the "Jeffersonian Principles" and give the government back to the people. Well, the people wouldn't know any more what to do with it than they did back in those days. Nothing would please the rich more than to have the government handed back to the people, for they would take it away from them so quick, the people wouldn't know what it looked like while they had it.

You know, the Democrat at heart is just naturally an amiable fellow. He would rather talk with you anytime than make a dollar off you. He just loves politics, not for what he can get out of 'em, for he never has received much of a dividend on his political investments, but he just wants to be known as a politician. Now a Republican don't, he just wants politics to be known as a side line. He is sorter ashamed of it. He wants to work at it, but he wants people to believe he don't have to.

Yes, the old Democrat, he is still so old-fashioned that he thinks politics is one of the honored professions. Just let him head a few committees, and make a few speeches every once in a while, and he is in his glory. He will miss his supper to explain to you what Jeffersonian Principles are. He don't know what they are, but he has heard 'em spoken of so often in speeches that he knows no speech is complete without wishing that we would return to those Principles, and the only thing that keeps us from not returning to them is that very reason that we don't know what they were. Jackson is another life saver in their legends. You take him out of there, and you would just about lessen Democratic conversation 50 per cent.

I thought at the time of this Jackson Day Dinner that the Democrats were going mighty far back to find some hero that they could worship. But I happened to be in Cuba when President Coolidge delivered his speech to the Latins, and the Republicans had to go even further back than the Democrats did for Jackson. Coolidge went back to Columbus. I had never known, or even heard Columbus's political faith discussed before. But he must have been a Republican the way Cal was boosting him. Anyhow, you see, neither party hasn't got much when they have to reach back that far to find some one to boost.

But I was telling you about this Jackson Day Dinner. I went there with a speech prepared about Jackson, telling how "he stood like a Stone Wall," and there it wasn't that Jackson that they were using as an alibi to give the dinner to. It was old "Andy" Jackson!

Well, to tell you the truth, I am not so sweet on old Andy. He is the one that run us Cherokees out of Georgia and North Carolina. I ate the Jackson Day Dinner on him, but I didn't enjoy it.

Old Andy, every time he couldn't find any one to jump on, would come back and pounce onto us Indians. Course, he licked the English down in New Orleans, but he didn't do it till the war had been over two weeks, so he really just fought them as an encore. Then he would go to Florida, and shoot up the Seminoles. That was before there was a single bathing suit in Palm Beach. Then he would have a row with the government, and they would take his liquor away from him, and he would come back and sick himself onto us Cherokees again.

He was the first one to think up the idea to promise everybody that if they will vote for you, why, you will give them an office when you get in, and the more times they vote for you, the bigger the office you will give them. That was the real start of the Democratic Party. "If he ain't of your Party," old Andy used to say, "give him nothing! Charity begins at the polls!" Then he would go back home, if he happened to have been defeated, pounce on the Indians and take it out on them. An Indian had no more right to live, according to old Andrew, than a Republican to hold a job during the Democratic administration.

Then the Republicans came along and improved on Jackson's idea by giving them money, instead of promises for jobs. In that way you got paid whether your man was elected, or not. Nobody with any business sense wants to wait till after the election to see if they get something. They liked the Republican idea of "paying as you go."

But old Andy made the White House. You see, he got in before the Republicans got their scheme working. Even the Indians wanted him in there, so he would let us alone for a while. Andy stayed two terms; the Indians wanted him to serve a third term, but Andy had to get back to his regular business, which was shooting at Indians.

They sent the Indians to Oklahoma. They had a treaty that said: "You shall have this land as long as grass grows and water flows." It was not only a good rhyme, but looked like a good treaty; and it was, till they struck oil. Then the government took it away from us again. They said the treaty only refers to "water and grass; it don't say anything about oil!"

So the Indians lost another bet. The first one was to Andy Jackson, and the second was to the oil companies. But years later, when the Cherokees went back and saw where they used to live in Georgia, North Carolina and Alabama, why, we always felt that Andy had unconsciously done us a favor. So we Cherokees can always kinder forgive old Andy for not knowing what he was doing.

But you got to give old Andrew credit, he fought duels when duels was duels, and not just the inconvenience of getting up before sunrise.

Anyhow, the dinner started at 7 o'clock and run til 3 a.m. We didn't eat that long, we only ate as long as they brought it. They run out of food about 8 p.m. From then on you had to subsist on speeches on "Liquor, with or without a license," and "Party Harmony!"

Each new speaker had to thank the previous one fast, before they had left the room. You see, there is a few peculiarities that apply to the Democrats that don't apply to any other sex. One is they will always leave as soon as they are through listening to themselves, and the other is they won't come unless they can speak.

The last speaker closed the show with "Corruption" at exactly 3 a.m. the next morning and held 'em in their seats. You know the Democrats can just naturally stand more oratory than any other race. But it was all mighty fine.

The Democrat is just naturally a better orator than the Republican. The Democrats have the best side; they are always attacking and the Republicans have to defend. The Democrats always have things to attack, for the Republicans furnish them plenty, and on the other hand, the Republicans haven't got much to defend with. Their only defense is "We are in; try to get us out!"

So if you ever get a chance don't miss one of these Jackson Day Dinners; they only hold 'em in election years; they save up four years' stuff to tell about Republicans, and it's sure worth the money.

North versus South

Back here in New York there is an awful lot of papers to read. But they are mostly pictures. New York newspapers don't have reporters, all they have is photographers. Everything is done by pictures. They wouldn't give a dime for the biggest story in the world, if there was no picture with it, for it would be no good, for their people couldn't read it. So I sure have read a lot of pictures since I have been back here.

And what they can't read in the pictures, why, New Yorkers hear over the radio, so there is no use knowing how to read any more.

There must be a kind of gentleman's agreement between the two presidential candidates. Al Smith and Herbert Hoover have divided up the air, so that Smith has it Mondays, Wednesdays, and Fridays, and Hoover on Tuesdays, Thursdays and Saturdays. Now you would think: Well, that gives us Sundays without having to listen to any politics!

Don't you believe it. That's when you get more politics than all the rest of the week combined. That's when the preachers start 'lectioneering. They all start out by saying: "The church should not enter into politics, BUT." Then they try to show how in their case it is different; that they are not entering politics, they are just advising; that people are so flighty nowadays, that if they are not advised properly, why, they are apt to be led astray by the opposition.

131

Smith started out a couple of weeks ago and made what I bet he thought was a trip around the world. I bet he had no more idea this country was that big, or he would never have had the nerve to say he would try to govern it. He hit Omaha first. He made a Farm Relief speech there. The poor farmers have had more oratorical relief, than monetary.

Smith brought out one pretty clever thing in that speech, that was showing that the Republican Farm Relief plank was exactly the same in the 1924 Convention and in the 1928. They hadn't even gone to enough trouble for the farmer to re-word their promise. It just looked like they said: Well, what did we promise him last election? Oh, we promised him relief? We'll do as well for him this time—promise it to him again. As long as we don't give it to him, we can keep on promising.

Well, Al Smith nailed 'em on that, but of course the Republicans will squirm out of it some way by saying they were just on the verge of giving the farmer relief, when something happened. But the old farmer up North, he will go right to the polls on November 6th, and vote the Republican ticket. And the old farmer down South will go and vote the Democratic ticket. Now will you tell me why those two should not be on the same side politically? What does the farmer in the North want that the Republican party can give him, that his brother in the South wants that the Democrats can give him? Why ain't they on the same side?

They both raise corn and oats; they both have to buy wagons and plows; they both want to sell what they raise for as much as they can get for it, and buy the same things for as little as they can. Now I don't know if they should be Republicans or Democrats, but it does look like they should be on the same side. The only reason I can see is, they fought against each other in 1865, so that made one a Democrat, and one a Republican. So if they still harbor that feeling, then there is no reason why they should get relief. When they can't agree among themselves, how do they ever expect to get anything? I don't blame the parties for not helping them.

Imagine, here is the Southern farmer lined up with New York's political machine, Tammany Hall! Now what have Tammany Hall and any farmer in common? And then, there is the Northern farmer lined up with Wall Street and Big Business. Now why should they be together? The farmer don't want to borrow any money. Borrowing is what put him in the hole he is in today. The government was always figuring out where he could borrow more. But they never figured out where he could pay something back.

Will Rogers as his fans knew him.

In 1913, with Eddie Cantor in
Winnipeg, Manitoba, Canada.

Theater program advertising
Midnight Frolic showing, though
not mentioning, Will Rogers. As he
was the only cowboy to appear
with the show, the illustration
must refer to him.

Ziegfeld Follies' program, 1916; Scene 10 is
"Will Rogers and His Educated Ropes."
Note Scene 12, featuring "William Fields,"
who became better known as W. C. Fields.

Photograph taken on Long Island, New York, 1917. This mule was dark lemon-colored with brown spots.

Betty, Mary, Will, Jr., and Will in Rogers, Arkansas, c. 1914.

Stunt riding for the photographer, Long Island, New York, 1917.

Florenz Ziegfeld, Jr., and his wife, famous actress Billie Burke.

Will, Jr., Mary, Betty, Jimmy, and Will on Goldwyn studio set, 1919.

Party on Clem Vann Rogers' ranch, 1906. *Second from left*, Betty Blake; *far right*, Will.

In *Ziegfeld Follies'* sketch with Brandon Tynan as David Belasco, Will as an aspiring actress. *Theatre Collection, Museum of the City of New York*

On set, Will tries to teach Charlie Chaplin the secrets of twirling a lariat.

Advertising layout for "Aerial Gardens Atop New Amsterdam Theatre," as Ziegfeld's *Midnight Frolic* was called. *Theatre Collection, Museum of the City of New York*

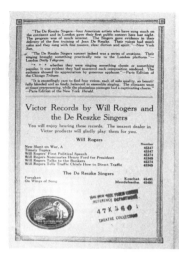

A 1925 program for Will's lecture in Newark, New Jersey. Note there was no rest, even on Sundays. The night before he had appeared in Lynchburg, Virginia; the next night he would be in Springfield, Massachusetts.

In *A Poor Relation*, 1921.

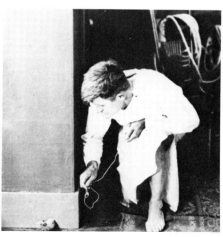

About to lasso a rat, in *The Ropin' Fool*, 1922.

With Brig. Gen. "Billy" Mitchell, Washington, D.C., 1925.

Will Rogers at home in Beverly Hills, California.

His Honor, the Mayor of Beverly Hills, tries out a street sweeper.

After a hard game of polo.
Theatre Collection, Museum of the City of New York

With David S. Ingalls, assistant secretary of the navy for aeronautics. In San
Diego, November 18, 1930.

After publicly kidding that the census takers
had missed him, Will is finally tracked down
on May 9, 1930.

Dressed up for *A Connecticut
Yankee*, 1931.

October 28, 1932. Will arriving at Newark, New Jersey, airport, returning from a trip to South America.

With Oklahoma's Governor "Alfalfa" Bill Murray, having lunch, February 3, 1931.

With Chic Sale at a Christmas benefit, December 18, 1933, Los Angeles.

With Janet Gaynor and Lew Ayres in *State Fair*, 1933.

Always slightly unorthodox, Will plays polo dressed somewhat less than traditionally.

June 29, 1932. At the Democratic National Convention in Chicago, Will took the speaker's stand while the orchestra played "Pony Boy." He pleaded with delegates to accept whoever was nominated and to work for his election.

Will receives a shiny new dime from John D. Rockefeller, Sr.

With Florence Desmond in *Mr. Skitch,* 1933.

On set of *Mr. Skitch,* 1933.

A toast and a wink, filming *Doctor Bull,* 1933.

At a benefit dinner, November 1934.

Studio publicity release, paraphrasing Will's famous "All I know is what I read in the papers."

Twentieth anniversary party for producer Hal Roach, Sr., December 10, 1933. *Left to right:* Roach, Theda Bara, Will, Charlie Chase.

Arriving in Los Angeles, 1935.

Using his car as a temporary office, Will pecks out his column.

Returning from Europe aboard the *Ile de France*, Will and Betty are caught on a stroll around the deck.

Will hurrying through the Kansas City airport, 1935.

Dressed in a pilot's suit on a stopover in Cleveland, 1935.

With Evelyn Venable in *The County Chairman*, 1935.

Left to right: Will, Irvin S. Cobb, and director John Ford.

With Sterling Holloway in *Doubting Thomas*, 1935.

Interior of Rogers' ranch-style home. Note the stuffed calf, which Will would use to practice roping indoors, until finally both ears wore off.

Left to right: Will Rogers, Jr., Will, Billie Burke, Wiley Post, and Fred Stone.

The plane in which Rogers would later die, when still owned by TWA and before Wiley Post's structural changes. Note the letter *C* as part of the license number, indicating approval for commercial use.

The same plane after Post's changes. Wiley is at the controls, and they are off to test-fly the plane, now equipped with pontoons. The letter *R* on the license number denotes restricted use only, which specifically forbids passengers. Will Rogers was considered "a member of the crew."

Wiley at Seattle, with the plane in the background.

Five months after the accident, the wreckage of the plane rests at Barrow, Alaska.

Now there is a real reason why farmers, or country people, should be in one political party, and city people in another. They have different interests, different needs, different things to sell, and hundreds of different wants and customs. But why the Northern farmer and the Northern city fellow should be allied against the Southern farmer and the Southern city fellow—that is beyond sane understanding.

What should be the legitimate alignment of politics, is the country against the city. Tariff don't divide the two parties any more. Smith is explaining his head off that if he gets in, they won't do away with the tariff, so it would drive a person pretty near crazy to dope out really what does divide the two political parties.

Outside of one being in and wanting to stay in, and the other being out and wanting to get in. Prohibition can't be the dividing line, for it is so arranged that both sides get all the liquor they want. Prosperity don't divide the two parties, for under either administration the poor get poorer, and the rich get richer. Prosperity is only a question of giving a guy time to get it.

So the whole thing, it looks like, goes back to the Civil War. The boys are still fighting it, and don't know it.

What the Farmer Needs

The question is, is either party going to do anything for the farmer? I can tell you in a few words what the farmer needs. He needs a punch in the jaw if he believes that either one of the parties cares about him after election. That's all the farmer needs—a punch in the jaw—and that's all he'll get.

Raid the Treasury

All the politicians are trying to stir up some excitement in their line of work. But I can't find much interest in their graft, outside the ones that are in it. The outside people have just about come to the conclusion that there ain't a worry's worth of difference in either one, and they just try to forget it, and lve it down if they ever did take any interest.

By the way, the way they are raiding the Treasury now, there don't look like it will do anybody any good to get elected. What's the use running your head off to get to a table where the food has just been all eaten up? If I was an office seeker, I would kinder be doubtful whether there was enough money left in there just to pay my regular salary, much less what I wanted to run for office for.

They sure are taking the old Treasury to a cleaning. None of this million, or five million dollar appropriation. It's a half billion, or nothing in a bill nowadays. It takes a man that can think in big numbers to introduce a bill in Congress nowadays. A bill under a hundred million would be so unusual that it wouldn't pass. "We can't spend our time voting on trifles!" He would be laughed out of Congress as a Small-Timer.

If you got a river near your house and the government hasn't dammed it up yet, why, it's because you haven't sent your Congressman a blueprint of where it is, and haven't asked them to put one in for you. If you got some land that nothing will grow on, and haven't had it irrigated, why, it's because you don't know your Congressman. Everybody wants land irrigated by the government. For, as anyone knows, new land with plenty of water will raise quite a bit. But so will OLD land, if it's fertilized! So why should the whole of the American taxpayers pay for water for newly irrigated land—any more than they should for fertilizer for old land? Both will do the same thing if you will put them on there. But it looks like nobody is ever original enough to think of a bill like that. They just think that water is the only thing that will help the land. Why, my lord, there is dozens of different things that will help the farmer on his land, besides water, or fertilizer, either. There is the interest on the first, and second mortgages. Why don't they introduce a bill in Congress to help the farmer by paying off his mortgages? That's what's eating him up on the farm, it's not lack of irrigation, or lack of fertilizer—it's abundance of interest payments; that's the baby that is there every minute of every day. Not when it is needed, or when you spread it, but every minute of every day and night. Talk and sing about "Old Man River," but it's old man "interest" that keeps the farmer running to town every few days. He has to have a bookkeeper to keep a set of books to keep track of when his various Notes and Mortgage interest comes due. It's the thought of the old mortgages that keep him awake at night.

But if you notice, they are always trying to put through some kind of bill in Congress, but nobody ever puts one through to do something about interest. No sir, you couldn't do that, because then you are getting into the business of the boys that really hold the hoops while the jumping is going on. You could no more get a bill through to whittle the old interest down, than you could get a politician to admit a mistake.

Notice they limit a Savings Bank from paying you over four or five per cent, but about eight is legal if you are the one to do the borrowing.

So you see, everybody has their racket, and everybody is looking to nick the old Treasury out of something, and on account of this being a Presidential year, that makes the nicking more juicy.

Convention Afterthoughts

All I know is just what I read in the papers, and what I can remember of days that passed lately at—what was, for lack of better names— Political Conventions.

It kinder made you wonder, Are we doing all this progressing that we talk about all the time? They say that practice makes perfect at anything. But I tell you, 'tain't so! No nation that was ever invented under the sun does as much practicing "talking," as we do, and if you think we are perfect at it, you just listen over the radio, or worse still, in person, to the speeches at the Political Conventions.

I am just getting over it. Two weeks straight of applesauce. "These are momentous times!" "The eyes of the world are on us!" "Let us act with foresight and deliberation!" Now you heard that by every speaker. Now just take 'em apart and see why they fall over, if you try and let 'em stand alone.

"These are momentous times!" Now what is momentous about 'em? Time is time, momentous things happen to individuals, not to everybody at once. What might be momentous to one, would just be wasting time to another. They are momentous times with the speaker. For if justice gets its due, it's the last time he will ever get to address a National Convention. The only guy a Convention is momentous with, is the bird that gets the nomination.

Then the prize bromo of all: "The eyes of the world are upon us!" Now if that is not insulting your intelligence! Whose eyes are on who? What's the world care what we are doing? What do we care what the world is doing? The eyes of the world are cockeyed as far as we are concerned. Why, the eyes of our own country are not even on us. They know the thing is just an ordinary routine. Somebody is going to be President. It don't make any difference who is in. None of them, from any party, are going to purposely ruin the country. They will do the best they can. If weather and crops, and no wars, and a fair share of prosperity is with them, they will go out of office having had a good administration. So the world is not paying any attention to us; the world is shortsighted as far as we are concerned.

Our public men take themselves so serious. It just looks like they are stoop-shouldered from carrying our country on their backs. And the women, poor souls, when they speak it seems they have paid more attention to the material in the dress, than they have to the material in the speech. They mean well and act awful sincere. It gets 'em out and gives 'em a chance to get away from home, but it just seems like they haven't added anything constructive to the art of politics. They haven't been able to harrow much of a row as far as cleaning up our national pastime is concerned. I think they take it too serious. I believe they would get further if they kinder ridiculed and kidded the men. They can do that in everything else, so why can't they do it in politics?

Personally, I think the camera has done more harm for politics than any other one faction. Everybody would rather get their picture than their ideas in the paper. What does the platform of a political party amount to compared to the photography? There are 10 cameras to every plank in the platform. There was more film wasted on the two Conventions than was wasted making "King of Kings." Speakers get up early in the morning, not to find out how their speech was received by the press, but how the pictures turned out.

And some means should be worked out whereby you could keep track of the same things said by various speakers over and over again. Each man just stands and repeats what has been said a thousand times before, and generally better than he is saying it.

The most terrible things were the nominating speeches. Every man would talk for half the time about what his state had done. For instance, a Wisconsin man gabbed for an hour, telling what Wisconsin had accomplished, including the milk and butter fat per cow. Now what's that got to do with Al Smith?

Another guy, one from Tennessee, was nominating somebody from perhaps Vermont, or Arizona—I forget which—and he went on for an age about what Andrew Jackson had done for the Commonwealth, and the records and traditions of his state. As a matter of fact, about all old Andrew was responsible for, was the system that made us all have to sit there and listen to such junk. Andrew was the one that said: "If you don't get out and work for the Party, you don't get in on the gravy after election!" So all these guys were lined up at the feed trough.

One thing these nominators dwelled on was their candidate's honesty. You would think—from the nominating speeches—that that was their outstanding qualification, honesty. They didn't exactly say so, but they casually insinuated that the candidate on the other side will perhaps steal the White House, if he is not carefully watched.

We did think that the Democratic Convention at Houston would improve on the Republicans at Kansas City. For we did think that the one thing that a Democrat had on a Republican, was that he was a better talker. For he, being out of office more, had more time to think up reasons why he should be in. But it's just as I told you, the speeches at the Democratic wake blew up higher than the Kansas City orgy.

One speaker started his speech with: "As I look into this sea of faces . . ." So that shows you about how far speech making has advanced. It was Noah, that first pulled that line when he looked over the bunch just before pulling in the gang plank.

Then the Democrats especially harped on "Corruption." Now they made that their battle slogan four years ago, when all the corruption and Tea Pot Dome oil scandal was at its height—and they were then beaten by eight million. So how can they win with it this year, when we are more used to corruption than we was four years ago?

In fact, what these nominators should say, is: "The man I am about to name, needs no naming!" Then he would have it right. The ones that were named, needed no naming. They should have been left to their own solitude. And the ones that did the nominating, just where do they dig them up? And do the men that are being nominated know of it in advance? I don't believe they do, or they would never allow them to go on. These nominators can't be friends of the men being nominated, or he would never go on and handicap them as they do.

You see, here is what has made bad speeches stand out so over what they used to be. Maybe in the old days speeches were just as idea-less. But they were only listened to by the delegates. And the man making the speech was a delegate, so he only had to appeal to intelligence as high as his own. But nowadays, this radio thing has changed all that. They are not just talking to a lot of politicians—they are talking to the world. And people are getting wise to the type of man that is supposed to be saving our country. Right away he compares the intelligence of their talk with the talk that he hears in other lines of business, and it just don't stand up. So the old radio is just about to give us a true line on our public servants. But speech making was never at a lower ebb in the history of the world than it is today here in America. A speech nowadays is just like bootleg liquor.

Nobody knows what all the junk is they put in it, but it tastes terrible and sounds worse.

But it's a great game, this Convention game is. I don't suppose there is a show in the world with as much sameness in it. You know exactly what each speaker is going to say before he says it. You know before you go who will be nominated. The platform will always be the same: promise everything, deliver nothing! You cuss yourself for sitting day in and day out, listening to such nonsense. So let's don't hold another Convention till some one can think of a new speech.

The Election Campaign

Every four years we have politics. Every seven years some people have the itch; in a malaria country, every other day people are scheduled to have a chill; every forty years France and Germany fight; and there is just hundreds of these calamities that hit us every once in a while. But of all of them, I think politics is really the most disastrous. It hits a country like a pestilence. There is no telling where it will hit. People that you would think was smart, and would know better, are sometimes struck. And when they are, they are as dumb as the dumb ones.

Course we have these things every four years, but we don't have 'em this bad. Most of the elections heretofore, it didn't matter much who was elected, except to the fellow drawing the salary, but this year we are due for a mental, moral and financial somersault. It just happened that by accident, they named two men who was pretty well known, to run this year. It generally takes to November to explain who each of the presidential candidates are. But this year each side went out and got a couple of headliners.

Hoover is known wherever calamities are known. A national catastrophe without Herbert Hoover wouldn't make the editorial page even. He has fed more hungry people than Child's restaurants. He has been in Coolidge's cabinet ever since Coolidge was old enough to have a cabinet. The Democrats even wanted to run him a few years ago on their side. But after looking them over, and finding that they had no side at that time, why, he just waited till he got a better offer.

And the Democrats, they went stark crazy this time and did the right thing by nominating a man "that needs no introduction," Al Smith. He is a man that has worked steady, even when his whole party was laying off. He seemed to have made himself so valuable that even the Republicans engage him. He was born under the shade of the Brooklyn Bridge, but he didn't set in the shade long. He went out and got himself a political office, and every time he would see a little higher one with nobody sitting in it, he would make a dive for it. And he has never had the chair pulled from under him yet. He is one immigrant in our country that makes no claim of having arrived on the Mayflower. His father was a truckman, and if he had lived he would have been kept busy moving his son's famous brown derby from one office to the next higher one. Al has defeated the Republicans in his home state so much, that they don't nominate a man to run against him any more—they draft him. They tell him: You are not a candidate, you are just a victim!

It's on account of us having these men run that we have all this excitement. Women are voting who haven't left a bridge table that long in years. The voting booth won't be ballot boxes, they will be fashion parades. Milliners will sell millions of hats, just to be voted in. School children this year know the candidates' names—children that ordinarily only know their fraternity's yell. Why, it don't seem like a political election, it seems more like a family quarrel. Thousands and thousands of new voters that don't know a ballot from a laundry slip, will be trying to write down their vote in November.

Both candidates are fine men, and would run the country perhaps equally as well. But, if you listen to either side you would think that for either opponent to get in, it would be a return of the whole country to Slavery, Free Silver, "empty dinner pails," Long Skirts, Bustles and Suspenders. So that's what makes this the prize calamity of all political times. You see, we got people that are really taking the whole thing serious. They think a President has got something to do with running the country.

So just sit back and watch the smoke fly. Money, that's the thing that is bringing the big response. The Democrats never had money before, while this year they are right in the market for A number 1 votes.

That's why the Democratic national chairman says, "Al Smith has the solid South, the mushy East, the cracked North, and a fighting chance in the cuckoo West."

The Republican chairman says that Al won't even carry his derby; that Hoover has the whole thing sewed up, and that the only reason they are going through with the election is just because they have the ballots printed, and it's a kind of holiday, anyway.

Now that is the way those birds rave on from day to day. You would think that everybody in America had gone to them and placed a bond and a guarantee the very way they were going to vote. Did you ever see such assurance in your life? Besides, the man that announces who he is going to vote for, generally is not registered, or perhaps his wife has not told him how he is to vote yet, anyway. Any of those fellows don't know any more about this election than the rest of us, and we don' know anything. If both sides were as sure as they claim, why are they working so hard, and spending so much money? Those guys like a dollar as well as the rest of us, and they wouldn't be handing anything out to the voters if they knew it was a cinch.

No sir, it's a tough race. The Democrats not only have a good candidate, but they got money, which it's better to have than a good candidate. When there is money in an election, it's always doubtful.

So somebody is going to make some money out of politics this year, besides the politicians, and that's just about what is making it an unusual political year.

So don't sell your vote too quick—wait till you hear from the Democrats.

1929

In the Soviet Union, Stalin continues to solidify his dictatorship by banishing Leon Trotsky from Russia on charges of antiparty activities. Next on the agenda is Nikolai Ivanovich Bukharin, editor of *Pravda* and called by Lenin "the most valuable and greatest theoretician of the party." Though Bukharin detests Stalin, he did support him against Trotsky, Zinoviev, and Kamenev. But in November it is his turn, and he is stripped of his Comintern and party positions and expelled from the Politbureau. Later, he will be arrested, put on trial, and shot.

Britain's unemployment rate reaches a disastrous 12.2 percent, and on May 20, the Labour party wins the general election. James Ramsay MacDonald returns as prime minister, and predictably, diplomatic relations with the Soviet Union are once more established.

In the United States, Herbert Clark Hoover takes office on March 4, as the thirty-first president. The stockmarket is going up, profits are climbing, dividends are increasing . . . yet 71 percent of America's families have an annual income below the $2,500 level that is considered the minimum for a family's decent standard of living. Writes Will Rogers: "Wall Street is in good shape, but Eighth Avenue was never as bad off."

Moral values too, are disintegrating. On May 20, Hoover appoints a commission—he likes appointing commissions—headed by former Attorney General George W. Wickersham, to investigate and report on "dominant national problems." And there are many of those. Widespread disregard of the laws of the land is demonstrated by bootlegging, hijacking, and kidnapping. America leads the "civilized" world in the negative statistics of homicides, burglaries, holdups, and graft. Citizens are terrorized by gangsters better equipped than the police charged to protect them; the underworld is able to incriminate or bribe those who are to enforce the law. Court records show that out of every one hundred apprehended and indicted, only three are convicted.

Gang warfare in Chicago again grabs the headlines with the "Saint Valentine's Day massacre." At 10:30 A.M. on February 14, seven members of the George ("Bugs") Moran gang are machine-gunned down in a garage on North Clark Street, which has also been used as a bootleg liquor warehouse. Al Capone's gang is suspected of the murders.

America has now more than 20 million telephones—twice as many as ten years before—and automobile production reaches a total of 5 million; but two decades will have to pass before America will produce that many cars again in a single year. Ford announces an increase in a day's wage—from six dollars to seven. Ford, too, is the first to introduce a "station wagon," actually a Model A with a wooden boxlike compartment. This is also the year in which the first mobile houselike trailer is offered to the public. And to go with all these cars, the first commercially successful car radio is introduced—unfortunately it is so enormously bulky that designers have trouble stowing tuner and speaker into available space.

Some of the most notable books of the year: *All Quiet on the Western Front,* by Erich Maria Remarque (translated from the German); *Look Homeward, Angel,* by Thomas Wolfe; *A Farewell to Arms,* by Ernest Hemingway; *The Magnificent Obsession,* by Lloyd Douglas; and *Dodsworth,* by Sinclair Lewis.

Among the films Americans see: *The Blue Angel,* with Marlene Dietrich and Emil Jannings; *Disraeli,* with George Arliss and for which he wins the Academy Award; and *The Virginian,* with Gary Cooper.

The year's most popular songs are: "Star Dust," by Hoagy Carmichael; "Honeysuckle Rose," by Thomas "Fats" Waller; "Button Up Your Overcoat," by Ray Henderson; "You Do Something to Me" and "What Is This Thing Called Love," both by Cole Porter.

Broadway's Pulitzer Prize winner is *Street Scene,* by Elmer Rice, featuring Erin O'Brien Moore and Beulah Bondi; other plays are: *Strictly Dishonorable,* by Preston Sturges; *Berkeley Square,* by John L. Baldridge, starring Leslie Howard.

"The Rise of the Goldbergs" joins the radio dramas; it stars

Gertrude Berg and will change its title to "The Goldbergs."

Dance-band leader Guy Lombardo and his Royal Canadians open at the Roosevelt Hotel in New York City, and his New Year's Eve broadcast becomes a national institution.

By mid-1929, the road to riches is paved with stock certificates, and the forecast is for clear and sunny skies. There is just one very small problem—most of these stock certificates are "bought" with just a minimum down payment. In fact, by July, 300 million shares are being carried on margin.

And in October, after a gathering of threatening clouds and some flashes of lightning, the market breaks. At first there is controlled alarm, as the existence of more sellers than buyers begins to depress the market—then there is fear, and then there is panic! On October 29, 16,410,000 shares flood the New York Stock Exchange in search of whatever the market will pay.

Between October 1 and October 30, a market value of between $30 billion and $45 billion is wiped out—most of it in a single week. To comprehend this amount, one should bear in mind that this loss is more money than the total U.S. cost of the Great War from April 5, 1917 to June 30, 1919.

In the early part of 1929, Will Rogers still appears with Dorothy Stone in *Three Cheers*. Mid-April, the show moves to Boston, and in May it plays in Philadelphia, Detroit, and Pittsburgh.

At the beginning of June, Will is home again for the first time in almost nine months. Will is welcomed by the Beverly Hills Chamber of Commerce, which honors him with a dinner at the Beverly Wilshire Hotel. Betty Rogers is presented with a cut-crystal and silver service from the citizens of Beverly Hills.

When Charles Lindbergh inaugurates the International Airmail Service to New York City, Will is the first to buy a ticket as a fare-paying passenger.

This is the year that Will Rogers takes on yet another task: the new talking pictures. Under contract to Fox Film Corporation, Will first films a cameo part in *Happy Days,* a film that is really a revue, featuring more than two dozen stars. Will's first feature film, *They Had to See Paris,* with Irene Rich, Marguerite Churchill, Owen Davis, Jr., and vivacious Canadian actress Fifi Dorsay, is based on a story by Homer Croy.

The premiere is held at the Fox Carthay Circle Theatre. But Will ducks out on attending his own premiere and grabs a plane for Oklahoma. He is not present to learn firsthand of his great success in this new medium.

Will Rogers

Will Has Read Another Book

You remember a few weeks ago I was telling you about starting in to improve myself with some book learning? Well, I started in a book "The Cradle of the Deep," by a girl that would just walk up and slap a shark in the face if he started pulling any wisecracks at her. Buying that book got me into a book store. Well, I had no idea there was as many books as there must be. Half the world that don't know what the other half is doing, why, they are writing books! Busy men that you would think would have something important to do, have got some book that they have written.

I heard in a roundabout way that Henry 8th was having a revival year, and as I was headed for Hollywood for a couple of years, I says to myself, I will read about old Henry, and see where all these movie gangs got their idea. I knew a little about him, for years ago in the Ziegfeld Follies, we had a Shakespeare revival. All the sketches were on things he had written about. Sam Hardy, the fellow that is so good out in talking pictures, he played Henry 8th, and we had six beautiful girls as his wives. Marion Davis, I remember, was one of them and she had one line to speak: "And a hell of a King was he!" And I always did say I am going to read about this old bird, if Congress will give me the time.

There was a fellow named Hackett, they said he had spent a lifetime in England (course, everybody has their own idea of what a lifetime is), just working on material for this book. I don't know how long he spent, but he sure come up with something! Talk about suppressing books! I would think they would extinguish this one in England. Not because the book is bad, but this old Henry, why, if the English nobility have gone down in a direct line, and if King Edward and George, and the Prince of Wales, are all direct descendants of that old reprobate, I would rise up and say: Folks, you got me wrong, I am not of that strain at all. He was no forefather of mine.

Why, if somebody told all those things about one of my ancestors, I would take it up with the Al Capone gang, and I wouldn't care how much it cost me to extinguish him, I'd do it.

This old Henry was just an old fat, big-footed, chuckle-headed baby! He had an older brother named Arthur. Older brothers got everything in those days, a younger brother was just like a Democrat—he had to take what was left. This Arthur wasn't well, and he didn't know much, even when he felt good. England wasn't much of a

144

country; it stood just about like the Red Sox in the American League. They wanted to marry this Prince Arthur off to somebody with a pedigree. They looked in the stud book, and found there had been a filly colt sired in Spain a few years ahead of Arthur, but that this mating might add to the fast slipping organization.

So they got hold of Queen Isabella of Spain. There was a King along with her, I think it was Ferdinand; but they kept him sitting on the bench, season after season. This Isabella is the same one that this Italian come and got her to back the first non-stop flight of the Atlantic. This fellow, Columbus, went in for safety, he wanted a three-motored job, he wouldn't take a chance on one ship going dead on him. So he made her fix him up with three. He missed the whole of the American continent, but found San Domingo.

Well, this Isabella not only had jewels to pawn to back these cross-ocean tours, but she had children to distribute around where they would bring in the most revenue. She had landed one in France as a king's wife, and one in Rome (who ever had it that day). When nations in those days had nothing else to do, they would take Rome, then sit and pray for somebody to come and take it off their hands.

Well, they had a daughter Catherine, so about the best they could do with her, was an offer from England. That was kinder like slumming for it didn't mean much to Spain, who was the General Motors in those days. But they sent her over and married her to Arthur, who, I think, was about fourteen years old. They wanted to get him settled down before he had a chance to start running around too much. Well, Arthur was disgusted with the whole proceedings, and to get even with all of them, he just died.

Well, that brought this old, round fat-headed boy Henry into the proceedings. For a second son in England only has one chance in the world, and that's for the older one to die. So that was Henry's first good break early in life. He not only inherited the direct line to the King, but he took over all of Prince Arthur's estate, including a wife.

In order for Henry not to marry a widow, why, they dug up a guy named Wolsey. He was a lobbyist to Rome, and the Pope, and anything like old marriage ceremonies, or dates, or deeds, why, he could arrange and change them to fit the times. So he thought of the bright idea of saying that Prince Arthur and Catherine were never married—that it was two other fellows. So Henry took her over. I think he was about twelve. He had to start in marrying early, for he had a lot of marrying to do. About all you could say for him, was that he was big. If he had lived in our time, he would have been a wrestler, or a doorman outside some New York hotel.

Catherine couldn't speak English, and he couldn't speak Spanish, so there was no chance of an argument. Henry's father, whoever it was, I forget his number, (you know they have numbers on these kings, like they do on a race horse), well, I forget whether it was a George the 7th, or Edward the 11th, well, anyhow, he died, and left young King Henry a disease in one leg, and Cardinal Wolsey. That's the only two things he willed him. Now Catherine seemed to have been all right as a wife for a Prince of Wales, but for a king, well, she just wasn't the type. No male heir had been born, and of course, everybody was to blame, but Henry. To have a baby girl in those days was not only a total loss, but practically a social disaster. It wasn't that boys were any more comfort to you, but if there was no male heir to follow you up, the graft might slip out of your family's hands, and into some other. It was the days of high ideals and square dealings.

Well, now the story is getting hot; it's about Anne Boleyn, the local vamp, and how she took Henry, how she made all his fat go to his head, it's about love, graft, corruption, murders, wars, and beheadings, galore.

There was Henry's first wife, Catherine of Aragon. This "Aragon" translated from our old college days' Latin, means: Somewhere in Spain. Well, Henry just lost "his taste for Catherine." He was trying to raise him a bunch of boy babies, and Catherine's inclination ran more to the effeminate.

Now we get to Anne Boleyn, she was the Greta Garbo, Peggy Joyce, type. You see Catherine was a devout Catholic, and didn't believe in a divorce, but Anne could regulate her religion and her morals to fit the situation. She just said: "If this big fat round-headed bird is going to start in on a series of promiscuous weddings, why I better get in early, while he is really only an amateur."

But wait a minute. Before we get to Anne, we got to stop and do something for Mary Boleyn, Anne's sister four years older. Mary had a husband named Carey, but what's a husband between friends? Henry give him a job, it says, at the Court, where he could see his own wife and Henry. I don't know what job Mary had at the court, but it was nothing trivial for her and Henry to raise a baby boy. Carey was still around there, but Henry was the "Head Man."

Now Anne comes in; Anne was nineteen, Henry was 35. Catherine, his wife, was 41. Now which of the two will win? You said it!

Anne had already been stuck on a young noble, named Percy, but he was kinder of the drug store type. This Cardinal Wolsey, he was the one that King Henry kept promising that he would see that he would be made Pope, at the next vacancy. Wolsey had the backing of

Hen, but he lacked the vote of some 55 Cardinals. If it hadn't been for that little oversight, he might have been elected. Hen was for Wolsey, on the platform of "Divorce Relief." Clement, the Pope, couldn't see any reason why Henry should have a spare wife, when he already had one. But if Henry could make Wolsey Pope, he could have given him a Bill-of-Sale to go out and marry who, and what he wanted. Why, there is practically no telling who all Henry would have married. No woman would have been safe from becoming Queen of England.

Wolsey would go to Rome when a Pope would die, with what Henry thought would be enough Doubloons, to buy enough votes, but some other king, from France or Spain, would send an entry with more Doubloons. And before poor old Wolsey could communicate with Henry to make another Campaign Contribution, why, the new Pope would be elected. Radio, or even a good bicycle, would have been a Godsend to Wolsey in those trying hours. But it just looked like Wolsey was a Democrat in a Republican administration. So when Henry the 8th saw that Rome was going to veto his divorce bills, why Henry and Wolsey started a religion of their own.

It wasn't exactly a free love religion, but they would listen to reason in case some "Gentleman" run onto a younger lady friend. Had Rome given Henry a divorce, there would have been no Church of England. For Henry wasn't particular about what religion it was, all he wanted was "bigger and better Divorces!" So this Anne Boleyn really should be their Patron Saint. She not only started a row, but a Religion.

Hen kinder suggested to Anne that there really didn't have to be any marriage ceremony, but this Anne had seen where her sister Mary finished, when there had been no wedding bells. She just kindly informed the old king that there would be a session with the Justice of the Peace, before he started any of his funny business. This Anne lived in 1529, but boy, she knew her onions. She not only knew her onions, but she knew her king.

Henry started a couple of wars, thinking maybe that would attract some attention to him and his country, and make it look so important that Rome would have to listen to reason. That's when he issued that famous historical statement: "My Kingdom, My Kingdom, for a divorce!" Anne stood pat, and the Catholic church lost England, which was of such little importance to them that it was about like a presidential candidate losing Rhode Island. Martin Luther, over in Germany, was kinder kicking for a minority religion at this same time, and I guess that's really where Henry got his idea from. Luther didn't want to get married again, he just wanted to get free.

Well, when Henry got his own Court, and made his own laws, why,

147

of course, he said that Catherine was not married to him. He had it annulled on the grounds that he had never seen Anne Boleyn when he married Catherine. Mistaken Identity!

So he grabs off Anne, and leaves Catherine, and his daughter Mary, marries Anne and in five months she has a baby, and it's a girl, so he starts looking around again. This baby was Elizabeth, that we are later to hear so much of. What happened to Anne? The ax! What had she done? Why, nothing, but Henry had run into Jane Seymour, and in the meantime Catherine had died of a broken heart; so his batting average was: met two, defeated two. Here is what Anne Boleyn said: "I heard say the executioner is very good, and I have a little neck." That night Henry give her a big party, he had found a better way to divorce 'em. He married Jane, who didn't have much to recommend her, outside of just being of the female gender. Well, they hadn't any more than got home from the church, till they had a baby, and it was a boy, and Jane died at once, which was fortunate for her, for Henry was already in communication with Germany, to import a new wife from over there. Her name was Anne of Cleves. His ministers had picked her from a Holbein portrait, so they brought her over. I will say one thing for old Henry; he had no conscience, but he did have judgement.

Henry went to the docks to meet Anne from Germany, and got one flash at her, and chopped off Cromwell's head for being such a bad judge of beauty. But it looked like it would strengthen the kingdom with Europe, if he married her, so he shut his eyes and went at it. She had been, what the Japanese call "a picture bride." All they see is the picture. But Holbein was a painter, not a camera. If cameras had been in use, it would have saved Henry that marriage. One snap shot with a Brownie of her, would have kept her right at home. She had a lot of breeding, but no class. She was a princess, 31 years old, and made up in virtue what she lacked in charm. Well, Henry had never been very high on virtue; what he wanted was beauty, and HOW! The only English word she could say was "Ja, Ja." and Henry didn't know what that was. Neither do I.

Cromwell said, "Yes, my Lord, but she hath a Queenly manner." And Hen wisecracked back, "Well, she don't need it to protect her." She missed beheading, by him divorcing her and sending her home.

Now we get Catherine Howard, a cousin of Anne Boleyn. She went to the block with these kind words: "I die Queen of England, but I would rather die the wife of a Culpepper." (I wonder if he was any relation to the Virginia Culpeppers, who owned a Court House?)

Well, that didn't make Henry feel any too good, to know that he wasn't in as good favor as Culpepper, so he just hunted up that Culpepper, and off with his bean. Oh what a cheerful little ancestor our folks that come over on the Mayflower had in this gentleman Henry.

Henry sure was death on Catherines, and he gets another one. This last one is Catherine Parr. She was a motherly kind of soul, and they do say, (and all hoped that it was true), that she poisoned him. Anyhow, she beats him to the ax. She had been married twice before, and you got to learn something in that time. Of course, Henry had her 6 to 3, but her and that English grog, bumped him off before he could get to her. She buried him and then married the man of her choice, which was No. 4 for her. And then we say: "What's our country coming to, we are getting worse and worse!"

Well, it looks to me like the only safe man in those days was the ax man. So I just want to meet some Colonial Dame now that likes to claim she can trace her ancestors back to the Tudors.

The Prince of Wales Marries?

What do you know about the Prince of Wales getting married? Looks like the kid is going to settle down. These titled birds seem to have one tradition that they are pretty jealous of, and that is to try and cop off a princess, if possible. Some times they go out among the plebians and take a wife. This one is a beautiful, lovely girl, 19 years old, who perhaps is in love with some nice young man of her own age, but the old heads must keep up the prestige of this marrying business, and find somebody that will do royalty the most good.

It's just like Queen Isabella told all her children, when she was doling them out to Henry the 8th, and King Charles. "It's not a princess' place to love, it's a princess' place to breed." She sure sent 'em out to marry for their country.

A thoroughbred race horse breeding establishment is more in line with royal marriages than anything I know of, only they are more careful to never inbreed; but as far as love is concerned, that's a lot of hooey. They think it brings nations closer to each other, to have royal families married to each other. Well, it didn't do much for Germany and England, but anyhow, let's get the Prince of Wales married off and let the girls all over the world get their minds on somebody else. It's wonderful, I reckon, to be a prince, but they pay for it.

The Dinner

Scene: The White House, Washington, D.C.
Time: Sunday Night, March 3rd, 1929—The evening before the
  Inauguration.
Play produced under the management of the U.S. Government.

Characters in the order of their appearance:

> Calvin. . . . . Mr. Coolidge
> Grace . . . . Mrs. Coolidge
> Lou . . . . Mrs. Hoover
> Herb . . . . Mr. Hoover

Supers in mob scene, Congressmen and Senators.

CALVIN: Grace, I bet you gone and packed my shirt front!
GRACE: No, I didn't, Calvin, I didn't touch your old thing. You probably endorsed it and sent it back with those other bills to Congress.
CALVIN: Well, what am I going to do for a shirt tonight?
GRACE: Wear the one you are going to wear to the Inauguration tomorrow.
CALVIN: I am not going to wear any to the Inauguration tomorrow. It's not my Inauguration. Hoover will have on enough for both of us.
GRACE: Well, for land's sake, hurry up! They will be coming in a few minutes, cause he is noted for being on time.
CALVIN: From what I hear, he is noted for about everything. Where is my other sock? I bet you packed it around that painting.
GRACE: Calvin, I didn't see your old sock. Put on your cowboy chaps and they won't notice you having one sock missing.
CALVIN: What would I want to put on my chaps for? I am not running for anything.
GRACE: You are running for this train tomorrow, ain't you? You claim you are in such a hurry to get out of town. Hurry up now, they will be here any minute. They are just the kind that will be on time.
CALVIN: Now I lost my collar buttons. What truck did you pack them on? I had 'em laid out right here. They was the pair that Tom Heflin, the senator from Alabama, brought me from Rome.
GRACE: Well I do wish you would hurry up. I want to straighten this room after you get out, for she will want to look around. By the way, who owns these sheets, us or the government?
CALVIN: U.S.

150

GRACE: I've got Emily Post's Book here on "What is proper to carry in and out of the White House."

CALVIN: Well, there is a precedent, I reckon. Half of Washington does nothing but study up "precedents." They can tell what color underwear that a retiring President should have on when he turns over the salary to his successful competitor. If the people of Washington obeyed as many laws as they do precedents, they wouldn't even need a jail in the whole town.

GRACE: Well, I know I want to leave the house in good shape. I had the whole place fumigated after those Senators breakfasts you had here.

CALVIN: Well, they shouldn't be so particular. They lived in a rented house all their lives, haven't they?

GRACE: Why no, they got a home.

CALVIN: But they was only there the night the election returns come in.

GRACE: Well where was you the night the election returns come in?

CALVIN: I was asleep.

GRACE: Well they have traveled around and seen a lot.

CALVIN: Well I seen a lot right here in Washington without traveling.

GRACE: Why he has been to Siberia!

CALVIN: Yes, and the first time he has a run-in with that Senate, he will wish he was back in Siberia.

GRACE: He is an engineer, he can do lots of things.

CALVIN: Well, he will wish he studied to be a conductor, instead.

GRACE: Listen, I hear 'em, or is that them?

CALVIN: It don't sound well enough organized for them.

GRACE: Yes, that's them. Hurry up! Fasten your suspenders. "Precedent" says we should both meet 'em at the door, and say in unison, "Welcome to your new home."

(LOU AND HERB IN HUDDLE, OUTSIDE OF DOOR)

HERB: Now let's don't stay here long, for I want to get home and rehearse some gestures on my speech for tomorrow. I bet they forgot this was the night we was coming.

GRACE: Hello, why it's you all! Come right in, Calvin will be down just as soon as he vetoes two more bills.

HERB: Nice place you got here.

GRACE: Yes, we think so—that is—we thought so. It's old but we have managed some way.

151

LOU: Where is the study? I want to fix up around Herbert's study.

GRACE: Well Calvin studied wherever he happened to be. He didn't have any regular place to study, when he studied. He used public dinners mostly.

LOU: How is the help? Are they dependable?

GRACE: Well, they are government help, and you been here long enough to know what that is, either in Kabinet, Kongress, or Kitchen.

LOU: Oh, but look at those cuspidors!

GRACE: You have to have those for Congressional receptions.

CALVIN: Hello Herb, glad you come to the wake.

HERB: Well, we thought we would walk over. Lou wanted to look the place over. The two trunks won't be over till tomorrow.

CALVIN: Oh, it's all right. But you can't get much of a steady lease on this place. The fellow just lets you have it on short term. Then lots of times he don't want to renew, and that's what makes it bad. Come in and sit down to dinner. We ain't got much, just kinder a little snack. Just sorter cleaning out what little was left in the ice box, we didn't want to get in anything more. We figured you was like most folks, you liked to come in with all your own stuff. There is a few half jars of some stuff that we didn't think hardly worth while packing, and maybe some butter left from breakfast, and lots of just little, small things like that, that we just thought we would leave. I expect there is a little flour in there, ain't there, Grace? She will give your wife the name and the phone of the grocer, and they will send you up what you will need for lunch tomorrow. Just run a charge account there, that's the way I did. But you got to watch the bills! This town is awful slick that way, they just live off such as you and me. You see, there is so many of these politicians that get away and don't pay their bills, that they have to make it up on those of us who do. Now I don't want to be telling you your business, but don't go and make the mistake I did and start feeding them Senators and Congressmen breakfast. They will eat you out of house and home, and then go right back up on the Hill, and vote against what you fed 'em for.

LOU: Come on, Herb, now we must be going and let these people get some rest. They got a long, hard trip in front of 'em tomorrow. Thanks for showing me the house, Grace. Herb has to get home and study up a new Cabinet, in case the Senate got wise to this one.

HERB and LOU: Well, goodnight, you all. Coming to the Inauguration tomorrow, ain't you? Maybe we will see you there. Thanks for the dinner. Just leave the key under the door mat, and leave your address and I will send you any little thing you might have left.

CALVIN and GRACE: Goodnight, thanks for coming. Hope you like the place. I will have to mail you our new address where we will be. Calvin can't make up his mind.

Will Rogers Had Wall Street by the Tail

This stock market thing has spoiled more appetites lately than bad cooking. Now that stock market is all a puzzle to me. I never did mess with it except one time in New York last year, when everybody was just raking in money with a shovel—or so they all told me. I was hearing that Eddie Cantor, the actor, was piling up a fortune that Rockefeller couldn't vault over. Now I had known and been a friend of Eddie's for many years, so I hold out some dough on Mrs. Rogers— out of the weekly stipend and I go over to the New Amsterdam Theatre one night and call on Eddie.

When I was admitted, I felt like a racketeer that had finally gained admission to J.P. Morgan's sanctum. Eddie thought I had come to persuade him to play a benefit for some improvident fellow actor (as I had often done with him in the past). But then I quietly whispered to him that I wanted him to make me a few dollars without telling jokes for them, or what went for jokes. I told him about the amount that I had been able by judicious scheming to nick from Mrs. Rogers. Knowing her, he wouldn't believe that I had been so shrewd, and he immediately said: "You don't need me. Just keep this thing up and grab it off from her. What does it matter whether you make it from Wall Street, or from her?"

But I told him that I wanted to get in on this skinning of Wall Street. Everybody was doing it and I wanted to be in at the killing. I didn't have anything particular against Wall Street, but knowing the geographical and physical attributes of the street, I knew that it was crooked. You can stand at the head of it and you can only see to the bend. It just won't let you see all of it at once, as short as it is. I just said to myself, I would like to be with the bunch that has the credit of straightening this alley out.

Well, Eddie had just that day made fifty thousand, according to closing odds on the last commodity. I says, show me the fifty. He then explained to me that he hadn't the money, that that's what he could have made if he had sold. But he hadn't sold, as tomorrow he should make at least another fifty, or even if he only made 49, why, it would help pay for burnt cork, which he uses for his make-up. Well, Eddie then explained the stock market to me in a mighty sensible way. He told me who had told him this and he repeated it very well, so I will repeat it all to you.

The stock market is just like a sieve (one of those pans with holes in it). Everything and everybody is put into it and it is shaken, and through the holes go all the small stuff. Then they load it up again and maybe hold it still for a little while, and then they start shaking again and all the little investors go through. They pick themselves up, turn bootlegger or do something to get some more money, and then they crawl back in the hopper, and away they go again.

Well, that made a pretty good scenario, but I said, that's only the boobs that go through the hole. I am going to grab a root and hang on with the big boys. Eddie didn't much want to take my money, knowing how hard I had worked for it, both from the theatre manager, and Mrs. Rogers. But I went on telling him I was 49 years, and had never in my life made a single dollar without having to chew some gum to get it. So he says, "Well, I will buy you some of my bank stock. It's selling mighty high, and with this little dab you got here, you won't get much of it, but it's bound to go up, for banks make money whether the market goes up or down. Even if it stands still, they are getting their interest while it's making up its mind what to do."

So Eddie said, "I will get you some of this stock. You don't need to pay me for it, just let it go. Put it away and forget about it. Then some day, when you want, you can send me a check for it."

Well, just think of that! Here I was going to break Wall Street on credit! Well, I shook hands, and I told him that I had always known, and said that he was the greatest comedian on stage, but now I knew that he was the best financier we had in our profession. Well, I went back to my own dressing room at my theatre, and I never was as funny in my life as I was that night. I had Wall Street by the tail, and a downhill run.

I stayed up the next night till the papers come out, to see what OUR bank had closed at, and after reading it I stayed up the rest of the night, wondering if Eddie could possibly be wrong. Well one little drop brought on another, till one day I received a letter from Eddie's broker, saying that my check would come in mighty handy, and for me to please remit undernamed amount.

Well, in the meantime I had used most of the money celebrating the fact that I had bought the stock. In fact, I had really spent most of it in advertising Eddie and his humanitarian qualities. Each night I began to get unfunnier and unfunnier. This strain of "being in the market," was telling on me. Eddie could laugh at a loss and still remain comical. But when there was minus signs before my lone stock, I just was not unctuous. I didn't want to tell Eddie, but finally I sent for his personal Aide de Camp, and told him that on the morrow, when the market opened, among those desiring to dispose, I would be among those present. I got out with a very moderate loss.

The next day that stock went up big. But the whole thing is no place for a weak-hearted comedian, and from now on when Eddie wants to help me, he can just give me some of his old jokes.

Whooping It Up for Wall Street

This Stock Market thing has kinder had the front page groggy here lately. They thought we had the thing just about as low as they possibly could get it, but it's been getting still worse. The old "margin" fellow, he has a mustard plaster on him all over. He can't take any good stocks of his to protect the weak ones, for there is no good ones; it's the good ones that are going down. England says our Market is all cockeyed, and it will eventually get so that everything will be based on just a fair percentage of what it earns. Folks been buying without even having any idea what they were earning. We been buying just alphabetically; the nearer "A" you could get, the more it seemed to be worth.

If the president of a concern was a good after-dinner speaker, and made a good appearance, why, his stock would go up. Nothing determined the worth of a stock but the fact that it was going up, and that it hadn't reached a thousand yet, and that there was no reason why it shouldn't keep going till it did.

Oh, it was a great game while it lasted. All you had to do was to buy and wait till the next morning and just pick up the paper and see how much you made—in print. But all that has changed. After all, everybody just can't live on gambling. Somebody has to do some work!

I haven't had much time to read the papers lately, on account as you know, that I have been trying my best to help the president and Wall Street to "Restore Confidence!" You take confidence, it's one of the hardest things in the world to get restored, once it gets out of bounds.

I have restored a lot of things in my time, such as cattle back to the home range. Herded Follies Girls toward the stage door, near show time. Helped to revive interest in National Political Conventions. Even assisted the Democrats in every forlorn pilgrimage, and a host of other worthy charities. But I tell you, this "Restoring Confidence," is the toughest drive I ever assisted in. When I took up the work, confidence was at a mighty low ebb, that is, so all the papers and speakers was saying.

Wall Street had gone into one tail spin after another. You would pick up a paper in the morning and read the stock report, and you wouldn't think there was that many "minus" signs in the world. Well, the effect of it was just like going to Monte Carlo, and hearing that everybody was betting on the Black, and the Red had been coming up continually for two days. That would just simply demoralize southern France, and the whole Riviera. Well, that's what this Market was doing here. It was just taking all the joy out of gambling. If it kept on like that, it would discourage gambling, and that of course would be bad for the country—that's what they said!

Course there was a lot of us dumb ones that couldn't understand it. We said: "Well, if somebody lost money here, why, somebody else must have made it. You can't just lose money to nobody, unless you drop it somewhere and nobody ever finds it."

Then they said a good deal of the money was "Lost on Paper." That it was just figures, that it wasn't real money. Well, I had done that. I could remember every contract I would get for a season's work on stage or screen, my wife and I would sit down and figure out what all we would have by the end of that season. Well at the end of the season we had the figures, but we couldn't find the money. So Wall Street had nothing on us.

In fact, I don't think it had anything on anybody. For we all can take a piece of paper, and if you give us enough pencil, we can figure ourselves out a pretty neat little fortune in no time, so when I heard that most of the money had been lost on "Paper Profits," why, I felt right at home with them.

But then everybody said it would have a demoralizing effect on the country for so many to have their paper profits all rubbed out at once. That it would have the effect of making people more careful with their money, and thereby make it bad for speculation. That if people didn't trade in stocks, Wall Street couldn't exist.

So I says, what can we do for 'em, so they will keep on existing? "Why, restore confidence!" And that's what I been doing for weeks, writing and talking. Course I haven't been buying anything myself. I wanted to give all the other folks a chance to have confidence first. There is none of the greedy pig about me. This confidence was for sale, and I wanted them to have the very first chance of buying it.

Course I never could understand what the price of the stock had to do with keeping the company working and turning out their product. For instance if "Consolidated Corn Salve" stock had all been sold, and the company had that money it had brought in, and was operating on that, what difference did it make to them if the stock was selling at a thousand bucks, or if people was using the stock to kindle their fire with? Their business was still to keep after those corns. In other words, they should be watching corns, instead of the Market. If the shares had sold for $564 one day, and $1.80 the next, what had happened during the night to the afflicted toes of the country? Well, I couldn't get that.

Course they explained it off some way. They said: "Trading was good for the country, and kept things a-circulating." So I finally went over to their side. I really did it for vanity, for I could see all the big men over there, and I felt flattered when I saw that I was to join 'em in this great work of getting people back to contribute to Wall Street again.

I can see that there is lots of them that it will take time to get them back. They not only lost confidence, but they lost money, some of them all their money. So we will have to wait till they get some money in some other business, perhaps in some business in which they really have no confidence. They will then be able to get back into the Market, not only with new confidence, but with new money.

But I am telling them that this country, as a whole, is sound, and that all those whose heads are solid, are bound to get back into the Market again. I tell 'em that this country is bigger than Wall Street, and if they don't believe it, I show 'em the map.

The Infallible Stock Market Tip

There is one rule that works in every calamity, be it pestilence, war, or famine. The rich get richer, and the poor get poorer. The poor even help arrange it. But it's just as I have been constantly telling you, "Don't gamble! Take all your savings and buy some good stocks, and hold it till it goes up. Then sell it."

"If it don't go up, don't buy it."

Who Runs the Stock Exchange?

The Lord was wise to the world, and He just wanted to show 'em that after all, He was running things, in spite of what the New York Stock Exchange thought.

Well, that was a terrible blow to finance, to learn that the Lord not only closed the stock market on Sundays, but that He could practically close it any day of the week.

1930

General, worldwide economic and emotional depression is beginning to settle in as trade declines, production falls, and unemployment rises.

In London, a conference on naval armament convenes, and ends three months later with an agreement by participants: the United States, Britain, France, Italy, and Japan. Submarine tonnage is to be limited, gun caliber is to be controlled, and certain warships are to be scrapped. While the United States has to physically destroy such warships, other nations simply refrain from building theirs.

The last Allied troops are withdrawn from the Saar and the Rhineland. In Benito Mussolini's Italy, Il Duce speaks out in favor of revising the Versailles Peace Treaty; he also decrees that abortions are a crime "against the integrity and the health of the race." Despite the threat of punishment, half a million abortions a year are performed illegally.

In Africa, Ethiopia's Empress Zawditu dies; Haile Selassie I will be proclaimed king of kings.

The world's population approaches the 2 billion mark, while the census in the United States shows that the population is nearing 123 million. Four million are unemployed here, and the national income drops drastically. During the year, 1,300 banks close, including the Bank of United States (a private bank, despite the official-sounding name) with sixty branch offices. The Smoot-Hawley Tariff Act passes Congress, and despite advice by over one thousand economists to the contrary, President Hoover signs it into law June 17. Tariffs are raised to their highest level ever, and in retaliation, other countries raise theirs against U.S. imports. To upset matters even further, the Soviet Union tries to sell grain at ten cents below the world price. And to add to the farmers' concerns, a most severe winter is followed by an unprecedented drought, which plagues and parches the South and Midwest.

Ford still sells 1 million Model A cars, but that figure shows a 50 percent drop from last year. The United States now has a total of 700,000 miles of paved roads, and 2.3 million miles of unpaved roads. Along all of them move 23 million American cars. By comparison, Japan has a total of just 50,000 cars.

In Long Island City, New York, German-born Max Schmeling wins the world heavyweight title on a foul by U.S. champion Jack Sharkey. American golfer Bobby Jones wins both open and amateur tournaments in the United States and Great Britain. When his yacht, *Shamrock V,* is defeated 4 to 0, Sir Thomas J. Lipton has lost his fifth and final attempt since 1899 to win the America's Cup. Called "The World's Best Loser" by Will Rogers in an *American Magazine* article, Will suggests in his daily squib of September 18 that "everybody send $1 apiece for a fund to buy a loving cup for Sir Thomas Lipton, bigger than the one he would have got if he had won." At noon on December 3, in New York, Sir Thomas is indeed presented with a gold cup, purchased with nationwide contributions. Knute Rockne, Notre Dame's head football coach since 1918, brings his team to Los Angeles to face the University of Southern California on December 6. The California team is heavily favored despite Rockne's awesome thirteen-year record of 102 wins, 12 losses, and 5 ties. Notre Dame wins, 27 to 0.

Radio, too, has come into its own. There are now 13.5 million radio sets, and American advertisers spend almost $60 million to hawk their products. A new drama has listeners spellbound at their sets. It started over station WXYZ in Detroit, and tells of a masked westerner and his Indian friend; it is called "The Lone Ranger." And a young newscaster begins a career that will last forty-six years. On September 29, Lowell Thomas reads his first summary of the day's events.

A young, mostly self-taught pilot named Wiley Post wins the first Bendix Trophy air race between Los Angeles and Chicago. He is flying a Lockheed Vega, owned by his employer, Floyd C. Hall; the plane is named *Winnie Mae,* after Hall's daughter.

Former President William Howard Taft resigns as chief justice of the Supreme Court on February 3 because of ill health; he dies March 8. Charles Evans Hughes, a former associate justice of the Supreme Court, who had resigned to run as Republican candidate for the presidency, is now named chief justice.

The Apple Shippers Association offers surplus apples on credit for unemployed men and women to sell on street corners. By year's end, some six thousand such apple sellers crowd New York City's main streets. Uncounted thousands try to sell apples in other cities. They will become a most familiar sight, and a symbol of the Depression.

Incredibly, authorities in New York City will consider them a nuisance and instruct police to order them off the streets.

A demonstration by the unemployed in New York City's Union Square, staged by the Communist party, is transformed by its organizers into an angry, fighting mob scene, as 35,000 battle with police. Scores are injured.

Despite harder times, U.S. movies report increased attendance, especially as all film companies rush into the new medium—talkies. A new process also widens the screen. Among the most memorable films of the year are: *Anna Christie,* with Greta Garbo and Charles Bickford; René Clair's *Under the Roofs of Paris;* Lewis Milestone's *All Quiet on the Western Front,* with Lew Ayres; *Outward Bound,* with Leslie Howard; *Min and Bill,* with Marie Dressler and Wallace Beery; Howard Hughes's *Hell's Angels,* with Jean Harlow and Ben Lyons; and *Little Caesar,* with Edward G. Robinson.

In an effort to display Prohibition enforcement, New York City police arrest eleven patrons, dressed in formal evening wear, of a well-known nightclub on Broadway. The eleven are found to be carrying hip flasks, and are therefore "in possession of intoxicating liquor in a public place." The U.S. Supreme Court rules, however, that the buyer of liquor commits no crime! The Court finds that the Volstead Act purposely ignored the purchaser. A bill is introduced in Congress to stipulate that the sale of up to one gallon of liquor be considered just a "minor violation."

Among the songs America sings are: "Georgia on My Mind," by Hoagy Carmichael; "Sleepy Lagoon," by Erich Coates; and "Three Little Words," by Harry Ruby.

Books on the best-seller list are: *East Wind: West Wind,* by Pearl S. Buck; *Destry Rides Again,* by Max Brand, and *The Maltese Falcon,* by Dashiell Hammett.

On the stage, these are among the popular plays of the season: *The Green Pastures,* by Marc Connelly; *The Barretts of Wimpole Street,* by Rudolf Besier; *Private Lives,* by Noel Coward; and *Grand Hotel,* by W. A. Drake, which is based on the novel by Vicki Baum.

Early in the twentieth century, noted U.S. astronomer Percival Lowell determined mathematically the existence of an unseen planet beyond Neptune. Having built the Lowell Observatory at Flagstaff, Arizona, in 1905 he organized a systematic search for that planet. Fourteen years after Lowell's death, Clyde William Tombaugh discovers the planet Pluto on February 18, 1930, at—fittingly—the Lowell Observatory.

On January 10, Will Rogers suddenly decides to take a firsthand look at the London Naval Conference. He leaves aboard the fast *Bremen* and returns February 6 aboard the *Ile de France.* While in England, Will visits at Cliveden, the famed Astor home. Waldorf Astor and his wife, Nancy, both American-born, are socially and politically prominent. A member of Parliament before succeeding to the family viscountcy, Waldorf had to relinquish his seat in the House of Commons. Nancy campaigned in his place and was elected, becoming the first woman to sit in the British House of Commons. A tireless fighter for women's interests, her activities are followed with great interest on both sides of the Atlantic. Arriving in New York City, Will's next stop is Washington, D.C., as usual, just to "see what the Boys we send there, are up to." On his way back to Beverly Hills, Will stops in Oklahoma to visit with the home folks.

In March, Will is the principal speaker at the dedication of Coolidge Dam at Globe, Arizona. In March, also, he signs a contract with E. R. Squibb & Sons to deliver twelve radio broadcasts.

In the summer, the Fred Stone family comes for a visit at the Santa Monica ranch. Fred is now mostly recovered. Though he will dance and perform again on the stage and in motion pictures, he will carry the scars of his plane crash for the rest of his life.

In August, the Fox Film Corporation crew goes on location to Lake Tahoe to shoot some scenes for the movie *Lightnin'.* Starring with Will in this production of the famous Winchell Smith and Frank Bacon play are Louise Dresser, Jason Robards, and a handsome newcomer, Joel McCrea. This is also the first film for Helen Cohan, daughter of George M. Cohan.

Will completes two other films in 1930: *So This Is London,* with Irene Rich, Maureen O'Sullivan, Frank Albertson, Lumsden Hare, and Bramwell Fletcher, and *A Connecticut Yankee,* directed by David Butler, with Myrna Loy, Maureen O'Sullivan, William Farnum, Frank Albertson, and Brandon Hurst.

Around the Astor Farm

Of all the places I visited on this last trip to England, the one that really was the most impressive, was the country place of Lord and Lady Astor. I had been lots of times at their London residence. But this one, out about an hour from London, was the real McCoy. It's got one of those long records that take you back and maybe was where old Henry the 8th did a big percentage of his marrying. I expect Caesar was registered there.

It's right on a hill, overlooking the winding Thames River. I don't know the acreage, but the chances are that old Cromwell filed on the original 160 acres, and then had all his hired help homestead on adjoining 160's, and then when they had improved on them, why, "Crommy" conveniently sent them off to some little Nicaraguan uprising. But before going he had them make their cross on some parchment, saying that in case of their not returning, the holdings of the said crossee, were entirely at the disposal of the party of the first part, which was Cromwell. So the Astors practically hold all the country lying east of the Thames.

The house is a modest bungalow, of not over seventy-five, or a hundred rooms. It's laid out a good deal like Westminster Abbey, only without the towers. It's rambling, but still kept within the bounds of good taste. There is a landing field in each wing, where you can take off and make the dining room by lunch. The ceilings are high enough that they give you plenty of altitude for taking off and landing. The first room you enter is kind of a cosy corner. It's about ten acres, cut off from the rest of the subdivision. But now they have made it a lovely, homely place.

It was a lovely Sunday afternoon, the sun shining bright, a kind of historic day for that time of the year near London. The door tender told me that Lady Astor was out in the tennis court, and she had left word for me to come out, and sure enough she was out there. She was going great guns. You know, she has more energy, can get more things done in one day, and has more to do than any creature, either male or female, that I ever saw. Well, she quit the tennis racket, and when I started in blowing about what a place it was, she said, "Come on, I will show you around."

We were then out in front of the main house, and I was gaping at it, and then she told me: "Right where you are standing, is where my old colored woman, that I brought with me from Virginia when I was married, got one look at the place, and said to me: 'Miss Nancy, is here where we all going to live?' Why, yes, Cynthia, here is our home. 'My Lord, Miss Nancy, you all done outmarried yourself.'" Well, what a kick she got out of repeating that old favorite of hers.

Then we started in to see this wonderful place. We walked for about three-quarters of an hour, then saw a little old car there, and she said: "come on, we will ride." I asked her, can you run this thing? Then we commenced on seeing the place right: a golf course, steeplechase course, beautiful colored pheasants running about, stables where he breeds his great thoroughbreds, and then we walked down a beautiful walk. There was a fine, big monument with names on it. It was all the men killed in the war that worked on the estate. Then on down on the side of a beautiful wooded bluff, or hillside, and there was a kind of a lovely sunken garden effect, about 100 feet long, and maybe forty wide, in oblong shape, with a marvelous statue of an angel-faced woman with arms outstretched and she standing at the back and over this garden effect, facing a wide strip of clearing through the trees away down below so you could see out across the river.

What was in this spot? You wouldn't guess in a million years. Well, during the great war they had given up their place for a great hospital. They had used a part of the house, and built, in addition, great temporary buildings. And here, in this garden were the graves of boys who had died in their place, boys that lived in almost every country— both in England and all overseas. The stones were laid flat over the graves, all of one shape and kind, with their names and homes; several of our boys, Canadians and Australians. There must have been as many as fifty in all, and she could stand at any grave and tell you about each boy. She knew them all personally. She had held the hands of many as they passed out.

She would move from grave to grave and tell you the characteristics of each. How she had promised one a wrist watch if he would live till she could go to London and buy it, and he did; and he had it on, smiling as he passed on. How she could go into a ward and say: "Now you boys either got to die, or get well, we are not going to have you sick here all the time." She is the greatest jollier in the world. If I was sick, and didn't even know her, I know of no one I would rather have come to see me. There she stood, with tears in her eyes, as she spoke of each boy, as though he had been her own, and related stories of them.

This woman that can get up in the House of Commons, and stand the "ragging" and "chaffing" of the roughest old politicians, an American-born woman, and first to sit in the great parliamentary halls of England, the center of every drawing room crowd, the famous Lady Astor, but here she was, just plain mother, all the fight, all the alertness of mind, all the social graces, all the wit and sparkle, gone. There, almost under the shade of her great house lay buried these lads she had tried to help, and learned to love. She was just walking among "her boys."

She had a great artist do the statue. It was symbolic of the mother looking across these graves to the west, as they had "gone west." The spot had been consecrated for those of the various religions that had asked for that. One woman knew of her son being buried there, and she wanted to move him. Lady Astor paid her way and had her come from Canada, and when she saw the spot, she said, "I wouldn't move him for the world. No spot could be more beautiful than this." How many will turn their beautiful estate into a burial ground?

And when I hear some political, or social opponent ever say aught of her, I won't even go to the trouble of telling them of her wonderful heart. I will just smile satisfyingly to myself, and rake up that vision of that woman walking among "her boys" with tears in her eyes, yet telling jokes of each one. So let no woman, mother, or son, ever say evil against her.

Then we come back to the house, and that's when I demanded the port wine, instead of the tea—and got it.

Everybody's Counting

When a man comes around to our house nowadays, or you get a letter, you don't know if it's a Census taker, a Literary Digest poll, or a bootlegger.

This is the year of the Census. We take a tally. That's what we used to call it when I was on a ranch, and we counted cattle. In other words, we run 'em by us and see how many we got. Well, Uncle Sam takes a tally every ten years. And it's a good thing, not that it means much to anybody to know how many other people there are. But it's an old Spanish custom, and it does give work to the ones that count, and that's what we got to do this year, is to do something that will give everybody something to do.

California is sure excited over this Census. Most places just take it as a matter of fact. But not out here. These babies take it as a business. They have instructed every one of us on just what assumed names to give to the different Census takers, and when we have registered under every name we can think of, then not to forget to use our right one. That's how far they are going out here. They are all excited over the fact that the more votes we show we have, the more Congressmen we will be allowed in the next Congress.

Well, of all the silly arguments! Who wants more Congressmen? But they seem to think the more we have, the more loot we will get from the national Treasury in the way of appropriations. Then the more we can advertise that we have out here, the better they think it will make us. I don't know about that. There ain't much quality in numbers. But there is not an editorial that don't tell us how valuable it is to register all we can.

The Literary Digest poll on Prohibition is causing a lot of talk. It's staying "Wet" a little longer than I thought. That might be on account of that most of the "Drys" can't write. But I think when the old back country gets going good, they will throw the thing the other way.

It's given the preachers something to talk about, anyway. They are getting out now, working like it was a regular election. I just heard a couple of them over the radio tonight. Well, it's a funny thing, that a so-called busy nation can take so much time to argue over Prohibition, that can't be changed now, no matter what happened. This is no election time, and all this talk will be for nothing. But we are that way. We can get more excited over something that can't be done anything about. The bootlegger is with us, and like the Sunday automobile accidents, it just looks like both will be with us for some time.

Then the old Disarmament Conference over in London is being slipped oxygen between gasps. I don't want to brag, but when I went there and heard the king make his opening, and then I came home, why I thought that I wouldn't miss a thing. Here is all these poor newspapermen over there all this time. There was four hundred visiting correspondents there, just waiting day after day, to find out something. And all the misunderstanding that they have there now could have easily been found out at home before they left—for none of them have changed. We wanted parity, and we were never going to get it. Italy wanted equality with France, and they were never going to get it. So these were things that should have been threshed out before anyone ever left home.

I have always claimed that any international conference does more harm than good, for they engender more hate than good will. It's hatred formed at conferences that causes the next war. If I don't meet you, and have any business dealings with you, I think you are perhaps o.k. But the minute I meet you day after day, and both of us are trying to do the best we can towards our own, why, that just shows up our shortcomings, and we go home, knowing the other fellow's weaknesses.

I tell you when you commence to talking war, you are on a pretty ticklish subject—and that's all that disarmament is. It's just talk about wars.

You can't discuss battleships without discussing what they are to each other in battle. Why, at this London conference, I was there and heard them for two weeks, and when they had each discussed publicly their needs, why, there wasn't a navy afloat that would have been adequate for them. Everybody got up and got to talking about the amount of coast line they had. Why, you had no idea that there was anywhere so much ocean front. Here in California, I had been putting what little money I had in ocean frontage, for the sole reason that there was only so much of it, and no more, and that they wasn't making any more. Then when I hear nation after nation arise and announce the amount of coast line they had, it sure was discouraging to me.

I tell you this old thing of telling another nation how to defend itself, is bad dope. Every man protects himself according to his own needs, and his best methods.

Say, old Wall Street is picking up again. The boys must have saved up and started to contributing again. They always did say that the heart of the American people was sound—in fact, it was sounder than most of the stocks that the sound heart bought.

A Harvard Cannibal

A couple of weeks ago, I wrote a Sunday article and it mentioned the Donner Party at Donner Lake as being our only case of cannibalism ever practiced in our abundant country. Well, then some man wrote me and told me of a case of a man named Packer, in Colorado, and so I wrote a Daily column:

> In a Sunday article I stated that the Donner Party was our only cannibalism. I was wrong, as usual, for I just learned of this case. Crossing the divide from Utah to Colorado, in 1872 a man named Packer evidently practiced it. He was convicted in Del Norte, Colorado, and the judge passed sentence as follows: "Packer, you have committed the world's most fiendish crime. You not only murdered your companions, but you ate up every Democrat in Hillsdale county. You are to be hung by the neck till you are dead, and may God have mercy on your Republican soul."

They lived off the Democrats, but this was the only one we could ever convict.

Now if this fellow Packer had just eaten up a Republican, why, the judge—a fine old-type Democrat from Arkansas—would have perhaps given him a pension, instead of a sentence. Well now, we got that much straight.

Well, now comes a long and very interesting letter from a man named N. E. Guyot, whose letterhead says Kingman, Arizona, and he gives me the exact details of this last case.

Now a lot of folks thought I was just kidding when I wrote of this Packer, and the story of the Democrats, but it was the Gospel truth. I certainly wouldn't make light of a thing so serious as eating a Democrat. We are reaching a time in our existence, when we need every Democrat we can muster. We got to get some prosperity mixed up in our national existence and as the coming November reaches the election day, Democrats are coming out in numbers that will astonish the natives. So I certainly was serious, and was relating an historical fact. But wait, let Mr. Guyot tell you:

It was in the north-western part of Colorado, San Juan mountains, ten miles from the town of Lake City, on a plateau that is called on government survey "Cannibal Plateau." It was here that Packer, through a severe snow storm murdered and devoured his prospector companions.

Now those are some mere facts, but here is the things I want you to get. It's the history of this fellow Packer, before he started in subsisting on the minority party. Packer was a Harvard graduate, and he graduated in 1866. He was a law student, and started practicing in Boston. What I am getting at, is that the only case of a person willfully devouring human flesh, was by the alumni of the great Harvard. So Harvard has not only produced the least understandable English in our fair land, but produced the only living cannibal.

Then, this Packer was a lawyer, that of course, seems natural. Their profession is an off-shoot of the cannibal profession. They generally skin 'em alive. Packer did have the good taste to destroy 'em and get 'em out of their misery; most lawyers delight in seeing their victims suffer. It was in the winter of '72 and '73. There was six companions, and they were all well equipped with provisions. But in the snow they got lost from their burros. Mr. Guyot, in his letter, says that it was the first time, and perhaps the last, that a lawyer was ever permitted to accompany a band of prospectors into the mountains. He always waits till they get out and find it, and then he gets his share by showing 'em where to sign their name. But Packer was afraid they would come back and find another lawyer, so he just went along with 'em. But ain't that strange, that a lawyer is never allowed out with prospectors?

Well, it seems there was dissension from the start over allowing him to come along, and in his trial afterwards, he said he had heard them plotting to kill and eat him. But that didn't go with the judge and jury. They knew no men could ever be so hungry that they would eat a lawyer.

Now I was wrong in one little misstatement about the case. I had heard that he was hung. He was not. Colorado was then a territory, and the game laws did not protect Democrats. Even to this day in some states it would not be considered illegal to eat one. So they gave Packer forty years in Canyon City jail. That was a little over 6 years for each one he ate. You would have to eat at least ten, or more, to get life—according to Colorado justice. But he didn't stay in there that long. Along in 1899, when civilization and the Denver Post hit us, why them and other papers started a campaign to release him. There was a tight election coming on, and them being Republicans, they wanted to let him out, hoping he would eat up some more Democrats before November 4th.

Then they brought up that the judge (you remember, originally of Arkansas, and a Democrat by birth and breeding) had been biased in the trial. That no Democratic judge should sit in a case, where it had been Democrats that had been eaten.

The editorials of the Denver papers of that time, all brought out this injustice—that it was a blot on the fair name of Colorado—that a Harvard man shouldn't be able to eat what he liked. Well, anyhow, the papers got him out, and the fair name of Colorado was saved. And since then they have never convicted, or even tried a man for murdering, robbing or otherwise maiming a Democrat. Viva, Democracy!

After this Packer fellow was released from jail, he went to Cripple Creek, and inserted an advertisement in the local papers, asking for men with means to accompany him on a prospecting trip. Not a soul went.

Oh, yes. I forgot to tell you he was the son of a missionary, and in his youth had spent some time in the South Sea islands. That's how he acquired his taste.

Imagine, a missionary, a lawyer, a Harvard graduate. I want to tell you, illiteracy is a blessing.

Will Rogers

The Days of Rockne

When your great-grandchildren are sitting around some penal institution at recreation time, they will talk of the time—away back—when their parents and grandparents used to tell about a certain man that flourished from around 1920 to 1940, and from then on. Children will be as they are today, they will have to be taught who was president around all that era. But the same as we do today remember Jesse James and Paul Revere, and a few of those without any particular aid from history, why, we will remember this man.

These confined grandchildren of ours, will say: "Yes, we have great coaches today, we have great teams, but dad says every play they know was originally done away back in his childhood by Knute Rockne, who founded Notre Dame."

This Notre Dame was just another stubble-field college. They cut down the tall grass, dammed up the creek, and made another one of those Indiana Institutions of Learning, that flourished practically on every quarter section throughout the state. Well, it was going along, it had a few old uniforms, and some second-hand footballs. But they had never played any further away from home than you could make in a day-coach. On Sunday the results of their games would be listed along with Harvard, Yale, Princeton, Penn, and Columbia, and all of that ilk. They had never made the headlines along with Alabama, Georgia, Northwestern, Army, Navy, and all the other big shots. Well, from what granddad says, this Rockne blew in there, and went to school. He was a Swede, or a Norwegian, or a Dane, or some of those ski jumping nations up in there. He didn't know a football from a footpad. But these pumpkin seed boys was kicking one around there and playing what they humorously referred to as football. They let him play with 'em just for comedy purposes, and for a Swede, or a Norwegian, or a Dane, he turned out to be mighty good. Along about then they started throwing forward passes, so to have some more fun, they got to throwing 'em to this Swede, or Norwegian, or Dane. Well, instead of this Swede, or Norwegian, or Dane dodging 'em, why, he got to catching 'em, and skiing over the line with them. Well, then he graduated, for they won't let you stay in one of these schools but four years—no matter how little you know. They got a rule: they make you graduate whether you want to or not. Then, when they graduated him, then came the problem—what was he going to do? He hadn't finished from Harvard, so he couldn't sell bonds. He was just a

Swede, or Norwegian, or Dane football player, and there wasn't a whole lot of market for a football player. That was back in the days when football was a recreation, and not a racket.

So he says to himself, why can't I coach? I have missed enough signals during my years on the team to entitle me to instruct others. So he found some boys that didn't know much more about the game than he did, and he started in coaching 'em. The first thing you know, he was helping to coach Notre Dame. Well, he didn't think he was much of a coach, till he got to seeing some of the others. Then the head coach got a job at what he thought was a real high goal University, and Knute took over the team. Well from that day football left the red, and started to making gains into the black side of the ledger.

When the graduating class would receive their invocation, he would ask to say a few words to 'em: Boys, what is your aim through life?

"Why, Sir, to make a living."

"No, it's not! It's to send football players to Notre Dame. That's your life's work! Send me a football player!"

And when the football players got to Notre Dame, he knew what to do with 'em. He told 'em that football was a game of the head, and not of the feet and hands. Well, it just wasn't no time till Notre Dame had got out of the weeds, and raised their scholastic standing half a dozen touchdowns, and you started reading about it. It wasn't just a buckwheat college, it was right up in the money. It was filling more stadiums than any of 'em.

He then originated the idea of playing a real team every Saturday, instead of about three a season. Then come his climax, as my old grandparents have told me. He was a great kidder. He was to play a game on the Coast against their best, and the sporting writers had boosted their west coast team up till it looked like practical death for Knute to even go on the field with 'em.

Well, he started in before they left Chicago, saying that his team didn't have a chance, that they would be beat as they had lost their only star player. Well, on the coast, they all fell for it, and when he got to Tucson, Arizona, to practice, why, he was supposed to have lost another star, a Mr. Mullins. The sporting writers come down to see who he was practicing in Mullins place and they noted a No. 31. They looked it up and it was a Mr. Hanley. But when the game started, a gent named O'Connor was the starter. Nobody had ever heard of him, but nobody will ever forget him. Then the news leaked out that during this Arizona practice, he had been wearing Hanley's sweater. But no sporting writer had ever thought of that. Well, he kidded 'em right up to game time, and even got great odds against his team. Well, grandpap says that when they kicked off, Notre Dame got ahold of the ball and never give it back to the other side all day. But the thing that grandpap laughed about was the way this fellow Rockne just kidded the pants off the whole Pacific coast from the time he left South Bend, till he got back.

P. T. Barnum, so grandpap says, in his balmiest days never made such a sucker out of folks with his side show, as this Knute fellow did singlehanded, outside of what his team did to the others. He even told 'em that next year, they would beat him that bad. Well, everybody was surprised to know that they would play 'em again next year. Nobody after the Great War ever heard the Kaiser wanting a return date.

But I have just heard grandpap sit by the hour and tell some of the comical things this Rockne did in his day. Yes, Sir, grandpap says he is the one that made Notre Dame more famous than Oxford and Cambridge, this Swede, or Norwegian, or Dane, or Lithuanian, or whatever he is.

Thoughts of War

There is some pretty big stuff in the papers nowadays, but it's kinder under cover. Did you ever kinder stop to figure it out, this world of ours as a whole is not sitting so pretty just at the present time. Did you know that there is an awful lot of parts of Europe that is just sitting on—what the old-time orators used to call—a powder keg? Well, it is.

We can't pick up a paper, that from one to a hundred don't prophesy that Prosperity is just around the corner. But let me tell you, war is nearer around the corner than Prosperity is. I don't mean so much for us, right here, but I mean over in Europe. That Russia is kicking up an awful lot of dust; and Germany is harboring a terrible lot of dissatisfaction. That Hitler has got 'em all stirred up over there. He made a speech last week, in which he advocated the breaking of the Versailles Treaty. He said that it was made by a lot of old men, who most of them were about ready to die, and now here was a lot of young men grown up and they had to carry all this burden, for which they were not directly to blame, and that it was only a matter of time till they just wouldn't do it. They would say: "Well, come on France! What are you going to do about it? We can't be any worse off if you come in and take over our country, than we are now."

Then those little Balkan nations, they are like a little mess of stray Terriers, anyhow; they just as well be fighting, as like they are. This has been the longest they have ever been between wars. I see the other day where Russia was just on the verge of invading Roumania. They have always had it in for them, and figured they only had to take a couple of days' rations and rounds of ammunition, and go over and take that country, anyhow.

Russia and Poland are always on the verge of war. I remember when I was over in both countries in the summer of 1926, why they were growling at each other like a couple of fat prima donnas on the same opera bill.

Then Italy is ranting around down there, trying to pick up some more country and outlet for their population. France is watching them with an eagle eye all the time, and that's just what Mussolini wants. He would rather worry France, than anything. France feels that she would have no trouble whipping Italy, but if she went down there to do it, Germany would take that opportunity to get at them, and she just don't want to have to take the chance. Then Czechoslovakia feels kinder hemmed in down their way, and of course the Turks—there is nothing that irks a Turk so much, as peace.

Austria, they just been so bad off since the last war that they know there would be no way that war wouldn't be welcome to them. Bulgaria has started all the rest of them, her and Serbia, and they don't want to lose their reputation. They want to go down in history as having started all the big ones.

This whole mess have no more love for each other than a litter of hyenas; they either lost, or gained territory during the last war, and they feel—those that did gain, that in another war they could grab off even more. And the ones that lost, can't see how they could possibly make that mistake again, and that if given a chance to play the same hole over again, they could make it in par the next time. I try to read all that those old world diplomats write over here, and there is not a line of it that is not in regard to another war. They just can't write a prescription without predicting what will happen in the next great war. Their whole mind is on it, and from all that I read of them, there is no two that seem to give anywhere near the same possible line-up. It's like the National and the American Baseball Leagues, when the time comes to play the World Series, they would just take all the players from all their clubs in their League, and then choose up and play the other side. No one knows where the thing will start, or with whom; no one knows how the line-up will be, for they don't know who will be fighting who. Some of them that hate Russia like poison, will want to join her on account of her strength. They will all want to wait

173

and see who looks like the winner. They did that in the last war, quite a few stayed out, waiting for the best offer.

Lots of pretty smart men think that one of the biggest contributing factors to our present state of economic unrest—this Depression—is that all big finance is afraid of what will happen in the near future, and they don't know where it will end up. That's why everybody is hanging on to what they got. There is more in the wind than just our little local condition over here. We got as much as we ever had; there is just as much money, as many to eat, and as many to feed, as many to buy. But still, our condition is uncertain. Why? Just because it's things outside our land that is worrying them. The whole thing is world-wide; we are affected by it less than anyone.

If we keep our nose clean, and don't start yapping about somebody else's honor, or what our moral obligations are, we might escape it. But it's going to take better statesmanship than we have been favored with heretofore. But the way we are now, we are mighty lucky to have nothing but a business Depression that is bothering us. Just think what those other poor devils are up against.

Too Smart to Be Happy?

Christmas is getting like one of our old-time western dances. They wait till the dancing is all over, and then they sorter sweep out to see how many was left laying around. During this Prohibition we are killing off some mighty good citizens with our "Xmas cheer," and it has been discussed quite openly as to whether the whole thing was worth the tallow, or not.

Since Santa Claus has been pretty thoroughly discredited by even our babes in arms, and on account of the Xmas costs to everybody, there has come up in this country quite a wide movement to just let the Yuletide go by default. Of course in the old days, when the Democrats were at their zenith, and the old reindeers and the jingling bells were considered official, why, there was cause for all this. But now, when they dress up some poor old fellow as Santa, why, the kids get one peep at him, and say: "Oh, look at the old geezer trying to fool the old folks!"

That's the trouble with the whole thing. Kids are getting too wise. Why, I was a big old chuckle-head—maybe ten years old, before I really even suspicioned that our old friend of the long whiskers, wasn't delivering into my stocking every Xmas morning the sack of candy, horn, and cap pistol. But nowadays, you start asking a baby what he wants Santa to bring him, and he will bounce his empty nursing bottle off your bean.

In other words, we just ain't fooling nobody, and are buying a lot of stuff and giving it to folks that don't understand why you was so half-witted as to get that particular object. It was the last thing on earth they'd want.

In fact, we ourselves have gotten so wise that even when we are buying it for them, we know it won't suit. But the etiquette of Christmas tells us we must get something. Of course, the whole thing started in a fine spirit. It was to give happiness to the young, and another holiday for the old, so it was relished by practically everybody. It was a great day, the presents were inexpensive, and received with much joy and gratification. It was a pleasure to see the innocent little souls as they rushed down to the big room with the fireplace on Christmas morning in their bare feet, and generally the back end of their little sleepers unbuttoned and a-dragging. They remembered right where they had hung their stocking, and they dived into it with great glee and anticipation. No matter what they dug out, it was great, it was just what they wanted him to bring, for they had confidence in him. The merest little toy was a boon to their young lives. And what a kick it was to the parents to have them rush back up to the bed room and show you "what Santa brought."

Then the mother would finally venture down and look into her big-top stocking to see what the sly old father had deposited during the night. Maybe it was just more cotton stockings. Maybe it was a new sofa. Maybe it was a new axe for wood splitting. Maybe a hot-water bottle. But whatever it was, it was the most acceptable thing in the world. It was what she wanted "her man" to get her. Ah! Them was the days, lads! When you could satisfy 'em with a squirrel muff, and a box of five cent cigars practically cinched your friendship with a male friend for the coming year. Then they talk about civilization. Say, there ain't no civilization where there ain't no satisfaction, and that's what's the trouble now; nobody is satisfied.

In the old days where a nice crayon picture would be just the thing as a present, why, now an unborn lamb would be unacceptable. They would wonder why you didn't send mink.

And a wife, why, she will sneeze at a Buick! If she don't find a new Cord auto in her short sock, why, you will be the cheapest husband she ever had. The whole prospectus of the thing has changed. We not only don't believe in Santa Claus, we don't believe in anything. Kids say they don't care anything about a "train that will run if you wind it up." They want an airplane that will fly—and not wound up, either.

You start talking about sending them a ten cent horn that will blow, and they want a saxophone that will annoy; and as for cap pistol and a dozen boxes of caps, why say, he wants a machine gun. He has read about the gangsters in Chicago. A football? "Is it regulation?" if it's not, you're wasting your time.

If it's a girl baby, and you are sending some pink sachet powder, you are all wet again. The "she" infant will rise up and demand an overnight bag, some nose paint and a lip stick, and when they get it, they will examine the brand.

So you wonder sometimes if the ones that want to abolish Christmas are not about half right. Everybody faces it with: "Oh my goodness, Xmas is coming and how I dread it!" Then you decide that the whole thing is bunk, and you will just send cards. Then about three days before Xmas you commence to get a few little boxes and remembrances for friends. So the whole thing is an uproar from about Thanksgiving on. In fact that is what they have Thanksgiving for—it's your last day of peace for that year.

Suppose along about a day or so after Xmas the merchant went to each house and said: "Now this is confidential, but what did you get for Xmas that you don't want?" They buy it for ten cents on the dollar then hold it over for next Xmas, and you are ten per cent ahead. It's worth thinking about, this doing away with Xmas. It would be all right if we could again believe in Santa Claus, but our smartness has defeated our own happiness.

1931

The economic depression continues to deepen across the industrialized world. Vienna's major financial institute, the Creditanstalt, goes into bankruptcy. In Germany, the Danatbank, too, declares itself bankrupt, precipitating a general closing of all banks until August 5. All German stock exchanges close "indefinitely." Britain must secure financial assistance through a Franco-American loan. Once again she must abandon the gold standard, and there are riots in several major cities against the government's economy measures—which include a 10 percent salary cut for all government employees. Naval units mutiny in protest against pay cutbacks. The discount rate jumps to 6 percent, and the pound sterling drops 28 percent in value. Japan, also, must forgo the gold standard. In the United States, three thousand banks will fail this year alone.

In response to America's higher tariffs, Canada raises her protective tariffs, cutting off two-thirds of the goods previously imported from the United States.

France and Italy terminate the naval agreement that has been in effect just one day short of a year.

Mussolini orders all Catholic clubs closed, their papers seized, and roads leading to the Vatican barred. Pope Pius XI cancels the planned Eucharistic Congress. The Fascist government of Italy lifts the passports of many of its citizens, among them maestro Arturo Toscanini, making them virtual prisoners of the state.

In view of Europe's disastrous financial condition, President

Hoover suggests a one-year moratorium on her debts and reparation payments. Congress concurs—they might just as well.

The U.S. wheat crop breaks records, but the surplus naturally depresses prices. Banks foreclose on farm mortgages. While some areas use their grain to feed cattle, millions elsewhere go hungry for lack of bread. In the midst of this, the Soviet Union attempts to depress world prices even further by trying to export goods for sale at far below market prices. Canada and the United States agree to bar imports from the USSR unless proof is furnished that these are products of free, rather than forced, labor.

The lowest price for a four-cylinder Ford is $430; a Plymouth sells for $535, and a six-cylinder Chevrolet sells for $475. But car sales slump, and the industry lays off another 100,000. Unemployment figures climb above 8 million. When hunger marchers demonstrate in front of the White House, asking for work at a minimum living wage, they are turned away.

In England, a small town in Arkansas, about five hundred farmers and their wives storm into the business section of town demanding food, which the merchants supply. In Arkansas alone, the Red Cross feeds 100,000.

In Oklahoma City, several hundred hungry rioters who raid a grocery store are dispersed by police using tear gas.

On a nationwide NBC radio network, President Hoover broadcasts an appeal for support for the Red Cross effort to raise $10 million for the drought-stricken states. The president calls the situation "a calamity" and appeals to the "heart of the nation." Others on the program: former President Coolidge, speaking from Northampton, Vermont; former New York governor Al Smith and Mary Pickford, speaking from New York City; Amos and Andy from Chicago; and Will Rogers from Little Rock, Arkansas. Before Will's appeal, it is announced that he has just donated $5,000, half from Betty Rogers toward the Arkansas quota, the other half from himself toward the Oklahoma quota. Will, with Captain Frank Hawkes as his pilot, is on a personal fund-raising tour.

The Wickersham commission at last submits its first report, naturally with divided opinions on Prohibition: Two members are for repeal, five are for changes, and four are for a further trial period. The report reads: "The Commission is of the opinion that there is yet no adequate observance or enforcement." It took eleven men eighteen months to determine that! Any child could have told them that in the first five minutes. If the commission needed any proof of what was going on, all they had to do was to read *The New York Times* of

February 17: "2 Police 'Collectors' Pick Up $400,000 from 125 Upper West Side Speakeasies."

Gangster and bootlegger Al Capone is tried on tax evasion. Wearing a "screaming green suit," he seems to enjoy his court appearance—up to a point. After deliberating eight hours, the jury finds him guilty on two misdemeanors and three felonies, while dismissing eighteen other counts. Capone is sentenced to eleven years in jail, $50,000 in fines, $137,328 in back taxes, plus court costs, estimated at $100,000.

After four unsuccessful attempts on his life, gangster Jack ("Legs") Diamond is executed in gangland style in his sleep by two assassins. Underworld boss Salvatore Maranzano is assassinated on orders of Charles ("Lucky") Luciano, who will organize the Mafia into "families."

In Scottsboro, Alabama, nine black youths are tried on charges of having raped two white women. They are defended by a reluctant, unprepared, court-appointed lawyer. After a trial lasting three days, eight of the defendants are sentenced to death, the ninth to life imprisonment. In years to come, the Supreme Court will twice set aside the verdicts and order new trials. In the third trial, some indictments are dropped, but again the nine are convicted. Death sentences will be commuted to life imprisonment. The nine will serve a total of 130 years in prison, with the last one to be paroled in 1951.

Pilot Wiley Post and navigator Harold Gatty circle the globe in 8 days, 15 hours, and 51 minutes—though their actual flying time is only 106 hours.

The Nobel Peace Prize is shared by Dr. Nicholas Murray Butler (president of Columbia University) and Jane Addams (head of Women's League for Peace and Freedom). Despite such recognition of women, New York City's bar association debates two hours, then votes it "inadvisable" to accept women for membership.

The U.S. Public Health Service issues a report that "the contamination of the atmosphere . . . has become a serious matter in several large cities." Hardly anybody bothers to read it.

Thomas Alva Edison, whose inventions and improvements have touched almost every American, dies in his eighty-fifth year. Anna Pavlova, the world's premier dancer, dies of pleurisy in Holland. Knute Rockne, head coach of the Notre Dame football team since 1918, dies in a plane crash in Kansas.

The building industry seems to be the only one busy, as the Chrysler Building is completed and can—for a very short time only—claim to be the world's tallest. The Waldorf-Astoria Hotel opens its doors to the notable, and others, provided they can afford it; the

Empire State Building will add a mooring tower, and be for four decades the world's tallest building. Costing $60 million, the George Washington Bridge is formally opened; stretching from Manhattan to New Jersey, it is the longest suspension bridge to date.

Best-selling books include: *The Good Earth,* by Pearl S. Buck; *Hatter's Castle,* by A. J. Cronin; and—unofficially—Henry Miller's *Tropic of Cancer,* which has been banned in the United States.

Green Grow the Lilacs, by Oklahoman Lynn Riggs, has only sixty-four performances on Broadway, but it will be seen again as the trend-setting musical *Oklahoma. Mourning Becomes Electra,* by Eugene O'Neill, and *Counsellor-at-Law,* by Elmer Rice are two of the most successful theatrical presentations of the season.

The motion picture screen offers *City Lights,* with Charlie Chaplin; *The Public Enemy,* with James Cagney and Jean Harlow, with the well-remembered scene of a startled Mae Clark getting half a grapefruit in her face; *An American Tragedy,* with Sylvia Sidney and Frances Dee; *Frankenstein,* with Boris Karloff; and *Trader Horn,* with Harry Carey and his wife, Olive Carey.

Among the most popular songs are: "Mood Indigo," by Duke Ellington; "Heartaches," by Al Hoffman; "Lady of Spain," by Tolchard Evans; and "Where the Blue of the Night Meets the Gold of the Day," by Fred Ahlert (a crooner named Bing Crosby will record it, and both will become famous).

And on March 3, Congress gets around to declaring "The Star Spangled Banner" the national anthem of the United States.

In 1931, Will Rogers makes his own "relief tour," collecting for the Red Cross and the needy of the drought-affected areas. He pays his own expenses, and usually starts the collection with a substantial personal check. When news is received in April of the devastation caused by a severe earthquake in Nicaragua, Will flies there at once to see what he can do to help. In recognition of his services, and the assistance he personally rendered, Nicaragua will issue a five-stamp set posthumously featuring Will.

In July, Will flies to Claremore to help dedicate its new airport, built to welcome Wiley Post and Harold Gatty.

In October, at the request of President Hoover, Will again speaks on a nationwide radio network. This time it is an appeal to help the unemployed, and Will's statement is published in *The Survey* under the title: *Bacon, Beans and Limousines.*

In November, Will sails from San Francisco aboard the *Empress of Russia* for the Orient, and on around the world. He will not return until the beginning of the following year.

Now on a regular production schedule at Fox Film Corporation, Will usually makes several films in quick succession, and then has time to attend to other things. In 1931, Will Rogers made three films: *Business and Pleasure,* an adaptation of Booth Tarkington's *The Plutocrat,* with Joel McCrea, Jetta Goudal, and Boris Karloff; *Ambassador Bill,* with Marguerite Churchill and a very young Ray Milland; and *Young as You Feel,* with Fifi Dorsay and Lucien Littlefield.

Fisticuffs in Portland

We was making a movie here the other week of Booth Tarkington's book and play "Plutocrat." That's what it was called. But it's liable to be released under the title "Riches Traded for Virtue," or "The Gangster's Lost Moll." Well, in the picture my family and I are on one of these Mediterranean cruises, and we got to Morocco, or some country there where it's hot and full of Arabs and camels and Riffs.

Well, I will say one thing for Hollywood. If you want a couple of hundred real Arabs in a scene, you just let the casting department know that you do, and you get that many real Arabs. Anything under the sun you want, it's in Hollywood. I believe you could round up a hundred Eskimos.

Now among these Arabs and Turks and Foreign Legions, and all, we needed a few big Colored men, in their bare skin. Out here there is an awful lot of prize fighters—and awful is right, and every old-time pug is here; and among them is a lot of Colored ex-fighters that work around the pictures.

Well, we had the greatest gang on this street scene in Algiers, or wherever it was. I was raised down south, by—and with—Colored folks. Claremore is full of Colored Rogers—their folks belonged to our family and they took the name, you know, when they was freed. They got more humor and good nature than anybody in the world. Well, there was two, or three of those old boys, one was Sam Baker, a pretty good fighter three or four years ago. He fought Wills, and was a trial sparring partner for Dempsey. Then there was, I think, Lester Albert Johnson and Vic Alexander.

Well, the director couldn't get me on the set for laughing at these birds kidding each other about fights. I believe Sam Baker talked the best fight of all. They got him to tell about the time he was sent to Portland, Oregon, to fight the big ... (name deleted through

friendship) when he was making his famous march through the
buckwheat belt, bowling 'em over in one and two rounds. So listen to
Sam Baker, and you will get an earful of modern fisticuffs:

I was working down here in Hollywood, wasn't bothering a soul. I
had me a big part, purty uniform, taking care of de front door at a
high hat night club. Dis gentleman had been assassinating
around all up and down, and it seemed like in Oakland, another
Colored boy was to go out in the fourth round, and didn't. He
stayed till the sixth and could a stayed for a week, but his seconds
throwed in a towel, when all that had happened to him was that
he was jes goin' against de rules. He jes wouldn't lay down. Well,
I had fit up around Portland and I had been a 'big shot' and eat
regular up around there, so they sent for me to come up to
Portland. Well, I ain't been trainin' on nothing but close-ups
down here in Hollywood, but they tell me they will fix things and
they sho had 'em fixed when I got there.

I is called on by a couple of gun men, who inform me that there
is one thousand dollars, and it's mine to keep, hold or destroy,
BUT, here the guns come into the scene—that I was to go out in
the first round. First round, understand! Not to get my dates
mixed and dive in the second, but the first! Another Colored boy
crossed us, and we been hunting for him for two weeks. But we
ain't going to hunt for you, you are right here where your body
will be found. If you carried all this out accordin' to de aforesaid,
you gets another thousand, and if you don't, you is carried out.
You ain't to hit dis gentleman in de face. He is got a movie
contract in view and he don't want to jepson his chances. You
play for his stomach, but you don't play hard. You make it look
like you is going somewhere, but you ain't. You's jes headed that
way, that's all.

Den they showed me they still had their guns, and then rubbed
'em under my nose, and axed me if I could smell 'em. I told 'em I
had a cold, but could get a sort of idea what was around. Den I
got to thinking to myself after dey is gone: here I am in my old
stampin' ground of Portland and I got a lot of folks that think I am
still the 'big shot,' so dey is liable to bet on me and if they sees me
taking a nose dive, they is liable to have some guns, too. So I call
'em back and ax 'em about this. Dey say, there ain't going to be
but two pistols in that hall that night, and these is both of 'em.
And you want to have that 6 foot 5 ready for a nap not later than
the first round, see!

Well, dey goes on out and I says to myself, there ain't no
sensible arguing against a thing like that. Sammy, you is out

now. I goes down to the gymnasium and makes out like I is training, but I is just hopping around, eating all I can get, sipping a little gin on the side. I ain't worrying about him any more than he is about me. He knows I is fixed, and I knows I is fixed. But I do wants to make it look like as good as I can. I been acting around here in these pictures, so I figure I can do me some Barrymore, when the time comes. Well it sho had come. If I was a actor, I sho was going to have to start acting.

When we get in de ring, his managers all comes over—one at a time, there was a dozen of 'em, and dey say: Remember! De gun men is getting in awful good shooting distance. No reason for a man missing me at that range.

The bell rings and I dashed out and does like I is rushin' like a bull; he uppercuts me and I have a terrible time falling. It looks jes as faky as it was. I ain't acting so good. So I gets up quick, and make it look like I maybe slipped. He hits me on top of the head and down I goes again. Dis time I fall a little better, cause I am getting some practice. Den he swings, and I think he is going to hit me a terrible blow, so I start falling early—but he misses me. Well, I couldn't stop the fall, so I had to keep on. Well, even Portland couldn't swallow that. So I arise amid boos.

But he is standing straddle of me all the time. So they had to laugh at that, and it got their minds off the fall. So I lets him knock me down as I am getting up, but it don't look like a good enough one to stay down on, so I ups and lets him hit me into the ropes. I makes out like I am falling backwards, and there I hang with both hands down. He steps in and starts belting me, one after the other.

If he could a hit hard, he would a killed me, for I was just laying on the top rope with both hands down. Den I sunk down easy, glanced over at the gun men, and stayed down. I wasn't going to make any mistake about the round, and here I is, back in Hollywood, safe and sound, and still jes as good a actor as Mr. John Barrymore.

You see, he acts when he don't have to. I acted when I had to act—or else.

Home Cooking

I been doing a lot of reading in the papers here lately, for that's all I could do. You know, the other day coming home from the big Claremore celebration, on the plane I either ate something that didn't agree with me, at lunch in El Paso, where we stopped, or it was the general effects of what I had stacked in while at home in Oklahoma. Anyhow, I got home sick.

We always have such good things to eat at my sister's in Chelsea. Beans, and what beans, kinder soupy navy beans cooked with plenty of real fat meat. Well, when I can't knock off a whole bowl of those myself, why, I am sick before I start. And then the ham, fried ham; they cure their own ham. Tom McSpadden, my brother-in-law, he is the prize ham curer of any I ever saw. Smoked 'em with the old hickory log fire, then salts 'em away for all this time. Then the cooking of all this has got a lot to do with it. Sister Sallie has got a Negro woman there, but she is more for arguing purposes. Sallie fixes it all up when I come home.

Then the cream gravy. You know, there is an awful lot of folks that don't know much about eating gravy? Why, not to be raised on gravy would be like never going swimming in the creek. They got their own cows and real cream. Ham gravy is just about the last word in gravies. Course, good beefsteak gravy is good. You know, we fry our beefsteak. It's cut in thin pieces, and say, let me tell you something. Did you know all this eating raw, bloody rare meat, like they order in these big hotels, and that city people like, well, that's just them. That ain't western folks. Ranch cooks and farm women fry steak thin and hard. That old raw junk goes for the high collars in cities, they are kinder cannibalistic, anyhow.

Well, you can get some awful good gravy by putting the old milk in the skillet after you fried a lot of good beefsteak. There's an awful lot of good gravies. A good old home cook can mix up a tasty batch of gravy just about out of anything. No sir, the old city eaters missed some mighty fine grub when they don't take advantage of making gravy one of their regular dishes at every meal.

Now then comes the corn bread. Not the corn bread like you mean. I mean corn pone, made with nothing but meal, and hot water and salt. My old Daddy always had that at every meal, said it was only the high-toned folks that eat biscuits, and light-bread, or loaves like you all eat now. He called that "wasp nest," and thought that was just for the heathens. Well, this corn pone is mighty hard to go hungry after. You see, I am just telling you my dishes that they have when I come. I am not telling you of what they have, cause they know I would rather have it than go out and kill the fatted calf, or kill a turkey, or some chickens.

Beans, corn bread, country ham, and gravy, and then just raw onions, either the young ones if they are in, or the sliced ones. Sallie had some dandy Bermudas that Tom had raised. He has the best garden in that part of the country. Well, these onions wasn't strong, so he was going to send me some in California. But I don't guess they would let them come in. No, that's one thing about California, if you raise anything better than they do, they got a law against it coming in. That's why it's awful hard to get good vegetables and fruits in California. They make you just use home talent.

Then for dessert? Don't have room for any dessert. If I had any more room, I would have ate some more beans.

Now then I go from there over to my old home place where I was raised at Oolagah, and there my sister's son, Herb, and his remarkable wife Madeline give you an encore on all this, and maybe it tastes better, for this is the house you was born in. So about all I do when I go to Oklahoma, is just shake hands, and eat.

So the day I left Chelsea, we come to the old ranch place and Madeline did have a fine dinner for us. Now she is out in the country, with no ice, electricity, or all that, and yet she has got things that she can make everything that you would have at a town dinner. She can even make ice cream. Yes, she's got some kind of a doodad that makes ice out of a hot water thing, and she can put up and can more things than you ever saw, and this girl learned all this in the last five years. She wasn't a rancher; she was from the city of Los Angeles, but brother, she made a real rancher's wife, and a good one. Looks like the city ones, when they have to, come through the best.

Well, the home place looked mighty fine. Bout all we got left to farms, is their beauty. Lays on the bend of the Verdigris River. My father settled it just after the Civil War—same old log house weatherboarded over. Most of the farmers are all raising 'em a good garden and getting ready to try and offset a tough winter. Lord knows what it will be, especially if we hit a tough winter.

Oh, yes, I started out to tell you about being sick. Well, I have been for a week or so, thought I was going to die. Something I ate either in El Paso, where the plane stopped for lunch, or the night before at Amon G. Carter's "Shady Oak Farm." I had dinner with him and the Gas Sextette, and there was an amateur Doctor Walker, that mixed up a batch there that's laid me low.

The doctors call it "Catarrhal Jaundice." I was the yellowest white man you ever saw. I never have heard who else died from this Carter dinner. The diet was: cove oysters—canned, then canned tomatoes, and raw onions, all in one mess.

If they was laying for me, they got me.

Wheat and Combines

Here the other week, why, out to my house one night to pay us a visit and break corn bread with us was a mighty interesting couple, Mr. Tom Campbell and his wife. Now right off-hand, if you are not a farmer, or a buyer of farm products, you might say, "What Tom Campbell?" for it's a rather common name. But to anyone that is up on his onions and wheat, why, he will know in a minute. It's the man we have in the past read so much about.

Don't you remember a big wheat man up in Montana that was drafted by the Soviet government of Russia to go over there, and show them how to put their big wheat farms on a big mechanical farming basis? Well, he is the man. He now lives over in Pasadena.

He don't belong to any Hoover Commission, but he advises them after they are appointed—that is if they have anything to do about farming. He had up there in Montana, 90 thousand acres of plowed ground. He would rotate the crops, and have about half that in wheat each year. I remember seeing pictures of it, where there would be eight and ten combines running, one right behind the other.

You town waddies know what a combine is? Well, to tell the truth, I don't either. When I was the best farmer on the west bank of the Verdigris River, "binders" was just coming in, and we was lucky to get to see one of them. As a kid I used to ride the lead horse, when we used five head, three behind and two leaders.

Then those "combines" come along, and they just rounded up a whole remuda full and hitched on all the horses they had harness for. I think from some of those pictures I have seen of 'em up in those northern states, they had a whole bunch of horses—thirty or forty head. Now they got these tractors, great big ones that pull the thing. But I haven't told you radiator folks what a combine is.

Well, here is what it does—just one machine, and in one trip over the ground. On the front end of it is an arrangement that makes a deal to take over the ground from the bank that is holding the mortgage. Then, right behind that gadget on this big machine, is a thing that grubs up the roots and herbs. Another thing, right behind that grinds up the roots and herbs into "Sagwa" Indian medicine, which is sold by a white man who says he was adopted into the Indian tribe. Then just a few feet behind that, all connected with the same machine, are the plows that plow the ground. Then right in the furrow is the seeder, then another plow that plows the furrow back where it was in the first place. Then comes the fertilizer, and then the sickle that cuts the grain. Then it's carried along a little platform into the threshing machine where it's threshed, then out and into sacks, and into the big grain elevator that is fastened onto the thing.

Then on, near the back end, is a stock market board, where a bunch of men that don't own the farm, the wheat, or the combine, buy it back and forth from each other. That is, if you have threshed a thousand bushels, why, they sell each other a million bushels of this thousand bushels which was actually threshed, then they announce to the farmer that on account of supply and demand, the wheat is only worth 25 cents. That's what you call a combine.

Well, this Campbell fellow is mighty interesting. He told me a lot about Russia. He says they are farming 90 million acres of wheat. He told Stalin when they had their first conference, that he didn't believe in Communism, and a dozen other things that Russia was practicing. Well, Stalin got up and shook hands with him very warmly, and told him: "We will get on fine, we at least understand each other. It's wheat we want to agree on, and not politics or religion."

It was a mighty interesting visit, and well worth what little spare ribs and sour kraut that I fed him.

Crime Made Easy

Los Angeles, which has been in the Bush League as far as racketeers are concerned, is getting right up in fast company. We pulled off a double header of a murder here a couple of weeks ago, that would do credit to a Chicago, or any of the big timers. The racketeers are mixed up with phases of the city government, just like a regular class A city. The killer here walked away, as usual.

In the old wild west days, the bandit had to back out shooting, and make it to his horse by the blaze of his guns. But nowadays, the robber, or killer, or whatever his day's work might be, why, he does it all casually, just in the regular routine of things. If there is a bank to rob, why, he just saunters in, and the only way he can possibly be noticed is that he will perhaps be dressed better than the banker.

Well, the young man simply walks up with no mask, no western hat, no big forty-five, just a little automatic which a baby can shoot as well as Billy, the Kid could—for all you do is point and keep the trigger pulled, and you hit everything in the place. There is no possible way you can miss any part of anyone in the building. The more nervous you are, the more you hit. If there is one thing that has increased crime, it's been the automatic pistol. It's made no practice necessary to be an outlaw. Give any young egotist two shots of dope, and an automatic, and he will hold up the government mint.

He goes in and gets his money quicker than you can get it with a bona fide check. Out he comes. His partner has the car running, and away they go—perhaps to their country home, or their golf club. The toughest part of robbing nowadays, is to find somebody that has something.

The minute a robber gets a clue to some loot, the rest is easy. Now that's about the routine of the modern robbery, and murder is about along the same routine—course it's a little more expensive on account of having to use a little ammunition.

But the fellow that's hiring the fellow to do the job, has to pay so much, AND ammunition. The fellow that kills you nowadays, why, he don't have it in for you. He don't even know you. You are not even pointed out to him till just before he bumps you off. That's all a business, done through an agency, just like any other agency. They can furnish killers for "Singles" or "Double Murders" or "Group." You get a special rate if you want several put out of commission. It's cheaper to have it all done at once. It's very little more trouble to shoot down a group, than it is one.

Oh, we are living in progress. All of our boasted inventions, like the auto and the automatic, and our increased dope output, terrible liquor, lost confidence in our Justice, graft from top to bottom, all these have made it possible to commit anything you can think of, and in about 80 per cent of the cases, get away with it. He can get away quick in a car. He can't miss with the gun he's got. If he is caught he knows it will be accidental. Then, if he is caught, his connections with his gangs get him out. So it's not a dangerous business, after all, from the looks of it.

But there is no use going on with what's happening out here in our town, Los Angeles, cause the same thing is happening in yours. So I don't want to be like all these Californians, and be accused of bragging.

Ziegfeld and the Lion

Well, Sir, every man that has ever done anything out of the ordinary, is a character. And I would call Florenz Ziegfeld a man that had done something out of the ordinary, plum out of the ordinary. He has given to the American public for Lord knows how many years, entertainment that must have given them more pleasure and happiness than any other, for they have paid more to see it than to any other man in the world. A circus has all its tremendous aggregation of assorted animals from the four corners of all the earth. Yet Mr. Florenz Ziegfeld can take just one breed—in fact just one half the breed, the "she" of the species and can assemble such a round-up of beauty, combined with the best there is to offer at that time in the amusement line, and he can concoct an evening's entertainment that you remember till the next year.

A funny thing about the Ziegfeld Follies all the years I was with it. In hearing people speak of the show that year, they never spoke of it in comparison to any other show. It was always: "It's better than last year's," or, "it's not as good as last year's." It always stood alone, for there was no other show that they could remember for a year. His hardest opposition has been himself. If he had been new every year, and that particular show was the very first, why, each one would have been heralded as a masterpiece. But naturally, they had to compete with each other. But it's not of his shows, or his hundred and one other things that anyone could write on by the hour that he has accomplished in the theatrical world, it's just of him that I want to tell you something.

The reason is, it's fresh in my mind. He was out on the coast a few weeks ago to visit his charming wife, Billie Burke, who was playing out here in one of the coast's most successful shows, and as I and my family are tremendously fond of him and his family, why, he was up to our little igloo some. One evening, at dinner, we got him started on old times, and we had a great evening. Here was the foremost of all revue producers of all time, telling about his barnstorming around the country in his early career.

His real start was with Sandow, the strong man, the first of the strong men—that is, the first strong man that was strong enough to make people pay to see how strong he was. Well, Mr. Ziegfeld dug him up over in Europe, and brought him over here. But let him tell it:

> I remember the first time I was out here on the west coast. It was on Sandow's first trip. We had a kind of a vaudeville show built around him, sorter like Harry Lauder carried, only a better show. One time, in Frisco, we had him billed to fight a lion. Just bare-handed. It created a lot of excitement, and we had a packed house. We were bringing ancient Rome to Frisco. It was not part

of our regular program, it was a special stunt that was arranged there. It wasn't framed, either. This fellow Sandow really thought he was better than a lion, so we got him a big old lion. Sandow entered the temporary colosseum with more bravado than any Christian in the early days ever faced one. The women kinder half hid their eyes, appearing like they didn't want it to be seen that they were looking at such a sight, but secretly hoping that something would happen. Instead of the lion making for Sandow, he had to make for the lion. Well, the old lion took to the outer edges. Sandow followed him, in fact, chased him.

The lion didn't pay any more attention to him, than a house cat would. Well, there wasn't much fight. Everybody hollered that the lion was doped, but he wasn't. I wouldn't even think of such a thing. I love lions, especially after I counted the house. Well, Sandow kept at him, at least he kept at him till I could get the money from the box office to a fast moving conveyance. It was a terrible shock to me to hear that the lion was not the king of the beasts, for I had read it all my life. Sandow dressed for his performances in a tiger skin, in fact he brought that style of raiment over here. Well, Sandow left the Arena de Lions not ahead of the lion, but ahead of the populace. He wore his tiger skin for pajamas during the rest of that night ride. He was as down-hearted about the lion as I was. I never went to Frisco till the year of their big Fair out here, when I took the Follies out. I thought the odor of the lion had vanished, but some of the newspapers had a memory, and said: "The man that arranged for a man to whip a lion one time, is in our midst again. We will watch him this time. If his Follies are doped, then give us some of the dope."

Did I tell you what happened when Sandow and I were on our way to the coast? Well, the train broke down, and a wheel come off a car. When they got the new one fixed, I got about 10 men to carry the broken one into our stateroom. When we arrived at Oakland, the press boys met us and I had them come in. They saw the wheel in the drawing room. "What in the world is this?" they wanted to know. "Oh, that is a wheel we broke off, and Sandow just picked it up and brought it in here." They photographed it, and it made a great story, when as a matter of fact, Sandow couldn't even have rolled it downhill. He was a great fellow, this Sandow, a very high class man, a fine man.

He was perhaps the strongest of them all, he had a most beautiful body and the women fell for him hard. An imitator was right ahead of us, claiming that he was the real Sandow. We finally had him brought to court, and as the case was progressing, all was argument as to who was which, and what, I suggested to our lawyer to tell the judge to test them, and see which was the real one. I had Sandow's big iron dumbbells brought in, and the judge asked the other fellow to lift it. He pulled a kidney loose, and couldn't even get it out of the box. Sandow then reached down, picked it up with one hand and was ready to make a forward pass with it out the back window. We won the case. I wish I had some way of testing all my imitators.

He has had a great experience, has Mr. Ziegfeld. He looks and is just the same as the days I went with him on his Midnight Frolic Roof (the first show) in 1915. Many a one of us got our start—our real start with him. Those were great old days, those Follies days, packed houses, wonderful audiences. He never bothered me as to what I was to do, or say, he never suggested anything, never asked me to cut something out.

And to think after 30 years of giving them the best in town, he still has the best show in New York. That shows it wasn't the performers that made Ziegfeld shows—for hundreds have come and gone—it was just Ziegfeld. I think he holds the record for being champion. He knew colors, and he knew beauty. He knew how to keep nudeness from being vulgar. His was a gift, and not an accomplishment.

Long live the old master.

This Philosophy Racket

I guess I get the usual amount of mail of anyone that writes junk for the papers, mostly from people that sho don't agree with anything you said in the papers, and showing you where you ought to be calling hogs instead somewhere. But this week I got some interesting letters. One I sure was surprised to get, was from Will Durant, a man that has studied philosophy like Mr. Coolidge has politics, and both have reached the height in their chosen professions. I met this Durant once. He is an awful nice fellow. I don't know much about what his "racket" is, this philosophy gag.

He wanted me to write him, and give him my version of "What Your Philosophy of Life" is? "I, who have lived philosophy for many years," he writes, "turn now from it back to life itself, and ask you, as one who has lived, to give me your version. Perhaps the version of those who have lived, is different from those who have merely thought. What keeps you going? What are the sources of your inspiration? And your energy? What is the goal or motive force of your toil? Where do you find your consolation and your happiness? Where is the last resort your treasure lies?"

He went on: "A copy of this letter is being sent to Hoover, MacDonald, Lloyd George, Mussolini, Marconi, Gandhi, Stalin, Trotsky, Tagore, Einstein, Edison, Ford, Eugene O'Neill, and Bernard Shaw," and three or four others that I had never seen in the weeklies.

Now I don't know if this guy Durant is kidding me, or not. If I got this kind of letter from somebody else, I would say it's a lot of "hooey" and wouldn't even finish reading it. But putting me in there with that class, why, I figured I better start looking into this philosophy thing.

I think what he is trying to get at in plain words—leaving all the philosophy out—is just how much better off, after all, is a highly educated man, than a dumb one? So that's how I figure is the way I got in that list. He knew that I was just as happy and contented as if I knew something, and he wanted to get the "dumb" angle, as well as the highbrow.

That education is sorter like a growing town. They get all excited when they start to get an increase, and they set a civic slogan of "Fifty Thousand by the End of Next Year!" Well, that's the guy that sets a college education as his goal. Then, when they get the fifty thousand, they want to go on and make it a hundred thousand; and the ambitious college graduate wants to go on and make it as a post graduate in some line, figuring he will just be about as smart as anyone, if he can just get that under his belt. And the town thinking that the hundred thousand will just put them by all the other competing towns, not figuring that while they are growing, all the rest are doing likewise, and maybe faster. When they get to a half million, New York will be twenty million, so they are no higher in the ladder comparatively than they were.

And the educated guy, he is the same. He finds when he gets his post graduate course, that all the other professors have got one too, and lots of 'em have a half a dozen. He begins to wonder if he hasn't spent all this time wondering if he knows anything, or not. He wishes he had took up some other line. He talks with an old, broad-minded man of the world of experience, and he feels lost. So I guess he gets to wondering what education really is. For there is nothing as stupid as an educated man, if you get him off the thing he was educated in.

Then right the same week, comes one from Bill Hanley of Oregon. I had read the most wonderful book of Hanley's called "Feeling Fine." It's got more real philosophy in it than any book today. I am going to send it on to Will Durant, and I want him to get this old bird's idea on a few things. It's the story of his life, not as he has lived, but as he has observed. He shows you a lesson of every day life in every little animal, or bird we have. Lord, what a wonder he would be to lecture in a college to boys. What confidence they would have in his knowledge. They would know that it come from a prairie, and not from under a lamp.

An educated man just teaches the things that he has been taught, and it's the same that everyone else has been taught that has read and studied the same books he has. But if these old fellows know anything, it come direct to them by experience, and not by the way of someone else. If I had Hanley's knowledge, I wouldn't give it for even Secretary of State's Hughes' and Columbia University's Nicholas Murray Butler's, combined—and I like 'em both personally, and think they are great men. But I would know I knew something, if I knew what one of these old cattlemen knew; and if I was as smart as Hughes or Butler, I would still be in doubt, because I would be educated so high that I would know that I only had a smattering of what I did have.

So I can't tell this doggone Durant anything. What all of us know put together, don't mean anything. Nothing don't mean anything. We are just here for a spell, and pass on. Any man that thinks civilization has advanced, is an egotist.

Fords and bathtubs have moved us and cleaned us, but we was just as ignorant when we got there. We know lots of things we used to didn't know but we don't know any way to prevent 'em from happening. Confucius perspired out more knowledge than the U.S. Senate has vocalized in the last 50 years.

We have got more tooth paste on the market, and more misery in our courts than at any time in our existence. There ain't nothing to life, but satisfaction. If you want to ship off fat beef cattle at the end of their existence, you got to have 'em satisfied on the range. Indians and primitive races were the highest civilized, because they were more satisfied, and they depended less on each other, and took less from each other. We couldn't live a day without depending on everybody. So our civilization has given us no liberty, or independence.

Suppose the other guy quits feeding us? The whole thing is a "racket." So get a few laughs, do the best you can, take nothing serious, for nothing is certainly depending on this generation. Each one lives in spite of the previous one, and not because of it. And don't start "seeking knowledge," for the more you seek, the nearer the "booby hatch" you get.

And don't have an ideal to work for. That's like riding towards a mirage of a lake. When you get there, it ain't there. Believe in something for another world, but don't be too set on what it is, and then you won't start out that life with a disappointment. Live your life so that whenever you lose, you are ahead.

A Poor Year for Leaders

Lots of Prime Ministers have passed under the bridge since I last broke news with you. Poor Mr. Ramsay MacDonald, he is still in there, but under another uniform. He was a very able, conscientious man, but just like all the leaders everywhere, the victim of the slump. Being President or leader of any country during the last two years, was like arriving at the railroad crossing just as the stop signal was against you. There is nothing you can do but just stand and watch and wait, till somebody switches something over which you have no control.

I don't suppose there is a leader today, who, if he had known what was in store for him, wouldn't have thrown the job right back in your face, when offered it. It's just an off season for leaders.

The Labor government come in when things looked bad over in England, and the people thought that they would do something for labor. Well, Mr. MacDonald, and Mr. Hoover, can't get you a job if nobody wants to hire you. They haven't any personal positions to put you in. So when things went fluey, why, they were the goats.

You see, over in England when you and your cabinet can't agree on some major issue, and everything is all cockeyed, why the Prime Minister is supposed to have lost control of his party, and he resigns and sends his resignation to the King. In fact, I think he takes it to the King. Well, then that generally means another election to put in some other party, but a general election costs a lot of money, and besides, it is sometimes unwise on account of conditions, to leave a thing to the people. They might not be in the mood to receive it like you would like to have them receive it. They can't have an election now in England, for there is so many unemployed, and so many dissatisfied, that they are liable to even vote further than for Labour, and go almost Bolsheviki. A hungry man is looking for immediate results, and not caring for future conditions.

You see, the whole thing come about over the "Dole." They were running short of money, and wanted to cut down on the amount given to the unemployed. Well, these have been getting that so long, that it's like saying: "Now here, you been eating three meals a day, but we got to cut you down to two."

The unemployed are not working, but they are in a position to dictate. Well, Ramsay wanted to cut the Dole in half. So instead, they just cut his authority in half. Then they said, in order to give him a kind of a dignified exit: You go form a coalition Cabinet, and see what you can do with it. That means he can take in a few from each party. So he got him three Conservatives, three Labour, and a couple of Liberals. The Liberals are the old Lloyd George Party, and they are the smallest Party, but neither of the others have a majority, so that leaves them like the Progressives in our Senate. They are the ones you have to deal with before you put anything over.

Well, the coalition got together, and they knew that their only hope was to cut some of the Dole, but they knew what had happened to Ramsay, when he wanted to nip off half of it. So they kinder studied and figured that if they proposed to slash off a third, would they still be able to retain their positions? Then they held another huddle, and decided that about ten per cent ought not to make 'em so mad that they would throw them—the coalition—out on their ear. So coalition really means being careful.

Now the English are going to pull through. They are that kind of people. They feel their loss of banking prestige worse than they do anything else. When you have been the world's money headquarters, why, it's sorter hard to see it slip away. But they got great—what do you call it—recuperative powers, or stick-to-it-iveness. They will juggle around and fit their business to present conditions.

You know, Mr. Hoover is sorter right about that Dole. He has seen what it has done for England, and he knows what it would do for this country. Of course, no country in its right mind would ever adopt the method that England did. That is, to just give people money that couldn't work, and not make them do something for it—just let them sit and draw enough to live on. It's got to be done by giving them something to do for the money. That's what ruined the whole plan over there.

I will never forget in one of the Arkansas towns that I visited with Frank Hawkes last year on our benefit tour. They had been feeding something like three hundred in their soup kitchen, and one night they announced that they had arranged so that everyone would be given work the next morning at about—I think it was—$1.50 a day. You could get a real meal in town for 25 cents, and after three meals that would have left you 75 cents. Well, the next morning there was less than seventy-five out of three hundred that showed up. So you see, that is where England pulled their boner.

You can't just give people something for nothing, you got to do something for what you get. Now big committees are working getting money for the coming fall and winter. Mr. Hoover is going to insist on the people taking care of each other as long as it is possible, and that will be a long time, for never was there as much money in the hands of the few, as now.

We been twenty years honoring and celebrating the inventor who could save a dollar by knocking somebody out of work; now we are paying for it. Machines are a great thing, but if one replaces a hundred men, it don't buy anything, it don't eat anything, while the hundred men spend their salaries back for food, shelter, and hundreds of commodities for them and their families. So they can have all the theories and plans they want, but till you get rid of something and put people back to work, you ain't going to be able to fix it. You can call it coalition, Republican, Democrat or Bolshevik—but folks got to have work.

1932

The Soviet Union begins its Second Five-Year Plan, setting delusory goals while trying to cover up that the goals from the last five-year plan had not been reached. Another, separate, five-year plan is to establish atheism in the Soviet Union. A target date is set, May 1—May Day—1937, when all places of worship are to be closed.

Elections in Germany forecast the future when Adolf Hitler's Nazi party makes enormous gains.

For the first time Britain, with 2.8 million unemployed, is forced to abandon free trade, and most imports are barred through new tariffs. Preferential treatment regarding imports is extended to colonies and commonwealth countries, such as Canada, Australia, South Africa, and New Zealand.

The British Union of Fascists is founded by a former Labour member of Parliament, Sir Oswald Mosley, who will become an ardent admirer of Adolf Hitler and Benito Mussolini and will advocate expulsion of all Jews from Britain.

In Holland, the draining of the Zuider Zee opens up much needed farmland, while in the Ukraine and the Caucasus, where farmland is already abundant, famine kills thousands.

In the United States, more Americans go to bed hungry every night than at any time in this country's history. Almost one million city dwellers return to the land to raise bare necessities. But U.S. farm prices keep falling to a low of 60 percent below 1929 levels. Wheat brings less than twenty-five cents a bushel, oats only ten cents, and sugar is three cents a pound. On August 9, Iowa farmers begin a thirty-day boycott to protest the low prices: "Stay at Home! Sell Nothing!" is their battle cry. At last the Federal Farm Bureau distributes 85 million bushels of wheat to the hungry.

By year's end, 34 million Americans are without an income, and for those lucky enough to be still employed the average weekly wage is seventeen dollars.

Wall Streeters will remember July 28, 1932. For on that day the Dow Jones Industrial Average falls to 41.22, the lowest it will go.

At 10:40 P.M. on March 1, Col. Charles Lindbergh telephones the New Jersey State Police headquarters at Trenton to report that his twenty-month-old son has been kidnapped from the family home at Hopewell. The small boy, investigation reveals, was taken some time between 8:30 and 10:00 P.M. through a second-story window. A ladder leaning against the window and muddy footprints leading to the child's bed clearly indicate the sequence.

A $50,000 ransom will be paid for the safe return of the child. Seventy-two days after the abduction, the body of the infant is found in a shallow grave, barely five miles from the Lindbergh home. It seems obvious that the child was killed on the night of the kidnapping.

Not until September 1934 will any of the ransom money surface. When it does, Bruno Richard Hauptmann will be arrested for passing the marked bills. He will claim to be innocent and to have received the money from a former business partner.

Starting in May, Great War veterans descend on Washington asking for the balance of a bonus voted them in 1924, but to be payable only in 1945. More than 20,000 Bonus Marchers—also dubbed BEF, Bonus Expeditionary Force—implore their government to prepay the bonus now, at a time when the money is desperately needed. Many veterans with wives and children find shelter only in packing cases, cartons, abandoned stores, city dump, or crates. On June 17, the Senate defeats the prepaid bonus bill by 62 to 18, but the veterans stay on, hoping somehow to move the legislators by their presence. On July 28, President Hoover orders 1,500 troops to evict the squatters. Under the direction of Army Chief of Staff Gen. Douglas MacArthur, cavalry, infantry using bayonets and tear gas, and tanks eject the veterans from their ramshackle "Hooverville." Then the torch is set to what had been the veterans' homes for the past two months. It is not one of this country's prouder moments. Other officers involved in this eviction: Maj. Dwight D. Eisenhower and Maj. George S. Patton, Jr.

There are many casualties, but President Hoover claims that "Red" agitators, rather than veterans, are responsible for the confrontation. It is true that more than thirty Communist leaders are arrested, including the Communist party's candidate for vice-president.

The Republican National Convention, held in Chicago, cannot possibly repudiate its own leadership, and incumbents Herbert Hoover and Charles Curtis are renominated.

The Democratic National Convention is also held in Chicago, and on the fourth day, June 30, nominations begin. Late at night, after other states' nominations and seconding speeches, Oklahoma places in nomination the name of Will Rogers as a gesture toward its favorite son, giving him all its twenty-two votes. Franklin Delano Roosevelt is nominated to be the Democratic presidential candidate and John Nance Garner to be vice-president.

In July, the Olympic Games open at Los Angeles, with 2,403 participants representing thirty-nine countries. Among American gold-medal winners: eighteen-year-old Mildred ("Babe") Didrikson in the javelin throw and the 80-meter hurdles, Clarence ("Buster") Crabbe for the 400-meter swim, and nineteen-year-old Eleanor Holm for the 100-meter backstroke.

Some of the books on the best-seller list are: *Death in the Afternoon,* by Ernest Hemingway; *Brave New World,* by Aldous Huxley; and *Tobacco Road,* by Erskine Caldwell.

One hundred twenty-seven sound films are made in the United States. Some of the best are: *The Sign of the Cross,* with Fredric March, Elissa Landi, Claudette Colbert, and Charles Laughton; *Grand Hotel,* with Greta Garbo, Joan Crawford, John and Lionel Barrymore, Wallace Beery, Lewis Stone, and Jean Hersholt; *King Kong,* with Fay Wray and Bruce Cabot; and *M,* directed by Fritz Lang, starring Peter Lorre.

The legitimate Broadway theaters feature, among others: *The Animal Kingdom,* by Philip Barry, with Leslie Howard, William Gargan, and Ilka Chase; *Dinner at Eight,* by George S. Kaufman and Edna Ferber, starring Constance Collier; at the Guild Theatre, Beatrice Lillie, Claude Rains, Leo G. Carroll, and Hope Williams, appear in a short-lived (57 performances) play called *Too True to Be Good,* by George Bernard Shaw.

The musical stage is more prolific this year, offering such triumphs as *Face the Music,* by Irving Berlin, including "Let's Have Another Cup of Coffee"; *Words and Music,* by Noel Coward, introducing the durable "Mad Dogs and Englishmen"; *Gay Divorcee,* with music and lyrics by Cole Porter, starring Fred Astaire, and his new dancing partner, Claire Luce, stopping the show with the ever popular "Night and Day"; *Earl Carroll's Vanities,* with Milton Berle and Helen Broderick; and *Americana,* which introduces the most poignant of all Depression songs: "Brother, Can You Spare a Dime."

Other songs popular this year are: "How Deep Is the Ocean?" by Irving Berlin; "I'm Getting Sentimental Over You," by George Bassman; "Don't Blame Me," by Jimmy McHugh; and Duke Ellington's "It Don't Mean a Thing If It Ain't Got That Swing."

And with money being scarce, families gather in front of radios to listen to such free programs as: "The Jack Benny Program," starring Jack Benny, who at this point is only thirty-eight years old. He will celebrate his thirty-ninth birthday the following year—and every year thereafter. Another newcomer is "The Fred Allen Show," which will change its name several times. And 1932 is the year in which the first installment is heard of a series that will go on for decades: "One Man's Family," the story of Henry and Fanny Barbour and their bewildering offsprings.

The 1932 election results are not exactly a surprise; only the magnitude of the landslide is. Roosevelt wins with 472 electoral votes over Hoover's 59. The Democrats also take control of a "wet" Congress.

And for those who may have been wondering about it, 1932 is the year an Oklahoman named Carl C. Magee invents the parking meter.

New Year's Eve 1931 finds Will Rogers aboard the S.S. *President Taft* headed for Hong Kong. He will proceed by plane and ship via Singapore, Penang, and Karachi to Cairo, on to Athens, Rome, Paris, and London, back to Paris and Geneva—most of this by plane—and arrive back in New York aboard the S.S. *Europe.* On to Washington—naturally—a quick stop with the folks in Oklahoma, and back in Los Angeles the last week of February. Will attends the two national conventions, which he covers in special syndicated columns.

In July, Will's longtime friend Florenz Ziegfeld dies after a long illness. Will delivers the eulogy at the funeral held in Los Angeles.

In October, the old wanderlust has Will firmly by the hand, and he is off again, this time to South America, and again by plane. Through Mexico to San Salvador, Ecuador, Peru, Chile, and Brazil, back to Puerto Rico and on to Florida. On November 7, election day, Will is back in his home in Santa Monica.

Will makes three films during 1932: *Down to Earth,* with Irene Rich and Dorothy Jordan; *Too Busy to Work,* based on the Ben Ames Williams' story *Jubilo,* with Marian Nixon and newcomer Dick Powell; and *State Fair,* with Janet Gaynor, Lew Ayres, Louise Dresser, and Victor Jory, which will be released in January 1933.

No Tax on Optimism—Yet

The tough part of our whole system is the amount of money they are spending—hundreds, thousands, practically millions that are working for the state, the city, the federal government. There is hundreds of different branches and bureaus, that everybody knows is not essential. But they were politically created to give jobs, and no politician has the nerve to do away with 'em. Lord, the money we do spend on government, and it's not a bit better than the government that we got for one-third the money twenty years ago. But we will do like the British, we will muddle through. We are kind of like China, we are so big that we get along in spite of all the bad management.

Gosh, wasn't we crazy there for awhile? Why the thought never entered our head that we wasn't the brightest, wisest, and most accomplished people that was ever on this earth. Hadn't we figured out "mass production"? Couldn't we make more things than anybody? Did the thought ever enter our bone head that the time might come when nobody would want all these things we were making? No, we had it all figured out that the more we made, the more they would want.

Honest, as we look back now, somebody ought to have taken each one of us and soaked our fat heads. We bought everything under the sun, if they would sell it on enough installments. Where was our payments going to come from if we lost our jobs? Why should we lose our jobs? Wasn't all our big men telling us things was even going to get better? Was our government, or our prominent men warning us? If we had had a "prominent" man he would have, but we just didn't have any. Each one of us, individually, as we look back, we can see what a mess we made, but the drunk is over, and this sobering up is terrible. But bad as it is, it's better than any other country. So cheer up! That's the only thing they don't tax you on.

A Night Phone Call

One night, out at my little ranch where I live, I was awakened out of my sleep about 2:30 in the morning by a telephone call. It was from New York and was from William Randolph Hearst, Jr.

I had been out to a dinner at the home of a neighbor, Oscar Lawler, Los Angeles' best lawyer, who had just won the biggest case the Standard Oil had ever won. It wasn't a celebration, for he is too modest for that. It was just a lot of friends gathered together to "blather" and eat.

So naturally no one turned on the radio, as everybody was pretty well fixed for tooth paste and mouth wash. So I went home about eleven, feeling that all was well with the world, outside of China, Japan, India, Manchuria, Russia, Germany, England, France, Italy, Spain, South America, Nicaragua, and the United States, including a two-and-a-half billion deficit in one year, and a worse year to come.

So I felt that the world was really sitting pretty, outside of everybody not working, and nobody buying anything, and nobody knowing what the morrow might bring forth, but even if it brought it forth, it wouldn't surprise us, for we were prepared for what we thought was the worst.

Well, the phone rings. You know how that scares you right away in the night? You think of the ones that are not there with you. Mrs. Rogers was with my sister in Chelsea, Oklahoma—about twenty miles from Claremore. She didn't fly home from the East with me. She don't mind short flights of a couple or three hours, but when they run into days, she believes that old man Pullman had a pretty good idea on how to cross this continent, and she has made it so much, she knows every jack rabbit, or coyote from California to Kansas. Her being away when the phone rang, and two boys scattered around in schools, of which we hadn't heard from since Christmas.

But when I am half asleep and nervously grabbed the phone, and it was young Bill Hearst from New York, I couldn't think what in the world it was. I had just been up to his father's ranch at San Simeon, about half way between Frisco and here, and I thought maybe I did something up there that I shouldn't. Maybe some of the silver is missing. Maybe there is an old William, the Conquerer tapestry misplaced.

In fact there is so much devilment up there that a country boy could do, that I couldn't think of what it was I had done. I remembered riding off horseback with the cattle boss, and spending the whole day, when I should have been, maybe, with the other guests at the castle. But there was lots of lawyers among the guests, and I knew cows better than I did lawyers. There is a way of studying a cow, and learning all about her, but a lawyer? There has never been any course at college devised where you can take in "What Makes A Lawyer Like He Is?"

This young Bill Hearst, Jr., is a mighty promising young fellow, and looks like he is going to pick up W. R.'s trail and keep the ink smearing over half the pulp wood of Canada. Then when he says,

"The Lindbergh's baby has been kidnapped," well that put a different complexion on life. What did General Honjo taking Manchuria amount to? We could give the whole mess of political candidates on both sides, for the return of the baby.

It was just one of those things that hit you right between the eyes. It was then five-thirty in the morning in New York, and he said they had been up all night, working on the case. He said that he had just had Arthur Brisbane, the fine columnist and editor, on the wire for a couple of hours down at his home in New Jersey, and Mr. Brisbane wanted him to get me, that I was the last newspaper man to have seen the child.

And would I tell 'em some more about it? So I told him what little I knew over the phone, which didn't take me long. It's as I have told you in my little daily blurb:

> Two weeks ago Sunday, Mrs. Rogers and I spent the day with the Lindberghs and the Morrow families. The whole family interest centered around the cute little fellow. He had his father's blond, curly hair, even more so than his dad's. It's almost golden, and all in little curls. His face is more of his mother's. He has her eyes exactly.
>
> His mother sat on the floor in the sun parlor, among all of us, and played blocks with him for an hour. His dad was pitching a soft sofa pillow at him as he was toddling around. The weight of it would knock him over. I asked Lindy if he was rehearsing him for forced landings.
>
> After about the fourth time of being knocked over, he did the cutest thing. He dropped of his own accord when he saw the pillow coming. He was just stumbling and jabbering around like any kid 20 months old.
>
> He crawled up in the back of the Morrow automobile that was going to take us home, and he howled like an Indian when they dragged him out.
>
> I wish we had taken him home with us and kept him.

We had spent the day out there, not at the Lindbergh home, but at the Morrow home, where the Lindberghs live most of the time. In fact, my wife and I discussed going home that evening as to whether the Lindberghs would ever live at their new home. You see, it was started before Ambassador Morrow's recent death. But that, of course had put a whole new complexion on all their lives. Mrs. Morrow is naturally crazy about the baby, as are all the family, and they have this great, lovely home at Englewood, New Jersey. And this baby, and the family all being there would just help to make up for some of the loss of Mr. Morrow. It is just a sad state of affairs, for here was this man Morrow, who was as sure to be one of the pillars in our destiny, as night was to follow day. You didn't find a public man like that but once in a lifetime. He had ability combined with common sense. Everything that came up, he just took all the hooey out of it and brought it down to just an every day problem. The bigger the problem, the easier it was to solve diplomatically with him, for he knew it only took square dealing on both sides, and the other fellow knowing how on the level Morrow was, why, naturally he turned "straight" too.

We all know a lot of these little old one-horse papers in New York have taken digs at Lindbergh. It made a lot of them sore because he didn't want their publicity. They can't understand anyone that don't want their name in the papers. He did his stunt, and he wanted to be let alone, and live his life the way he saw fit. But no! These birds must start tormenting him, when he don't do like they want him to, then the little scandal sheets started "gunning" for him.

Why, there is nothing that he has done since his flight that has not reflected credit on him, and the whole people who are proud of him. Heroes are made every little while, but only one in a million conduct themselves afterwards so that it makes us proud that we honored them at the time. As I have always argued, that fellow Lindbergh has a native intuition to do the right thing. In China, Japan, Mexico, France, or New Jersey, he hasn't made a wrong move yet. His wife has proven a lovely, sweet American girl. She has, at the risk of her own life, taken up her husband's profession, and anything said against them in any way, must come through nothing but jealousy.

Everything Fine with Nature

You would think that anyone living out here, this close to Hollywood, would see quite a bit. Lots of folks come from far and wide to look us over, but I think they go back kinder disappointed. Hollywood for real up and doing, is mighty delicatessen.

Depression has hit the devilment just like it has hit everything else. The pursuit of life and liberty has been checked by this slow return to "normalcy." So, as I say, I haven't seen much lately.

I have been keeping mighty close to home, riding the old ponies out in the hills and seeing how it was making out during this long spell of Republicanism. It just looks like everything is doing fine but humans.

Animals are having a great year, grass was never higher, flowers were never more in bloom, trees are throwing out an abundance of shade for us to loaf under. Everything the Lord has a hand in is going great; but the minute you notice anything that is in any way under the supervision of man, why, it's cockeyed.

And the more men have anything to do with trying to right a thing, why, the worse off it is. If every man was left absolutely to his own method of righting his own affairs, why, a big majority would get it done. But man cannot do that. The government has not only hundreds, but literally thousands in Washington, to see that no man can personally tend to his own business. They go there to do it for him, and a mob always gets panicky quicker than an individual. They hear so much of how bad things are, and that something should be done, and they immediately feel that it's up to them to do it. So they get up in the morning, determined to pass some bills that day that will attempt to do something. They were sent there to pass bills, so they get to passing them.

That was one of the great things about Coolidge. Coolidge never thought half the things that are wrong needed fixing. You knew that over half the things just needed leaving alone. It's kinder like writing a letter to everybody you hear from. He knew that if you leave nine-tenths of 'em alone, it didn't need answering.

Now here, a couple of weeks ago, Congress broke out, and they just gloried in their devilment. If some one could point out anyone that looked like a rich man going down the street, why, they just passed a search and seizure bill, and went out and not only plucked him, but added a little tar and feathers when they turned him loose. Well, they got everybody sore at 'em, and the big ones said: "Well, if they are going to confiscate what I may earn, I just won't earn anything! Why should I take a chance investing in something, when I will only be able to keep one-fourth of it when I win?"

Well, after Speaker Jack Garner got his strangle hold back on the boys again, and after they had sobered up, why, he showed 'em that the government was after all a sort of a co-operative affair, and that it wouldn't be a bad idea to sort of distribute the cost around in proportion. Course everybody knows that one of our great ills today, is the unequal distribution of wealth. You are either at a banquet in this country, or you are at a hot dog stand. There was no doubt that the ones with money were about the only ones that could pay anything, but, after all, these durn rich ones are the ones the rest of us got to live off of. If the government takes all their money in taxes, it don't leave any for the folks that work for 'em.

Then to add to the confusion of everything, Congress turned down the sales tax, then turned right around and had the same tax come up under a different name, and passed it. That's just like we do more things. Take the League of Nations, everybody agreed that we had no business in it, but the first thing, you know, here we were "advising" with 'em. Or the World Court; we wouldn't put on a cap and gown, but we would sit on the bench with 'em. We are always doing something through the kitchen door. We like the glory, but not the responsibilities.

But we are kicking along in spite of our handicaps. The East and the North have got to get like the South has been for years, poor, and used to it. Us folks down there have had to catch a catfish, or kill a possum, before we eat, for years. So the other parts of the country have got to learn to look to nature, and not to Wall Street for what goes in the pot.

They got to find some other way of making a living, besides looking at a list of names in the papers every day. Stocks and bonds have got so now, they don't go up and down, only when there is a reason, not like they used to go up and down when there was a wish on somebody's part.

If so many of 'em are not looking at our pictures as used to, we are mighty grateful to those that are. If they are not looking at us, it's because they are wise to us, and that's about the way it is with everything else.

The Secret of Education

Say, any of you that have kids in school, either grammar, high or college—it don't make any difference—but can any of you parents get head or tail of what they are doing, what they are taking, what they are learning? This modern education gag sure got me licked. I can't tell from talking to 'em what it's all about.

All the kids I know, either mine or anybody's, none of 'em can write so you can read it, none of 'em can spell. They can't figure and don't know geography, but they are always taking some of the darndest things like Political Science, International Relations, Drama, Buck Dancing, Sociology, Latin, Greek, Art—oh, Lord, the things they go in for runs by the hour!

But it is, as I say, not only our brood, but none of them that I have seen can write, spell, figure, or tell you what bounds Korea. Everybody has swimming pools, but nobody has got a plain old geography. Gymnasiums to the right of you, tennis courts to the left of you, but not a spelling book in a carload of schools.

Then they got another gag they call "credits." If you do anything thirty minutes twice a week, why, you get certain "credits." Maybe it's lampshade tinting, maybe it's singing, maybe it's a thing they call "music appreciation," that used to drive my cowboy son Jim pretty near nuts. He never could see how that would aid you to rope a calf. They give out these "credits" at schools for anything that anyone can think of. Some of 'em you get more "credits" than for others. If a thing is particularly useless, why, it gives you more credits. There is none at all for the things that we thought constituted school. You could write, read, spell, and give the capital of Rhode Island, and they wouldn't give you a credit in a year.

But you tell where a Latin word was originally located, and how it's been manhandled and orphanized down to the present day, and say, they will claim that you have the nucleus of a "thesis," and you are liable to get a horde of credits. Now who cares about the word, or what it has contributed to the welfare of nations? You have got yourself the family tree of a word. Course you can't go out and get a job on it, but these old professors value it mighty highly.

Some of these days they are going to remove so much of the punk and hooey and the thousands of things that the schools have become clogged up with, and we will find that we can educate our broods for about one-tenth the price, and at the same time learning 'em something they might accidentally use after they escaped.

But us poor old, dumb parents, we just string along, and do the best we can, and send 'em as long as we are able, because we want them to have the same handicaps the others have. We don't know what it's all about, we just have to take the teachers' word.

They all think that education is our salvation, but you could turn ten college presidents loose in a forest, with nothing to eat, or nothing to get it with, and then ten old so-called ignorant backwoodsmen, and your presidents wouldn't last a week. The smarter a nation, the more wars it has. The dumb ones are too smart to fight. Our schools teach us what the other fellow knows, but it don't teach us anything new for ourselves. Everybody is learning just one thing, not because they will know more, but because they have been taught that they won't have to work if they are educated. Well, we have so many educated now that there is not enough jobs for educated people. Most of our work is skilled and requires practice, and not education.

But none of these big professors will come out and tell you that our education might be lacking, that it might be shortened, that it might be improved. They know as it is now that it's a racket, and they are in on it. You couldn't get me to admit that making movies was the bunk, either. None of us will talk against our own graft. We all got us our "rackets," nowadays. There is just about as much hooey in everything, as there is merit. The heathens live with less effort, and less worry. Trying to live "past" our parents, and not "up to 'em" is one of our drawbacks. The old Chinese got the right idea along that line.

Anyhow, this education is just like everything else. You got to judge it by results. Here we are, better educated—according to educational methods—than we ever were, and we are worse off than we ever were. So it's not living up to its billing. It's over-rated, it's not worth the price. In fact, it's costing us more than it's worth. They got to devise some way of giving more for the money. All he is getting out with now is "credits," and nobody on the outside is cashing 'em.

A Day at the Republican Convention

They just played the National Anthem, and when they finished, they asked the band leader to play something else while the chairman was trying to think of something to say. They are still playing.

The whole show has degenerated into nothing but a dog fight for Vice President. If you are interested in Vice Presidents and such things, you will perhaps be interested in this convention. Nobody in the history of conventions ever saw a convention start out and end so quick. The "allies" stopped Hoover. Yea, they stopped him from being Secretary of Commerce.

Anyhow, the convention opened with a prayer, a very fervent prayer that Al Smith not be nominated. It was a keynote prayer. If the Lord can see his way clear to bless the Republican Party the way it's been carrying on, then the rest of us ought to get it without even asking for it.

Then they brought on Senator Simeon D. Fess, he delivered what is called the keynote speech. The crowd couldn't hear him and shouted for him to speak louder. Then, when he did speak louder and they did hear him, why, they got sorer than a boil and wanted him to speak low again.

He brought up Nicaragua, but he left our Marines down there. He said that he would protect American lives down there, even if we had to send some there to protect.

Now you all know that a keynote speech is just press notices by a party, written by its own members. Here are just a few things that I bet you didn't know the Republicans were responsible for: radio, telephone, baths, automobiles, savings accounts, law enforcement, workmen living in houses, and a living wage for Senators.

The Democrats had brought war, pestilence, debts, disease, boll weevil, gold teeth, need of farm relief, suspenders, floods, famines.

He told of so much money that we had saved, that I think if he had talked another hour, he would have paid us dividends.

When he got to Coolidge, I thought sure he was referring to Our Saviour, till they told me, "no, it was Coolidge." The way he rated 'em was, Coolidge, The Lord, and then Lincoln.

It was an impromptu address that he had been working on for only six months. He made no attempt at oratory. He just shouted. He dramatized figures. When he told how many millions we had saved, his voice raised, but when our savings had reached the billions, why, his voice reached a crescendo. All expenditures were spoken in an undertone.

Men who yesterday wouldn't allow their names to be even associated with the Vice Presidency, are today announcing they would consider being drafted. In fact, men who two days ago wouldn't even speak to a Vice President, are now trying to get to be one.

They have weeded the Vice Presidential candidates down now to just the following: ninety-six Senators, 435 Congressmen and forty-eight Governors.

If you haven't a room to stay in while here, you can get one now. There is six candidate headquarters that are to be sublet.

All we have done today is listen to Senator Fess explain what he forgot to say yesterday. It seems he left out Teddy Roosevelt's name yesterday, and it took him all day to alibi for it. I don't know who he forgot today that he will have to bring up tomorrow.

They had quite a time seating the Texas delegation, as there was no law in Texas to apply to a Republican primary. Texas never thought they would come to a point where there would ever be any Republicans there. They also have no law against the shooting out of season of reindeer or musk ox.

They adjourned till tomorrow for the sake of the hotels. They could have finished this convention in ten minutes today.

At the Democratic Convention

Ah! They was Democrats today, and we was all proud of 'em. They fought, they fit, they split and adjourned in a dandy wave of dissention. That's the old Democratic spirit! A whole day wasted and nothing done. I tell you, they are getting back to normal.

A whole day fighting over what? A President? No. A platform? No. Well, then, what did they take up eleven hundred delegates' and twelve thousand spectators' time for? Why, to see whether Huey Long, the Louisiana porcupine, was to sit on the floor or in the gallery. And the other four hours was fighting over who would be chairman of a convention that's already a week old.

The Democrats are the only known race of people that give a dinner and then won't decide who will be toastmaster till they all get to the dinner, and fight over it.

But to Huey Long goes the credit of being the first to split the party and get 'em acting like Democrats. I'll bet when Judgement Day comes, things will go along unusually quiet till all at once there will be the blamedest fight and it will be over what to do with Huey. But, by golly, he made a good speech today.

Now comes Senator Barkley with the keynote. What do you mean "note"? This was no note. This was in three volumes. Barkley leaves from here to go to the Olympic Games, to run in the marathon. He will win it, too, for that race only lasts three hours.

But it had to be a long speech, for when you start enumerating the things that the Republicans have got away with in the last years, you have cut yourself out a job. He touched on the highlights of their devilment. He did not have time to go into detail. This is one keynote speech you can forgive the length, for when you jot down our ills, you got to have a lot of paper. He had it all over the Republican keynoter, for this fellow was reading facts, while the other fellow had to read alibis.

That was yesterday. Nobody was asked to vote on anything today, so there was no fights. Half the Iowa delegation was still in the hospital from trying to count their own votes yesterday.

This is the third day of the convention. This is the day the Republicans adjourned. Adjourned! Why, the Democrats haven't done anything but meet and pray yet. How can you tell when a Democratic convention is adjourned, and when it's not? A Democrat never adjourns. He is born, becomes of voting age and starts right in arguing over something, and his first political adjournment is his date with the undertaker. Politics is business with the Democrat. He don't work at it, but he tells what he would do if he was working at it.

I am still trying to get the floor to nominate Coolidge at this Democratic convention. I know he was a Republican but Democrats did better with him than anybody we ever had in.

210

Politics ain't on the level. I was only in 'em for an hour but in that short space of time somebody stole 22 votes from me. I was sitting there in the press stand asleep—it was way past midnight—and I wasn't bothering a soul when they woke me up and said Oklahoma had started me on the way to the White House with 22 votes.

I thought to myself, well, there is no use going there this late in the night, so I dropped off to sleep again, and that's when somebody touched me for my whole roll, took the whole 22 votes, didn't even leave me a vote to get breakfast on.

Course I realize now that I should have stayed awake and protected my interest, but it was the only time I had ever entered national politics and I didn't look for the boys to nick me so quick. Course I should have had a manager, but the whole thing came on me so sudden and I was so sleepy. No man can listen to thirty-five nominating speeches and hold his head up. And I am sure some of these that did the nominating can never hold theirs up again.

Now I don't want you to think that I am belittling the importance of those 22 votes. They was worth something there at the time. Not in money, mind you, for there is not $2.80 in the whole convention. But they buy 'em with promises of offices.

I expect at that minute Franklin D. Roosevelt's bunch would have given me Secretary of State for that 22. And I could have sold them to Al Smith for maybe Mayor of New York. Governor Ritchie would have given me the whole state of Maryland, with the Vice Presidency thrown in just for amusement. Why, I could have taken those 22 votes and run Andy Mellon out of the embassy in England with 'em. I could have got that job with only 10 of the votes.

And what do I do—go to sleep and wake up without even the support of the Virgin Islands. They not only took my votes, but they got my hat and my typewriter. I not only lost my 22 delegates, but I woke up without even as much as an alternate. Now what am I? Just another ex-Democratic Presidential candidate. There's thousands of 'em. Well, the whole thing has been a terrible lesson to me and nothing to do but start in and live it down.

Say, did you ever parade at 6 o'clock in the morning? Course not, nobody ever did but the Democrats. I have been in circus parades and Wild West parades, but I had never entered a political parade. I had laughed at many a one, but I had never become looney enough to participate.

But this morning as dawn was breaking over the machine gun nests of Chicago, and you could just see the early peep of light down early-rising gangsters' rifle barrels, one of Oklahoma's ex-Governors arose and started to put in nomination a fellow ex-Governor. His melodious voice aroused me from my slumbers. It was a friend, Henry Johnston nominating my old friend Bill Murray. When he finished, the heavens broke loose, noise accompanied by bedlam, and wht dashes into the arena, not as you would expect at that hour of the morning, a milk wagon, but a band of beautiful little girls, all dressed in kilts, and thank goodness not playing bagpipes, but musical instruments. They had come all the way from Oklahoma City tò help "Our" Bill Murray's parade. Was I going to get in it? If I could get woke up, I was. I had no hat. Arthur Brisbane, the great newspaper-man, had been sleeping on mine during the nominating speeches. So Amon G. Carter, Texas' sole surviving dirt farmer whose farm is on the principal street of Dallas, acted as my unmounted outrider. He handed me a straw hat with the word "Texas" on the band, and for no reason at all—like Democrats do everything—somebody handed me a cane. I waved it till I almost hit Mrs. Woodrow Wilson in the eye.

Along the route of march, we picked up a couple of girls who had been stranded by some earlier demonstration. They evidently was just "thumbing" their way around the hall. I was against taking them on. But Amon thought perhaps they were maybe F.F.V.'s [First Families of Virginia] from the old Commonwealth of Virginia and were trying to make their way back to Governor Byrd's headquarters in the Culpeper corner of the hall.

Then as if by magic, the rising sun started creeping in through the stained glass windows of this great cathedral of liberty and justice, and I got the first real look at our traveling companions. The heels of their shoes were much run down, which we knew at a glance was the badge of the Republican Party. And then we realized that they were left-overs from the late Hoover uprising in the same hall a few weeks ago.

Some kindly soul that had temporarily escaped depression, handed me a box of popcorn, so I had rations through the biggest part of the pilgrimage. The hall runs about three miles to the lap. The journey got us no votes, but like all these half-witted convention parades, it kept anyone else from getting any votes, or rest, either, until every marcher has become thoroughly disgusted with himself.

I am glad Chicago's children didn't come by on their way to school this morning and see how this wonderful system of choosing our country's leaders was conducted. They would never again have asked: "What's the matter with the country?"

Thoughts during Keynote Speeches

The Democrats are trying to change the "two-thirds voting rule." It takes two-thirds to change it. If two-thirds of the Democrats agreed, they wouldn't be Democrats.

The loudspeaker system didn't work and half of the delegates couldn't hear the keynote speech. They got mad and got to leave—but not as quick as those that was sitting nearer and could hear it.

My press seat was near an exit, just ideal. The show ran for about an hour. Then somebody happened to tell that an invocation had not been delivered, and that if the Republicans hoped to corral the church vote, they had better have a little prayer. So they prayed just ahead of Senator Dickinson's speech, but it didn't have any effect on the Lord, or Dickinson, either, for the Lord just let it go on, and so did Dickinson. So the prayer was a total loss.

Listening to a keynote speech is like listening to a Chautauqua lecture, when you could have gone to the Ziegfeld Follies. The lobbyists have taken the whole convention. They give you a badge and a drink. Lots of us don't know what to do with the badge.

Election Post Mortem

Well, all I know is just what I read in the papers, and what I hear as I listen to Democrats like mockingbirds in the treetops. I kinder thought that when the votes were counted, that we had closed the arguments, but we seem to have just started 'em; so, as they are still going over 'em, we might just as well join in. You can never be too late with a post mortem, cause the corpse will always stay dead—that's one accommodating thing about a corpse.

Now let's start from the beginning. What chance did Mr. Hoover have at any time, even before the nominations? Everybody admitted "That if things don't pick up a whole lot, why Mr. Hoover hasn't got a ghost of a chance."

Well, things didn't pick up, everybody knew that. So why did they run him, or I mean rather, why did he run himself? Naturally he would be called upon by the party to run. They never care for the individual. It's always the old hooey: "For the good of the Party!"

Now if Mr. Hoover had just said: "Now boys, I have done all I can for the good of the old party. I have struggled with it, fought every type of hard luck that was ever invented, including some invented by my own party. Now I know the tide is against me, so why lead me to the slaughter? If people want a change, as they evidently seem to, why, maybe we can lead them to accept a change in our own party, so just let me drop out. In fact, I don't care for another term."

Now you see where he would have been. Course you will say, "Yes, Will, but this is a second guess you are making. It's easy to tell after it's all over, what might have been done." But it's not a second guess. It was plain to him and all of them all the time. The whole thing hinged on "things picking up." Well, what was to make 'em pick up? If they hadn't picked up in three years, why were they going to pick up this fall? A slight gain wouldn't have meant a thing. It would have had to rained dollars to make everybody think that the real turn had come.

Away before the Convention in Chicago, I used to ask: "Well, why does Mr. Hoover run? You all say that if the election was tomorrow, that he would be overwhelmingly defeated, that the people just want a change. Why don't he step out and let 'em nominate somebody else in his place, and save that beating?"

Well, they would always tell me: "Well, Will, don't you see that would be admitting that the Party had failed? And we couldn't do that."

You see, it all gets back to the Party. They couldn't have the Party admit anything. No sir, he must run, whether he wants to, or not. "We must stand for our principles!"

So another good man was sent out to bite the dust. I'll bet you that Mr. Coolidge would have ducked 'em if he had been in there under the same conditions. He would have "Not Choosed" right in their face. He would have told 'em, "The running don't look good, and I am not going in just for the sake of running second." The "Good of the Party" could have gone and jumped in the lake, as far as he would have been concerned. They wouldn't have made a Roman Holiday out of him. He would have said: "Boys, throw some other good Republican Christian to the lions. I see the handwriting on the wall in electric letters."

You see you could get over some resignation as this: "Citizens, I am afraid that my administration has not been entirely to your satisfaction, and there seems to be a decided element in favor of a change. I have no alibi to offer, I have no excuses, I have done my very best. It seems that I should have done more. So, for the good of all concerned, I decline to be a candidate for re-election. Yours, Herbert Hoover."

But the Party wouldn't have allowed such a sane and sensible course. It would have put them in the hole, instead of Mr. Hoover. He would have had the sympathy of everyone, but the Party kept hanging on to the idea that "Things" might pick up. They did. Democratic support picked up.

But on the other hand, there just seems to be something about running for president that you can never get out of a fellow's head. He never seems to figure his chances. If can be an "Off Year" or an "On Year" or a "Leap Year," just nominate him, and he is perfectly tickled to death. That he will wind up by being just a defeated candidate never seems to enter his head. That the time is not ripe for it, is as foreign to his thoughts, as the moon.

But it's over, Franklin Delano Roosevelt has been elected, and I guess everybody did the best they could according to what they had to do with. But I did hate to see a man that had been as conscientious as Mr. Hoover had, take a beating like that. He didn't deserve it, he deserved a straight forward declination to run again.

1933

After an eleven-day fishing cruise, President-elect Franklin D. Roosevelt lands at Miami, Florida. Seconds after addressing a crowd in Bay Front Park, a bricklayer from Hackensack, New Jersey, fires five shots in his direction. Two women and three men are shot; one of them, Chicago's Mayor Anton Joseph Cermak, will die of his wounds.

On February 27, fire destroys the German Reichstag (parliament) building in Berlin. The Nazis accuse the Communists of having started the fire, and as "proof" fabricate a case against Marinus van der Lubbe, a twenty-three-year-old Dutch Communist; he will be executed January 10, 1934. But rumors are persistent that the Nazis themselves set the fire under the direction of Nazi leader Hermann Göring, to manipulate public opinion against Germany's large Communist party just six days before the national election.

On March 4, Franklin D. Roosevelt is sworn in as the thirty-second president. In his inaugural address, he says: "This is preeminently the time to speak the truth . . . so first of all, let me assert my firm belief that the only thing we have to fear is fear itself." And thus begins a presidency that will last twelve years, and see the world change.

The next day, March 5, Germany holds an election, and after having repressed and intimidated opponents, Chancellor Adolf Hitler emerges with his Nazi party in full control. And thus begins a dictatorship that will last twelve years, and force the world to change.

Changes begin in Germany almost at once. April 1 is designated as official Anti-Semitic Day, starting the systematic persecution of German Jews. Even visiting Americans are attacked in Berlin as Nazi storm troopers roam the streets raiding and looting stores and homes owned by Jews. On Hitler's demand the Reichstag—the legislative assembly—grants him the dictatorial power to make laws by decree. After that, the Reichstag adjourns—permanently. By May, all trade unions are suppressed; attacks on the church follow.

At the World Economic Conference in London, Germany states that it now wants the return of its former colonies in Africa, and "some further territory"—unidentified, but presumably in Europe—for the "settlement of Germany's active race and for the construction of great works of peace."

In October, Germany walks out of the Geneva Disarmament Conference and leaves the League of Nations. Japan, too, announces intentions to leave the league, but not until 1935.

Famine is reported in Russia; collectivization has so far shown that it works only on paper. There are partly corroborated reports of widespread unrest in the Soviet Union. Tokyo reports that a mob attacked Stalin's residence; troops had to drive off the demonstrators, killing four hundred. In the north, farmers are in revolt. At Irkutsk, for example, 80,000 men are said to have banded together in revolt, and are being joined by Communists and even "Red" soldiers.

Foreign Commissar Maxim Litvinov is received at the White House. It is the first official link between the two countries since the Russian Revolution. Ten days later, the United States formally recognizes the Soviet Union, on the condition that "the Soviet Government pledges itself not to disseminate Communist propaganda in this country, nor attempt in any way to overthrow American institutions." It seems rather a strange commitment to have to ask of a new "friend."

Litvinov vows "Soviet friendship and cooperation for peace." To make the new friendship seem advantageous, it is announced that the Russians are willing to place orders for manufactured items and agricultural products totaling some $520 million—provided U.S. government credit can be arranged—after all, the Soviet Union is a good risk.

After almost fourteen years of Prohibition, in April Congress legalizes the sale of 3.2 percent beer, and President Roosevelt signs the bill into law. The various states must now ratify the Twenty-first Amendment to the Constitution, which calls for repeal of the Eighteenth Amendment—namely Prohibition. While New York State votes 20 to 1 in favor of repeal, New York City is far more enthusiastic: The margin is 41 to 1 in favor of a legal drink. But it is Utah, the thirty-sixth state to ratify repeal, that makes Prohibition a thing of the past. By the time the vote is taken in Salt Lake City, it is 5:32 P.M. local time, and in the East most people are at home. But the news spreads fast, and celebrators are about in search of a drink. There is just one minor trouble: Now that the sale of liquor is legal, there is no legal liquor to be found; but bootleggers and speakeasies are more than eager to dispose of their illegal stock, which will now be reduced to just another item on a shopping list.

Roosevelt's "New Deal" seems to make some progress. Agencies are formed and funded to help the needy, extend credit, and manage farm production. By June more than 1.7 million new jobs are created. The spirit of the country is up, even though the economy is still down.

Some prices of staples: bread, 5¢ a loaf; eggs, 29¢ a dozen; milk, 10¢ a quart; gasoline, 18¢ a gallon; and items bought by the pound: butter, 28¢; rice, 6¢; potatoes, 2¢; pork chops, 20¢; rib roast, 22¢. Average wages: professor, $3,100; doctor, $3,300; construction worker, $900; congressman, $8,660.

Wiley Post, again flying the *Winnie Mae,* attempts to break his round-the-world flight record. This time he has an automatic pilot and will fly alone. He leaves Floyd Bennett Field on Long Island on Saturday, July 15, at 5:10 A.M. and returns 7 days, 18 hours, and 49½ minutes later, having cut 21 hours off his previous time. Wiley says he is "disgusted," since he had hoped to make a much better time. "I had only three hours of good weather, all the way around the world."

The World's Fair at Chicago is a huge success. Its motto: "A Century of Progress," and while there are spectacular exhibits marking progress, people will talk mostly of Sally Rand and her fan dance.

On November 26, in San Jose, California, a mob breaks into the local jail, forces the release of two acknowledged kidnappers, and lynches both men.

Best-selling books of the year include: *God's Little Acre,* by Erskine Caldwell; *The Last Adam,* by James Gould Cozzens; and *Lost Horizon,* by James Hilton.

In the theater, *Tobacco Road,* adapted from Erskine Caldwell's novel by Jack Kirkland, opens and will run 3,182 performances into 1940, breaking the record set by *Abie's Irish Rose.* Some other plays: Noel Coward's *Design for Living,* Ben Hecht and Charles MacArthur's *Twentieth Century,* and Eugene O'Neill's *Ah, Wilderness!*

Radio adds a variety of new entertainment: "Ma Perkins," "The

Romance of Helen Trent," "Jack Armstrong, the All-American Boy," and Don McNeill's "Breakfast Club."

And the motion picture palaces, so grandiose and impressive-looking, attract crowds with: *The Private Life of Henry VIII,* with Charles Laughton; *Little Women,* with Katharine Hepburn, Joan Bennett, Frances Dee, Jean Parker, and Paul Lukas; *The Invisible Man,* with Claude Rains; and *I'm No Angel,* with Mae West and Cary Grant.

Among the tunes most often played on radio, or by those who can afford phonograph records, are "Basin Street Blues," "It's Only a Paper Moon," "Stormy Weather," "Sophisticated Lady," and Cab Calloway's "Minnie the Moocher."

Will Rogers is busy with broadcasts for Gulf Oil and films for Fox; there is no time for trips abroad. He does, however, cross the continent several times. On April 30, Will is in Washington, D.C., broadcasting before the Gridiron Club at a dinner honoring President Roosevelt. Will calls it "President's Day." The next day, Will visits the White House, and stays overnight as a guest of the new president. On the way to California, he stops in Chicago, where he gets a guided tour through the not-quite-finished exhibits of the World's Fair, due to open in two weeks. Will writes: "You can see the whole thing for fifty cents, and the way this Roosevelt is going, by then we will have the fifty cents."

He is back in Chicago the day the fair opens: "It had to open on time, to give everybody making those long speeches a chance to get 'em over before it closed. They had thousands of policemen to block you off at every street to see that you didn't get into it. At that there was 40,000 got by the police, and got in."

Will's films in 1933: *Doctor Bull,* directed by John Ford, with Vera Allen, Marian Nixon, Rochelle Hudson, Louise Dresser, Ralph Morgan, and Andy Devine, and *Mr. Skitch,* directed by James Cruze, with Florence Desmond, Zasu Pitts, Sterling Holloway, and Rochelle Hudson.

President's Day

This is President's Day. We generally recognize everything by a week. We have Apple Week, and Potato Week, and Don't-Murder-Your-Wife Week, and Smile Week—with everybody going around smiling like a possum for no reason at all. So somebody hit upon the bright idea and said, "Here, if Prunes are worth a Week, the President ought to be worth something, anyhow." So they figured out that while they couldn't give him a Week, they could compromise on a Day. Now the reason we gave him only a Day, was that he cut down on everybody. We're very generous that way. We're wonderful with our Presidents. When the sun is shining, we cheer him; but let it start raining, and if he don't furnish us with umbrellas and galoshes, well boy, we give him the boot right then.

The man we're here to pay our respects to—on account of it being President's Day—has no precedent for accomplishments in the seven weeks he's been in now. That bird has done more for us in seven weeks than we have done for ourselves in seven years. We elected him because he was a Democrat, now we honor him because he's a magician. He's the Houdini of Hyde Park. He's a fast worker. He was inaugurated at noon in Washington, and started the inaugural parade down Pennsylvania Avenue, and before it got half-way down there, he closed every bank in the United States. Now a Republican would have never thought of a thing like that; no, he would have let the depositors close 'em. Mind you, Mr. Roosevelt was just two days ahead of the depositors. Then he took the Democrats out of the ranks of the unemployed and he made Post Masters out of them—and he's made Christians out of the Republicans. All but former Secretary of the Treasury Ogden Mills; he's really subsidized by the Democratic Party, to kinder put up the appearance of an organized minority.

When Roosevelt first joined the Democratic Party, it looked like he wasn't going to draw any dividends. Did you notice that the first part of Roosevelt's career was spent in doing nothing but nominating N.Y. Governor Al Smith for President? You could wake him up in the middle of the night, I'll bet, and he would nominate Al. He made some fine speeches nominating Al, because he was nominating a fine man, but of course, the country wasn't ready for Democracy, because it wasn't broke yet.

You speak about sweeping the country, Roosevelt swept the country like a new toothpaste. They rushed up and voted for him like buying tickets for some new Hollywood sex drama. Then look at Wickersham, the former chairman of the National Commission on Law Observance and Enforcement. He worked two years and spent two million dollars to find out how effective Prohibition was, and what did he do with his report? He turned in a report that said: "I - won't - be - sure - and - I - can't - get - the - absolute - proof - but - I - think - there - is - a - little - drinking - going - on - around - the - country."

Roosevelt said I'll do all that with just three words, just give me three words: LET 'EM DRINK! And he collected 10 million dollars in revenue in the first two weeks. And if he had good beer, he would have paid off the national debt by now. Yes sir, Wickersham turned in a lot of figures and things, and Roosevelt said: NO! Just give me two figures, and I'll show you some results. Just give me 3 and 2, just 3 point 2 per cent beer.

You know, commissions are fine. They turn in a lot of data, but what's the good of having a lot of statistics and data on something, if you don't know what to do with 'em. It's kinder like garbage; what's the good of collecting it if you ain't got nowhere to put it. Appointing a commission is not a crime; it's been considered a very fine way of handling anything. But it just seems like a Presidential commission don't get anything done, you know. They don't really earn the breakfast that they give them at the White House the day that they appoint them.

Now Mr. Hoover didn't get results because he asked Congress to do something, that's where he made a mistake. Mr. Roosevelt, he just sends a thing up there every morning, and says: "Here's your menu, you guys, sign it!" Mr. Roosevelt just kids them, he never scolds 'em. Now Mr. Coolidge handled this thing altogether different. He paid no attention to them at all, he wouldn't mess with them. If the fish wasn't biting in the Columbia River, and the Abyssinians wasn't practicing birth control, why, Mr. Coolidge never messed with them at all—he just let it go along.

It seems funny for me to be telling all these Democratic things. I told some Republican industrialists before: How about it? I am going to get up and say naturally something complimentary about the Democrats. So they said: "It'll be o.k. Will. We'd rather have been saved by a Republican, but we will take a Democrat, anyhow."

So, Mr. Roosevelt, we have turned everything over to you. We have given you more power than we ever gave any man. We tried to run the country, but we gummed it up. So you take it and run it, and do anything, just so you get us a dollar, or two, every now and then. So you're our lawyer, we don't know what it's all about; so you take it, and God bless you, Mr. Roosevelt.

Support the President!

America hasn't been as happy in three years as they are today. No money, no banks, no work, no nothing, but they know they got a man in the White House who is wise to Congress, wise to our big bankers, and wise to our so-called big men. The whole country is with him. Even if what he does is wrong, they are with him. Just so he does something. If he burned down the Capitol, we would cheer him and say, Well, at least he got a fire started, anyhow.

We have had years of "Don't rock the boat!" Sink it, Mr. President. We just as well be swimming, as like the way we are.

Mike Donlin's Exit

One of the pleasant things connected with working in the movies is that you are all the time running into actors and friends from the stage days, folks you haven't seen in maybe years, but that you used to know and play on the bill with in vaudeville, or in a show. There is just any number of them live out here in California, for you wiped out a whole industry, the greatest creative branch that amusement ever produced. No line of entertainment ever enjoyed the enthusiastic endorsement of audiences that vaudeville did. Hammerstein's Victoria on 42nd Street and Broadway, was the peer of them all in those days, they, and the Percy Williams houses in New York. But Hammerstein's had a following and a type of audience that no theatre before, or since, had. It knew its vaudeville, like a cow knows its calf. Acts that were favorites year in and out, big importations from Europe, and all the world.

In my last released picture, called "Dr. Bull," worked with me an old timer, one of the unique characters of not only one amusement line, but two. He was not of the stage, he was drafted from another line of recreation. He had become the best known baseball player of his generation. It was he who really introduced so-called "color" into our national pastime. A ball player was just a man with a suit on, and a bat, but when Mike Donlin joined the New York Giants, away along about 1904, or thereabouts, he was the Babe Ruth of his time. He couldn't knock as many balls out of the park as Babe, but he could knock more men out of it. He could take a short arm jab, and bunt some boisterous spectator from the front row to the last.

In those days of the McGraw team, you played one inning, and you fought two. When you slid into a base, you slid into a fight. An umpire waved you out with one hand, and warded off a swinging bat with the other. When an umpire yelled "You're out!" he had to look quick, to tell who was out, him or the player.

College degrees hadn't entered baseball then, but degrees in language had. Well, that was when Mike Donlin was supreme, he was a quiet, orderly fellow, but he has licked more men than the First Division did in France.

We had a great stage comedienne in those days, Mabel Hite. I think Mabel was from Kansas City originally. Well, there is few funny women. Come to think about it, there is few funny men, but there has always been a scarcity of women comediennes. Mabel was a big favorite, in musical comedy the greatest of her time. She fell in love with Mike at the height of his wonderful career. She had a sketch in vaudeville with Walter Jones, a splendid comedian. I played on the bill with them with my old pony, and Buck McKee, an ex-Oklahoma sheriff that rode the pony across the stage, for me to rope at.

I hadn't married Mrs. Rogers then—she was still a girl of sound mind, living in Rogers, Arkansas. Mike and Mabel married. America's most popular comedienne, to America's most popular ball player. It was the most popular wedding New York ever had. She put him on the stage in a vaudeville act. I saw their opening at Hammerstein's Theatre on a Monday afternoon. In my 30 years in all branches of show business, I never heard such a reception. It's always lingered in my memory; and when dear old Mike was playing with me in my last picture "Dr. Bull," I used to tell him about it.

Along about that time, Betty Blake down in Rogers, Arkansas, had a mental relapse, and said "yes" after several solid years of "no's." She threw her lot with Buck, and me, and the pony "Teddy." From cheap hotels to dark stage entrances, she trudged her way. We met Mabel and Mike. We played on the bill with 'em, they the big headliners and drawing cards.

Now my wife reminded me of this the other night. They invited us up to their apartment in New York. It was the first time we had ever been in a swell apartment. It was the first time big actors had ever invited us out. We went up on the street car. This was in the winter of 1908. We had just been married, but I had been on the stage since 1905. Mabel liked my wife. An awful lot of people do. She showed her, so Betty was telling me the other night, beautiful dresses, and a fur coat that cost, I think, it was maybe two thousand dollars. It was a fairyland night for the rope-throwing Rogers.

Mabel is dead. Died just a few years after that, at the height of her career, but my wife will never forget her kindness to us, for you must remember there was "class" in vaudeville, as well as in society, and for an "act" to visit a headliner, was an event.

Mike carried on as best he could. Bad health, bad luck, but always that something that made him the real fighter. He was tremendously fortunate in his next marriage. A girl much younger, beautiful girl, daughter of one of the stage's shining lights of their day, a great vaudeville team, Ross and Fenton. She stuck with Mike through many ups and downs, and an awful lot of downs among the few ups. He did some splendid things on the stage. He was always natural in anything he did.

He has been out here in pictures for years. Everybody liked him. Everybody used him when they had a chance. Everything he did was o.k. To see him sitting around, day after day on our set, there was sometimes maybe a hundred people there with him, all kinds and all types of folks on a movie set; yet there he sat, joking and laughing. Health very bad, maybe in actual pain. There was out of that hundred perhaps ninety, or more people that never heard one speck of applause for them personally in their lives. Yet here sat this fellow, who maybe meant nothing to them, who had day after day, year after year had thousands rise when he come to bat, who had audiences cheer for actual minutes when he come on the stage.

Here he was, looking for no sympathy, offering no alibis, not sore at the world, not sore at anybody. Just a kindly soul who hadn't raised his hands in combat in thirty years. Peace on Earth, Mike Donlin, that was your motto. You lived game, and you died game.

Caviar and Vodka

Well, the United States has recognized Russia, but you would be surprised at the number of people that are not going there to settle. Their big importation is caviar—that's a kind of gooey mess of fish eggs that, I suppose, is without a doubt the poorest fodder in the world. But it costs a lot, and the rich just lap it up, like they do grand opera, when they can't understand a line.

But as long as a fish has gone to the trouble to lay eggs—especially when they go away up in Russia to lay them—we got fish here that must lay eggs, but we don't pay any attention to them, any more than we would to an American lecturer. The eggs our fish lay are just home talent. They are just a kind of local egg. But if the same fish went west in Russia, and layed those same eggs, why, then they become important eggs. Instead of just a setting of eggs, they become "caviar."

Caviar is a thing that you are supposed to eat before a meal. Now if you got a good meal coming, what's the idea of eating something before it? If it was good, it would spoil your meal, for you would eat too much of it, and if it's not any good, it will spoil your meal anyhow. So it just looks like we recognized Russia in order to give the Russian fish that want to lay eggs, a chance.

Now, of course, there is some parts of the world where there is certain fish that are better, but you wouldn't hardly think there was anywhere eggs that are better, especially fish eggs. But of course, being a Democrat, and not a caviar eater, I don't know anything about it. I like the cocktails though, that they put with 'em—that's about all I can see in caviar.

The next big importation that we will get from Russia, outside of a setting of these eggs, is a thing called Vodka. Now Vodka is just as different from fish eggs as a man's ideas that did get a government appropriation for a post office, from the one that didn't get one.

Vodka is a fluid, but it's what could be rightly classed as a deceptive fluid. It's as harmless a looking thing as a nice gourd full of branch water. But there the comparison stops. It's made from fermented Russian wheat, corn, oats, barley, alfalfa, or jimsonweed, just which ever one of these they happen to have handy. Now any one of them, as I say, is the ground work. Then they start adding the ingredients. Potato peelings is one of them, then Russian boot tops. You know over here, we have the tops of carrots, and onions, and all those; well, over there they all wear these high boots, so you just take the tops of as many Russian boots as you can get, when the men are asleep. You harvest them just above the ankle, you shock 'em up like wheat. Then bring one of those Russian carts along, where there is a high yoke over the horse's neck. You know a Russian horse always looks like he is going under an Arch de Triumph.

The next ingredient—the Russians always deny this to me, but I have always believed it's true—is the whiskers. They say that they don't put 'em in Vodka, that they are only used in that soup called Borsch.

Now then you add all these things and it's got to ferment. Well, it don't take long for anything to ferment in Russia. They are a nation that can start stewing before you know it. Now then you get this Vodka built up, and if it's concocted by a good architect, it's just as clear and innocent looking as a stein of gin. That is, it is before you start sampling it. Well, when you do, your eyes begin expanding, and your ears begin flopping like a mule's. It's the only drink where you drink and try to grit your teeth at the same time. It gives the most immediate results of any libation ever concocted, you don't have to wait for it to act. By the time it reaches the adam's apple, it has acted. A man stepping on a red hot poker could show no more immediate animation. It's the only drink where you can fall on the man that handed it to you, before he can possibly get away. It pays quicker dividends than any libation ever assembled. You don't go through that period where people say: "Silas is getting tight."

Say, brother, when Silas lifts that glass, Silas is not getting tight, Silas is out.

It's a time saver. It should especially appeal to Americans. There is nothing so dull in American life as that period when a drinker is just at that annoying stage. He is a pest to everybody. But Vodka eliminates that, you are never at that pest period.

So we haven't started to realize the benefits we got from recognizing Russia, till the caviar and the Vodka start coming in.

James J. Mattern, Aviator

Not long ago when I was back in Chicago to see the West beat the East at polo, I run onto Jimmy Mattern. I had met him before he made this last round-the-world flight, but this was the first time I had met him since he got back from just about the greatest adventure that any aviator ever had. They have all had some pretty queer ones, and are a great gang, these aviators. Just about the most interesting fellows to talk to of any bunch of men I ever saw. Lindbergh, Post, Hawkes, Doolittle, Al Williams, Roscoe Turner, and dozens of others that have really done things.

Well, this guy Mattern—oh, Boy!—if he didn't have some time when he set that old Lockheed down in Siberia. Just about a drive and two niblick shots from the North Pole. That's twice he has started on a round-the-world trip, and been grounded in Russia.

If I was Jimmy, the next time I made a trip around-the-world, I would go around Russia. But Russia is just about as tough to go around, as it is to go through. Well, he said that one of the things that got him off to a bad start was the rough weather crossing the Atlantic. The first trip crossing the Atlantic, he and his pardner had a joy ride, so he just figured the old Atlantic was duck soup—and that's just what it was this trip, duck soup! Just as thick all the way across. He couldn't see the sky, and he couldn't see the ocean. His altimeter showed nothing, so he must have been flying right on the water. But he never saw it, when he went up, his wings coated with ice. So he had to stay low.

Well, he says he took such a beating crossing the Atlantic that he was really all in from then on. He never did really recover his strength. He claims that the whole thing of making a record flight around-the-world is a case of physical endurance. Well, that was news because most of us had come to look on it as a case of mechanical luck, but he says it's mostly physical endurance. He claims that if he had been lucky enough to have had a fair trip across the Atlantic, he would not have been so tired, and done a lot of things that afterwards his fatigue and dopiness made him do.

He paid a fine compliment to Wiley Post. He says, "Wiley is plenty tough. He has got the endurance of a burro." And he has, too, I tell you. I met him after he and Gatty made their wonderful trip, and he is tough as a boot physically, and as determined as a bull. But this Mattern guy, along with an adventurous spirit, has some internal spunk there that is not all just tripe, either.

But the best part of Jimmy Mattern's trip was after he landed and joined the Eskimos. His fuel line froze on him. His plane, he said, was never going better, and he had plenty of oil and gas, but here was this fuel stopped and he had the Bering Sea to cross to make Nome, Alaska. Well, for thousands of miles it was this tundra—bumpy, mossy growth. So he did quite a stunt, I claim, he put on full power and brought the plane close to the ground and knocked his undercarriage off. That is, he did it purposely. When he felt the crash back against the body of his plane, he took her up off the ground again, and then brought her down with no wheels to hinder him. In that way when he landed, he didn't nose over. Now I claim that was pretty hot aviating. Spraining his ankle in landing, was his worst injury.

It was about two miles down to a river, and he went down there and built him a kind of brush hut. He stayed there 14 days, on three chocolate bars, not only quite an accomplishment, but the best ad I ever heard for chocolate. I suppose along with Jimmy and his other bad luck, it was some Russian brand chocolate, and he can't get anything out of the advertising.

Well, then some Eskimos come floating down the river, picked him up and didn't seem the least interested in how he got there, what he was, or anything. They spent the next two weeks doing nothing day and night, but playing with the zippers on Jimmy's flying suit. Laying in the hut, or igloo, at night, they would be zipping 'em up and down his legs and arms. In fact, it looked like they had saved him entirely for his zippers. They would have preferred saving the zippers, and letting him go.

Then he had some rubber bands around some maps. Well, when they saw those bands, what little interest they had previously showed in him, was off. They snapped rubber bands and pulled zippers for two weeks steady. Sounds silly, don't it? Just about as silly as spending the same time on bridge and golf.

Then they took him down the river to Anadir (that's the only town in Russia with a short name). Sixty white people there, that is if you want to be lenient and call Russians "white." According to their constitution now, they are supposed to be "red." None could talk English, so they started playing with the zippers. So Siberia is just a-zipping and a-snapping, and having the time of their lives. Nobody ever asked how he got there, or why, or when—they just figured he was an advance agent for zippers and rubber bands.

So if you are going to see the Eskimos, don't take gum drops, that's old stuff. Take zippers and rubber bands, and you can come back with all the white fox skins in the Bering Sea area. Their minds are just as simple as ours. You would think they would get civilized, and learn to sit all day working a cross-word puzzle. Something ought to be done about these "primitive" people who live in various parts of the world, and don't know a thing but to live off what nature provides. You would think they would get civilized, and learn to live off each other, like us civilized folks do.

Mr. Hal Roach Celebrates

Been doing a little prowling around here lately, kind of broke out socially. Mr. Hal Roach, an old employer (don't that mean the guy that hires you? I never could get those two words straight—employer and employee) well, which ever it is that does the work, why, I was him. Roach dug up the money, and I expect sometimes when I hadn't earned it. (Maybe all the time.)

Mr. Roach is the man that makes the very fine comedies. In the early days he was the producer of Harold Lloyd's films. Harold was there the other night. Our business, or anybody's business don't stable a better or finer fellow than Harold Lloyd. Everybody likes him, he is a grand young fellow that has not gone Hollywood, or anything, he is still just Lloyd. He and Hal have always remained great friends. They have a great deal in common, for Hal is another that has not been led haywire by the applause.

It was the 20th anniversary of his entry into pictures. I think he entered pictures as a cowboy, not because he was one, but he had a Bull Durham tobacco sack hanging out of his shirt pocket, so the casting director naturally thought that constituted a cowboy. In those days, if you played in pictures at all, you played a cowboy—for that's all there was to 'em. A cowboy running down hill, and having a fight at the bottom. Hal at that time couldn't ride, especially down hill, he has since learned, and plays an excellent game of polo. But in those days he must have played the rancher whose daughter was stolen, and he stayed at home and pointed out which way they went. You remember, there was always one fellow left just to point.

Lloyd, I think, played characters. He had got hold of a beard somewhere, perhaps he worked in a barber shop, but anyhow I have seen old pictures of Harold when he had on a beard. I can figure how he got the beard, but I can't dope out where he got the mucilage from, for I think there was times in those days, when he would have eaten the mucilage. As Lloyd and Roach got to producing their own, they mostly used policemen for characters. They didn't use horses, for a horse got more than an actor in those days, and you had to feed a horse. But a man playing the policeman, he would just eat the buttons off.

Twenty years of furnishing the entire world with laughs is not a bad epitaph on anybody's tombstone. Especially, when you have like him, never resorted to smut of any nature. It was a grand party, the biggest I ever saw. It would take me three columns to tell you who all was there. The list reads like one of those "who's delinquent in their income tax."

I run into Groucho Marx. He was out by one of the orchestras. I say "one of the orchestras" for there was orchestras for you to get out of your car by, another for you to check your hat by, another to dance by. Why, every couple had their own orchestra.

Well, this one I am talking about, was Hawaiian, and it was playing "The Last Round-Up." Groucho suggested that a cowboy tenor voice would be just about what was lacking in this whole musical set-up. So, having just gotten quite a few compliments on my tenor singing in the choir scene of "Dr. Bull," why, I told him if he would play it, I would sing it, if he would join me with his alto voice. Now here is a funny thing about these Marx Brothers. Groucho can play as good on the guitar as Harpo can on the harp, or Chico on the piano, but he never does. So he is really what I call an "ideal musician," he can play, but don't.

In New York, when I was playing with Miss Dorothy Stone, he even tried to learn me to play the guitar. He would come over to my dressing room before our two respective shows started, and he would play, and we would sing these old songs, and so this thing was really nothing new we was pulling. But it was new to the gang. "The Last Round-up" instead of us dying off, why, that gave us encouragement, and for half an hour we totally ruined (musically) Mr. Roach's party. Course lots of folks joined us in the singing, to try and drown us out I guess, but they couldn't.

The next night, Mrs. Rogers and I had dinner over at Groucho's, and we took up right where we had left off, only he played the piano that night.

I love to sing old songs, and any time anybody will start any, I am the loudest, and if they won't start 'em, I will myself. But we did have a good time at Hal's party, and I believe everybody did.

And when Hal celebrates 40 years in pictures, I am going to go to another party for him. Roach says he will hire Groucho and me the next time, but the songs we sing now will never become "old" songs; no one will remember 'em that long.

The Wrong Impression of Women

I had never met—until the other day—Mr. Robert R. McCormick that owns and runs the great Chicago Tribune. He is an awful nice fellow, and of course, awful well informed. He said I got him in trouble one time for quoting him in my little daily "blab" when he was talking about war in Europe. I had written:

> And talking about what people said, this McCormick of Chicago, who has just returned from Germany, editor of the great Chicago Tribune (no, I don't write for it), says very astonishingly, but no doubt truthfully: "Along with the youth of Germany in this war spirit is the women. When bigger wars are made, women will make 'em, as always."

Well, he says they sure hopped him.

Now I don't want to bring any more "she" condemnation down on him, but out here in California a couple of months ago, when they put on that lynching, women were the rooting section, and the original encouragement of the thing came from the "she" sex. So I guess, Mr. McCormick was about right at that. Many a man has got a licking because his wife has said: Go on, get him, John, you ain't a-going to let him say that, are you?

She will not only egg the thing on, but by golly, she will go in and join. Women are not the weak, frail, little flowers that they are advertised. They love to say that women don't want war, and they have to bear the brunt of it, which of course, they really do, but if you ever noticed all their speeches, and denunciations of war is after it's over—they never do it in the making of one. And that's a fine spirit, more power to 'em. They got more nerve than men.

They enter a thing with more spirit and enthusiasm. You let a woman get up at a recruiting meeting and denounce the whole thing, and defy the boys to join up, and I will lay you a bet that the first fifty hands that tore her asunder, would belong to the fair sex. No sir, the whole thing about the women is, they just love to be misunderstood. They always want you to have the wrong impression about what's in their minds, and not the right one. There has never been anything invented yet, including war, that a man would enter into, that a woman wouldn't too.

But here is the thing. You must never let 'em know but what you think they are just doing everything in their power to prevent war, when as a matter of fact, six or eight women could prevent any war.

The wives of the Prime Ministers, Diplomats and Presidents would only have to say: "If you allow war to come to this country, I will leave you, so help me."

But history records no record of one having been left for that reason, though left for everything else. But when he comes home some day, and says: "Honey, I guess you saw the extras on the street, I had to declare war," she says: "I know it, darling, and we will lick the very pants off the other old mean nation."

And when the recruiting starts, she will make the first speech, and she will work her head off from then to the finish at anything, no matter how tiring and dangerous. Then, when it is over, she will say: "We women must prevent war." But that's the way it should be, and that's the way we want it.

But how in the world did I get started off on all this, which I know absolutely nothing about? I started in to tell you about some interesting people that come out to Los Angeles, started in with Mr. McCormick, and get switched off on all this mess. It's like a dinner party. You settle down to have a nice evening, and somebody brings up what the price of the dollar should be, and the fight is on the rest of the night. Now here I am, and have used up all my space and have told nothing, done nothing, but maybe make a lot of fine ladies mad, but not as mad as they let on. Women are as proud of their war records, as men that fought in battle.

All the wars in the world, even if you won 'em, can't repay one mother for the loss of one son. But even at that, when she says to you: "That's my oldest boy's picture. He was lost in the war," there is behind that mist in her eyes a shine of pride.

231

Now any argument, or any letters in regard to the negative in this debate, please send to Mr. McCormick, owner and proprietor of the Chicago Tribune. He has plenty of secretaries. I answer no mail. Even if it's a good letter, I don't answer it. And I sho don't want to get into any argument with any women, for they like to argue just like they like to go to war. So leave me out, and go after McCormick again. Another good hiding would do him good. He deserves it for saying women help start wars. That's slander, saying women help to start 'em. Boy, women start 'em without any HELP.

Remember the address: Tribune Building, Chicago. Send postage if you wish an answer. No serious consideration given to anonymous letters.

P.S. I am certainly glad I had nothing to do with this argument, and am out of it.

P.P.S. Good luck, Mr. McCormick.

About the Churches

A preacher named Reverend Grant of Simpson Methodist Church of Minneapolis, Minnesota, wrote me: "I am speaking on you and your life's philosophy at a Sunday evening vesper service in our great church of two thousand members. Is there any word of greeting? I would appreciate it. Yours, A. Raymond Grant, pastor."

Well, that same night I answered his letter, I had to write my weekly Sunday article. So I couldn't see why one "greeting" or "alibi" wouldn't do for both. He had been mighty nice, and I appreciated it. So I got strung out and in my long winded way, I sounded like a preacher without a stop signal.

Dear Reverend Grant:

I got your letter saying you was "speaking on me." But you didn't say why? There is an awful lot of different ways to speak on me, and all of 'em pretty near true, at that.

My life has got more angles than a cat. You may be one of those Republicans (as most ministers have gone into politics), you may be one of those Democrats who blamed me for electing Mr. Hoover four years ago.

This is kinder the public season to jump on me if anything has gone wrong, everything from a scarcity of skunk hides in the north-west, to a predominating amount of girl babies in Pennsylvania. You see, Reverend Grant, I think I am as independent as anyone writing. I have as many Republican as Democratic papers, as many readers that can't read, as can. The editorial policies of these great dailies mean nothing to me, I am going to call 'em as I see 'em.

I think I have complimented many a worthy thing in my time, and I have taken a shot at a lot of hooey. I am not against it, mind you, as it just seems that it takes so much of it in every business. And they are all my friends, I am proud of the fact there is not a human being that I have got it in for. I never met a man I didn't like.

I got no philosophy. I don't even know what the word means. The Fourth Reader—McGuffey's is as far as I ever got in schools. I am not bragging on it. I am thoroughly ashamed of it, for I had every opportunity. Everything I have done has been by luck, no move was premeditated. I just stumbled from one thing to another. It might have been up, it might have been down. I didn't know it at the time, and I don't know it yet. For I don't know what "up" is. I may be lower than I ever was, I don't know. I may be making the wrong use of any little talent (if any) that I accidentally have. I don't know.

I was raised predominantly a Methodist, but I have traveled so much, mixed with so many people in all parts of the world, I don't know just what I am. I know I have never been a non-believer. But I can honestly tell you that I don't think that any religion is *the* religion.

If I am broad-minded in any way—and I hope I am in many—I do know that I am broad-minded in a religious way. Which way you serve your God will never get one word of argument, or condemnation, out of me. There has been times when I wished there had been as much real religion among some of our creeds as there has been vanity, but that's not in any way a criticism.

I feel mighty proud that you will discuss me in your tabernacle. The joke is more on you, than on me. I thought the only time I would ever make the pulpit as a conversational subject, was when I finished, and then only by one minister whose charges for kind words would be deducted from the estate.

I feel like I did the other day, when they told me I was in the British "Who's Who." There was no way I could sue 'em, or make 'em retract, and there is no way to keep you from gabbing around about anything you like. I heard a fellow preach one time on Jesse James, the outlaw, and I left the church wanting to hold up everything and everybody I run into.

So if you are such a persuasive preacher, you are liable to turn out a flock of Swedish comedians, up around Minneapolis. Don't make the life too rosy, for with the politicians horning in, our comedian business is over-crowded as it is. I preached one time in a church in Cleveland, Ohio, but the collection didn't warrant me carrying it on as

233

a steady profession. Preaching should not only be done by a preacher, but by a man like Mahatma Gandhi, who can do fasting when necessary, for it will be necessary.

Minneapolis has always been one of my pet cities. They have been good to me on every occasion I was ever there. They have not only laughed at me, but paid to laugh at me.

Love to all your congregation, including the ones that are not paid up. It's just hard times. They mean well, parson. They got just as much religion, as the paid up ones. So you will just have to trust 'em, and give 'em a little preaching "on time."

You see, preaching is one of the few things that folks have never been able to dope out exactly what it's worth, anyhow. Some preachers ought to pay admission to get into the church, themselves, but as a rule, preachers do a mighty good job, and are under-paid.

But there is a lot of dignity about the clerical profession that you would have to work years for in any other line. But you are sympathetic, useful, instructive, and the most worth-while profession ever invented.

I wish your church a happy and charitable 1933, or any other years. No use being stingy in our wishes. Pick out as many years as you want, and I will wish you good luck with all of 'em.

Yours,
Will.

1934

In January, amid great ceremony, Germany and Poland sign a ten-year nonaggression pact. After only five years, this pact will be unceremoniously broken on September 1, 1939, when German troops invade Poland to start World War II.

The Soviet Union, too, signs a ten-year nonaggression extension of an existing pact with her little neighbor, Finland. This pact, too, will be violated after five years, when Russia attacks Finland in November 1939.

In a purge of those who have outlived their usefulness, Hitler has some seventy-seven followers killed for an alleged plot, including Ernst Roehm and Kurt von Schleicher. The event will be remembered as the "Night of the Long Knives."

German President Paul von Hindenburg dies. In a plebiscite, 88 percent of the voters "elect" Hitler president. But he prefers the title Der Fuehrer—The Leader.

In an apparent attempt to expand the German Reich, Austrian Nazis murder Austrian dictator Engelbert Dollfuss. The coup fails, and Kurt von Schuschnigg takes over the regime.

The assassination of Sergeo Mironovich Kirov, Stalin's close collaborator, leads to Stalin-directed "treason trials" and a thorough purge.

Violence also reaches France. In Marseilles, visiting King Alexander I of Yugoslavia and French Foreign Minister Louis Barthou are assassinated.

In China, after disagreement with Chiang Kai-shek, the Communists under Mao Tse-tung begin the "Long March" to north China.

On November 28, in the British House of Commons, Winston Churchill warns an almost empty House—and a deaf world—of the German menace.

The United States goes off the gold standard, and by presidential proclamation the American dollar is revalued at 59.06 cents, and gold is set at $35 a troy ounce, at which it will remain for about four decades.

Dust storms blow an estimated 300 million tons of Kansas, Colorado, Texas, and Oklahoma topsoil away. Some 50 million acres lose all their topsoil; millions of acres are seriously damaged. One explanation: imprudent land management during the Great War, when farmers plowed virgin land to make money when wheat prices were high. Vast areas of bare soil, formerly covered by prairie grasses, were thus fully exposed to the strong, prevailing winds. In the next five years, 350,000 Okies and Arkies from the Dust Bowl will leave their useless land and trek to California.

Harry L. Hopkins, named relief administrator, reports that 4.7 million American families are on relief. And yet, workers in San Francisco will go out on a general strike in sympathy for 12,000 striking longshoremen led by Harry Bridges. Minneapolis, too, has a strike, and fifty are shot when police fire on strikers.

Schemes to help the needy abound. Louisiana's Senator Huey Long seriously suggests to the Senate his "Share-the-Wealth Program," which would make every man an instant king. Upton Sinclair, writer and Socialist, campaigns as a Democratic candidate for governor of California on his EPIC platform: *End Poverty In California*. Long Beach, California, doctor Francis E. Townsend urges an old-age revolving pension plan, which would assure two hundred dollars a month for every unemployed American over the age of sixty. And in Royal Oak, Michigan, radio priest Father Charles E. Coughlin, already famous for his broadcasts marked by racial and religious bigotry, now organizes a National Union for Social Justice. His scheme for America's recovery is somehow based on what he terms radical inflation.

Among those engaged in illegal self-help, Bonnie Parker and Clyde Barrow—known as Bonnie and Clyde—die in a police ambush on a quiet road in Louisiana. In their two-year career, they have killed twelve people in Texas, Oklahoma, Missouri, and Iowa, yet their most successful robbery netted them only $3,500.

George ("Baby-Face") Nelson is slain by two federal agents when he decides to shoot it out. Seventeen bullets are found in his body.

And public enemy number one, John Dillinger, is shot to death leaving the Biograph Theatre in Chicago, having been identified to the FBI by the "Lady in Red." During his eleven-year career of terrorizing the Middle West, he has killed sixteen.

The Securities and Exchange Commission (SEC) is created to police the securities industry. Wall Street speculator Joseph Patrick Kennedy is chosen in July to head the commission, despite strong opposition from New Dealers and several leading newspapers. Kennedy will hold this post for 431 days, then be transferred to head the U.S. Maritime Commission.

In Fort Worth, Texas, an enterprising J. F. Cantrell has set up four laundry washing machines, calls the store a "Washeteria," and charges customers by the hour.

In Callander, Ontario, Canada, Emilie, Yvonne, Cecile, Marie, and Annette Dionne are born, weighing in at an average of two pounds, eleven ounces. And during the year, Sir Edward Elgar, the composer, and Marie Curie, the scientist and twice Nobel Laureate, die.

Max Baer knocks out Primo Carnera in the eleventh round and becomes world heavyweight boxing champion. The Saint Louis Cardinals win the World Series by defeating the Detroit Tigers, 4 games to 2. And the U.S. yacht *Rainbow* successfully defends the America's Cup by defeating England's *Endeavour,* 4 races to 2.

In the world of motion pictures, these were picked among the best: Frank Capra's *It Happened One Night,* starring Clark Gable and Claudette Colbert, winner of Academy Awards for the two stars, the director, and as the best film of the year; *Twentieth Century,* with John Barrymore and Carole Lombard; *The Count of Monte Cristo,* with Robert Donat; *Death Takes a Holiday,* with Fredric March and Evelyn Venable; and *Of Human Bondage,* with Bette Davis, Leslie Howard, and Frances Dee.

A six-year-old Shirley Temple makes her first full-length film, and steals the show. The film is *Stand Up and Cheer,* and credit is being given to writers Will Rogers, Philip Klein, and Lew Brown.

Two newcomers to radio delight audiences: the "Lux Radio Theatre," and "The Aldrich Family," which features Ezra Stone as son Henry.

At New York's Wintergarden Theatre, *The New Ziegfeld Follies* opens with Fanny Brice, Jane Frohman, Vilma and Buddy Ebsen, and Eugene and Willie Howard. The production is staged by Florenz Ziegfeld's widow, Billie Burke. Lillian Hellman's *Children's Hour* is the hit of the Broadway season. Ballet news is made when George Balanchine establishes the School of American Ballet.

There is a long list of popular songs in 1934, ranging from "Beer Barrel Polka" to "Tumbling Tumbleweed." In between are: "Blue Moon," "Deep Purple," "Winter Wonderland," "You Ought to Be in Pictures," "The Very Thought of You," and "I Only Have Eyes for You."

Among the most-read books of the year: Robert Graves' *I Claudius,* Dashiell Hammett's *The Thin Man,* Agatha Christie's *Murder on the Orient Express,* Dorothy L. Sayer's *The Nine Tailors,* and John O'Hara's *Appointment in Samarra.*

There are also some new comic strips that first appear in the newspapers this year. There is Al Capp's *Li'l Abner,* Milton Caniff's *Terry and the Pirates,* and Alex Raymond's *Flash Gordon.*

Will Rogers has four fixed obligations. There is the "Daily Telegram," the short, topical squib, which has to be wired six days a week; then there is the "Weekly Article," which has to be filed once a week, with a two-week lead—meaning that the column has to be submitted two weeks before publication. Then there are the radio broadcasts for Gulf Oil. Those are live, on Sundays. And last, of course, there are the movies for Fox. Any plans Will Rogers makes must be made around these firm commitments.

Toward the end of January, Will flies east, stops off in Oklahoma, then on to Washington to attend President Roosevelt's March of Dimes Party for Infantile Paralysis. On this trip, Will's radio broadcast is made from the studios in New York City.

In March, Will is the master of ceremonies for the Academy Awards. In April, he appears in the play *Ah, Wilderness!* by Eugene O'Neill, with Ann Shoemaker. The play opens at the Curran Theatre in San Francisco to rave notices, and then moves on to Los Angeles.

By July, Will is ready for a trip around the world. Since Mary, Will's only daughter, is appearing in summer stock in Skowhegan, Maine, she will be the only one not coming along. Will and Betty, and the two sons, Will, Jr., and Jim, are aboard the S.S. *Malolo* when it steams out of San Francisco harbor on July 22.

First stop is Hawaii, where President Roosevelt is vacationing. Betty and Will have dinner with the president. Then it is on to Tokyo, through Russia aboard the Trans-Siberian Railroad, then to the Scandinavian countries, on to England, and aboard the *Ile de France* for their return in late September.

Will is back in time to see some of the World Series games between Saint Louis and Detroit. The series becomes so exciting that Will, who is now visiting Amon Carter in Fort Worth, hires a plane and pilot and flies to Detroit to see the final game on October 8.

238

In late December, Will begins to make plans with Helen Keller, the famous blind and deaf author and lecturer, for a benefit broadcast that is to help in the production of so-called talking books.

During 1934, Will works on four films: *David Harum,* directed by James Cruze, with Kent Taylor, Evelyn Venable, Louise Dresser, Stepin Fetchit, and Noah Beery, Sr.; *Handy Andy,* directed by David Butler, with Peggy Wood, Mary Carlisle, and a young Robert Taylor; *Judge Priest,* directed by John Ford, with Tom Brown, Anita Louise, Stepin Fetchit, Rochelle Hudson, Charley Grapewin, Berton Churchill, Henry B. Walthall, Hattie McDaniels, and David Landau.

And on November 30, Will begins *The County Chairman,* directed by John G. Blystone, with Kent Taylor, Evelyn Venable, Louise Dresser, and Mickey Rooney. The film will be released in 1935.

The Mission of San Juan Capistrano

Walking Monday afternoon through one of the most famous of the historical California missions, San Juan Capistrano, half-way to San Diego, and who should I find in meditation before a wonderful old picture depicting the joy of the harvest, and the merrymaking at the sale of the crops? It was Secretary of Agriculture Wallace.

Tears were in his eyes, and he kept murmuring lowly, as he turned to the altar, "Oh, what have I done, Father, that I couldn't have been Secretary of Agriculture in days like those?"

Well, it was no made up joke. You see, he had been out here on a speaking and inspection tour, and he was naturally doing a little sight-seeing on the side. Well, I had been down to La Jolla to the funeral of a friend. One should never pass any of these missions without stopping and going in. They are among the great historical spots of our country. This one was built in 1776. That's the year our last World Series was over with England. I don't know much history, but I have looked at many a one of those pictures labelled "Spirit of 1776." It stirs the spirit of you. I expect it's a terrible bad painting, and maybe worse music, but it's a heroic looking group. One has his head tied up, I remember, one's got a flute, and I believe the little fellow has a drum. It, and Washington standing up in that boat crossing (I think it was the Delaware), those two constitute all the art they had in those days. Nothing being painted now will ever live that long.

We tore ourselves loose from England in that year, and it's quite a question of who it was a better deal for. There was an awful lot of things before 1776 that we wasn't "blessed" with when we were under England. Just mention any problem that's facing our country today, and it wasn't with us before 1776. Do you realize there was no Senate, and no Congress? Then you talk about freedom. No inflation! No deflation, reforestation, sophistication!

The only thing like today was that we had no money—but we had no debts. Course you had a little Indian trouble, about one-tenth as much as you do today with kidnappers. If any trouble showed up, why, you had Paul Revere to saddle old "Ned" and come down the valley, and holler "The Sioux, or Blackfeet are coming!" And Paul was more sure-fire than a telephone.

Suppose the fellow that wants to warn you that somebody is coming after you hasn't got a nickel. Well, he can't warn you. But in those days everybody had a horse. They must have been great old days, at that. The tax in those days that they fought to do away with, must have amounted to at least five per cent of what it is today. They were very religious people that come over here from the old country. They were very human. They would shoot a couple of Indians on the way to every prayer meeting.

But what's all that got to do with what was happening out here on the west side of Uncle Sam? An old priest had come up into the country, Father Junipero Serra, and he built missions and schools, and taught the Indians trades; and the churches were run like big ranches. They each had thousands of cattle, and horses and sheep. He was an odd old fellow. He could pray without shooting an Indian first. He was a greater humanitarian than all the Pilgrims combined, including the 3 million that come on the Mayflower. No such man ever set foot on the eastern shore. He civilized with a Bible, and the old Pilgrim boys did it with a blunderbuss. There was never a church in the east built for Indians to worship in.

So, as I accidentally run onto Secretary Wallace in San Juan Capistrano, 65 miles out of Los Angeles, although perhaps like me not of that faith, he viewed it with great reverence. Each community farmed and raised everything, and remember that these missions were not in a great watered country—but they did it all; no overproduction, no underconsumption, no tariffs, no processing tax, no birth control with hogs, no plowing under every third row. Thousands lived in each of these valleys until the Gringos come. They gummed it up proper.

So I think Mr. Wallace's thoughts must have been on the way these people did the things that all our civilization seems to say we can't do. Wallace knows there is a way, because he stood on the very ground where it worked.

Thoughts on Agriculture

I hope they don't irrigate more land, so they can raise more things that they can't sell, and will have to plow up more rows, kill more pigs to keep 'em from becoming hogs.

What Henry Wallace, our Secretary of Agriculture, is trying to do is to teach farmers acreage control, and the hogs birth control, and one is just as hard to make understand, as the other.

Expert Planning

These old boys with a pair of specs and a tablet and pencil can sit and figure out just how much wheat, corn and oats can be raised each year in order to sell each bushel of it at a profit.

Then along comes a guy called "elements." This bird "elements" never went to college, and he has never been called an expert. But when this guy "elements" breaks out, he can make a sucker out of more experts than anybody.

The 59-Cent Dollar

Congress has been behaving itself now for a short period, and that hurt the news—course it helped the country. Then the "Silver" question has been pretty good there for a while.

I am about like a lot of others, I don't know just what silver being made a money, will do to us. It seems like it ought to help. But that's what we pay those birds in Washington ten thousand a year for, is to argue over such non-settleable things. Money and women are the most sought after and the least known about of any two things we have.

Now going off the gold standard may have been a necessity, and I guess it was the best thing, for you can't stand on it and have all these other nations off. For they gang up on you and take it all away from you. You see, they get a-hold of your paper money and it says right on there "Payable in Gold." Well, we always knew it said that, but we didn't try to make the government prove it every time we got a-hold of a ten dollar bill. But these Europeans, every time they got their clutches on some of our dough, they took that inscription on there serious, and our Treasury had to shell out the hard money; and they took it home and planted it in their Treasuries, or under their feather beds. As far as getting the gold back, that was impossible. Now you can't stay in a game where you are paying off with dough, and the others are paying off in I.O.U.'s.

But on the other hand, lowering the price of money from a dollar to 59 cents didn't have quite the effect that the economists thought it would. They had figured that it would raise prices forty cents on the dollar. Well, it was just one of those theories that worked fine with a pencil, but didn't work with money. I can sit in a grandstand with a race program and a good sharp pencil (well, I have even done it with a dull one) and I can write down the winning horse, and what he is thinking about as he crosses the line. But the minute I walk under the stands, and reach for a five dollar bill—instead of a pencil, that horse just seems to know it, and runs differently.

And that's one of the drawbacks to a professor. His work is entirely with a pencil. But the minute that pencil is traded for coin of the realm, and the dealings are with somebody else, and not just with a tablet, why, life takes on an entirely different outlook.

It's like driving a car. If you are the only one on the streets, you are like the professor with the pencil. You can have things pretty much your own way. But when they commence to coming from every way, all making for the same corner, no man living can tell just exactly what will happen—and it's the same with money. You can take 40 cents off the American dollar in terms of foreign money, but the old boy here at home that's not going to Europe still thinks it's a dollar.

You can't sit with a pencil and figure what a man with a dollar will do with it. About the only way I see for prices to go up, is for more people to want something, and about the only thing that I know of that everybody wants more of—is money. And as long as the people that have already got it are going to hang on to it, about the only way of getting these others any, is to print 'em some.

Course the question arises: "Just where can you stop?" Well, let the boys with the pencils, and the Senators with the worn-seated trousers figure that one out.

Goodbye to a Great Friend

We both come from Oklahoma. I went to Madison Square Garden in New York in 1905. Then went on the stage. He didn't come till 1915, ten years later.

I first saw him at a town in Connecticut, I think it was Westport. I liked him, and he come home with me, and I think he liked me. And the whole family liked him, and he lived with us all these years, up to a few days ago, when he left us, and it made us all sad, very sad. He was one of the family, he had helped raise our children.

He came to our house the same time Jim, our youngest, did. I was working in Ziegfeld's famous Midnight Frolic. We were living in a little home we had rented across the road from Fred Stone's lovely Summer home at Amityville, Long Island. We went there to be near Fred and his family. We had a wonderful time that summer. Jim and Dopey came that summer. Jim was a baby boy, and Dopey was a little round bodied coal-black pony, with glass eyes; the gentlest and greatest pony for grown-ups or children anyone ever saw. I don't know why we called him Dopey. I guess it was because he was always so gentle and just the least bit lazy. Anyhow, we meant no disrespect to him.

Outside of a pony I had in the Indian Territory when I was a boy, and that put me in the exhibition roping business, why, along pretty near next to him in affection, was Dopey.

Dopey belonged to the family. Our children learned to ride at two, and during his lifetime, he never did a wrong thing to throw one off, or do a wrong thing after they had fallen off. He couldn't pick 'em up, but he would stand there and look at 'em with a disgusted look for being so clumsy as to fall off. He never kicked or stepped on one of them in his life, and he was a young horse when I first got him. But he was always naturally gentle, and intelligent.

I used to sit on him by the hour, yes, by the year, and try new rope tricks, and he never batted an eye. Then I learned some trick riding, such as vaulting, and drags, and all that. In fact, he was the only one I could ever do it on. Then in 1919, we went to California to go in the movies. Dopey and another pet pony we had acquired for Mary, they occupied the best palace horse car by Express. Then I would come back to New York, to work another year for Mr. Ziegfeld in his Follies, and the first thing loaded would be Dopey. Then after a year in New York, back to the movies again, and back would go Dopey.

243

One year I took Dopey in a Follies baggage car, on the whole tour with the show, and I kept him in riding academies and practiced roping every day with him. Charley Aldrich, a cowboy, used to ride him, and run by for my fancy roping tricks. Dopey has been missed with a loop more times, and maybe caught more times, than any horse living. In a little picture, called "The Ropin' Fool," where I did all my little fancy catches in slow motion, he was the pony that run for them. He was coal black, and I had my ropes whitened and the catches showed up fine.

In a private tan bark ring we had in our Beverly Hills home, all the children learned trick riding on him; standing up on him running, vaulting, and they would use him to ride Roman style. It was all allowed, because I knew they were on a gentle pony.

He has been set free for four or five years, hasn't had a bridle on him. Fat as a pig. When nineteen years of your and your children's life is linked so closely with a horse, you can sorter imagine our feelings. We still have quite a few old favorites left, but Dopey was different. He was one of the family. He raised our children. He learned 'em to ride. He never hurt one in his life. He did everything right. That's a reputation that no human can die with.

Another Friend Has Gone

I have often thought my friend O. O. McIntyre gave more space in his column to his little dog than I do to the United States Senate.

But it does show that he knows human nature better than I do. He knows that everybody at heart loves a dog, while I have to try and make converts to the senate.

In London, five years ago, old Lord Dewar, a great humorist and character, and the biggest whiskey maker in the world, gave the children a little white dog, a Sealyham, saying: "If this dog knew how well bred he was, he wouldn't speak to any of us."

We have petted him, complained on him, called him a nuisance, but when we buried him yesterday, we couldn't think of a wrong thing he had ever done. His bravery was his undoing. He lost to a rattlesnake, but his face was towards it.

My Little Red Bag

Here I am getting all ready to make the big hop around the world. Now to get ready for that would take me about as long as it would most people to get ready to drive to town Saturday afternoon, and stay for the picture show that night. I got one little old soft, flat, red grip, or bag, that, if I tell it when I am leaving, will pack itself.

A few old white shirts with the collars attached, and a little batch of underwear, and sox, now all these you can replenish at any store, anywhere. I know, for I have done it, then throw the old ones away. You don't figure on laundry at all. And it's cheaper, for when you start paying excess weight on these aeroplanes, brother, till then you haven't seen any excess. So me and my little red bag and typewriter, one extra suit in it. It's always packed the same, no matter if it's to New York, or to Singapore.

But this time it was different. There was women folks along. Ma was going along, and she said I couldn't be trooping along with her unless I looked the part. So with all the fussing, and buying, and packing, the Rogers ranch was in a mess for days and days, tromping on dress makers, cutters and fitters. Then the boys, Bill and Jim, were both away at schools, and she felt she had to dress them by remote control to get them ready.

We got a fellow named Emil. He has got some other name but you can't pronounce it. Emil, is all I know. Well, he kinder runs the Rogers household. He is of that capable tribe called the Swiss. He can speak anything, and can do anything.

Well, it seems that there was concocted a scheme before we all embarked on this present enterprise, that the master—HA HA—meaning me, should be decked out as never before. They started dragging in Palm Beach suits to fit onto me, when I should have been roping calves. They dragged me in from the polo field where I would be working a green horse, to try some white shoes on me. Well, they might have just as well put them on the horse. He would have felt more comfortable.

And then, the new baggage commenced to arrive. Now we are a race of people that have lived in grips and trunks, all our lives, but it seems the old baggage was kinder rusty, and that Honolulu and Japan would turn up its nose, if the Rogers came in with old, soiled portmanteaus.

Now these Palm Beach suits. I don't care how hot it gets in these

245

so-called tropics around Honolulu, we ought to have sent those suits to our friends back in Arkansas and Oklahoma. There is your tropics for you this summer, or in fact any part of the old U.S. (I don't want to get in wrong with any particular part of the country; it's better to get in wrong with all of it.) Then besides, a Palm Beach suit is not supposed to fit. If it does, it's uncomfortable. Ma Rogers argued that she hadn't been anywhere in so long, that she just was plum out of clothes. (Any of you boys ever heard that talk before?) She had shortly before returned from New York, but she just didn't call that "anywhere," and she had been to Honolulu two summers ago. Anyhow, she had to get something light enough for Honolulu, and something else a shade heavier for Japan.

Well, I have never been to Japan in the summer time, but summer time anywhere is not a lot different—only San Francisco at night, then it snows.

So with all the fitting and trying on, stores have a habit now. If you have been keeping your bills pretty well paid up, they will just send you out a few loads of plunder, then you pick over it, and you are allowed to return 80 per cent. Of course, if there is a party, or picnic, or barbecue in the mean time, you can use those clothes for that— just so you don't soil the price mark.

Well, I was trying to pick out my 20 per cent, so the store could salvage the rest. Emil had an old-fashioned idea—it's an old Swiss idea—that you must have one dozen of everything. The last time I had a dozen of everything was when they packed me off to Kemper Military Academy at Boonville, Missouri in 1896. And my education didn't last long enough to wear them out.

Well, Emil would pack in the daytime, and I would come in and unpack at night. At one packing, he had a bath robe in there. Well that was the last straw. You only wear them when you are getting well from an operation. And that's where this one had come from.

Anyhow, we got off, and if we had had some horses with us, I would know we was taking away more than we were leaving.

The first airplane trip we make, I am going to let her pay for the excess baggage—that will cure her. And it will cure that Emil, too, if I charge part of it against him. What in the world do people want to lug so much junk around for?

If you just follow this family, you could pick up a lot of new, unworn things across Manchuria, and Siberia, and Moscow, and Finland, and Denmark, and Sweden, and Norway. I just slipped one grip full to a bellboy in Honolulu just now. It's going to take a long time to get rid of all of it. But I will come into New York harbor with the little red bag, the old blue serge suit, and my typewriter.

Report on Russia

I have been asked to speak to you tonight in the first of a series of intellectual and unreliable talks on Russia. It's not a new subject by any means. But explaining Russia, well, you can't do it. Everybody has already got their minds made up, and anything you say is not going to change it. Besides, Russia is a country that don't care what you say about 'em. They figure they've been knocked by better men than you, anyhow, and it don't make any difference. And they are still doing business, so they don't care.

Trying to tell what Russia is like, is trying to tell the difference between a conservative Democrat and a progressive Republican. It's too complicated. Just stop and think a minute, and suppose somebody come to you tomorrow and said: Tell us about America! Now how are you going to tell anybody about America? And what would you tell them about America?

I read a book called "The Heart of Russia." Now suppose someone tried to write one called "The Heart of America." Why, we can't even keep track of the toe of Maine, or the heel of California—much less the heart. My Lord, Maine's gone Democratic, and California's gone nuts. Now if you can't tell about America, how are you going to do it about Russia, a country that's so much bigger than ours, that we'd rattle around inside of it like an idea in Congress.

Everything in the world we do, every viewpoint we have, every matter of fact way of looking at anything, is entirely different in Russia. I was surprised they didn't walk on their hands, instead of their feet—just to be different from Capitalistic nations.

In the first place, the government owns everything. Well, that ain't so different than it is over here. The banks own it over here. But in Russia, everything belongs to the government—hotels, taxi cabs, restaurants. Why, I went to a race meeting one day and all the race horses belonged to the government—every one of them. I guess, any time the government needs a little extra money, all they have to do is to go down to the jockey on the favorite horse, and say: Comrade—when they want something from another brother, they say "Comrade"—Comrade, for the good of the Soviet Bolshevik system, you'd

247

better pull that old hound you're on, and run about third! And if you don't, your next race is liable to be ridden in Siberia.

Now that may be exaggerated a bit, but it would be possible over there. They own the opera, they own all the shows, the actors and singers, all work for the government. They own all the making of the movies. They are all propaganda.

Knowing that I was interested in the movies, they showed us a new and not quite finished film. It's called "The Three Songs of Lenin." The most elaborate and expensive moving picture that was ever made in Russia. In it they have embraced all the news reel shots that were ever taken during Lenin's life. The title "The Three Songs of Lenin," comes from the three stages of his career. First, the Song of Freedom to the Working Man; then the Song of the Revolution; then the Song of Industrial and Commercial Accomplishments. Then it shows his burial in Red Square in a blizzard when it was 35 below zero, and thousands standing there almost freezing. The picture is tremendous propaganda.

The one thing that impressed me most—it kinder makes you think—is that every person in Russia works. Either working, or going to school. Men and women—women digging subways, women carrying bricks, women climbing up the ladders with the bricks, and the men standing there, laying the bricks. Women working on the railway right-of-ways. Any of your women over here that keep telling American women that they should have equality—real equality with men, like they do in Russia—well, the difference as I could see in Russian equality was that the women had a pick and shovel, and the men didn't.

All along the Trans-Siberian Railway, the women would be harvesting the crops, and the men would be down to watch the train come in. I tell you, them old Bolsheviks are just plumb smart. They sure found out how to handle women.

Now the main question everybody asks me, is: Are they happy? Now that's a tough one to answer. There's a hundred and seventy million people in Russia, and I couldn't talk their language, so I naturally couldn't go around asking: Are you happy? It's awful hard to look at a person and tell just how happy they are. Now we looked at them for eight days at hundreds of stations crossing on the Trans-Siberian Railway, and we could see people come down to the trains, and just stand there with a dull, blank expression on their faces—no joy, no smile. They just looked like they didn't know what the future held in store for them. But I've sat in the gallery of the Senate, and in the gallery of the House of Representatives in Washington, and I've seen that same dull, blank expression.

Have the people got anything to say about the government? That's another thing they all ask me. I have an answer to that. Yes, they have! But they must say it to themselves, and under their breaths.

You know, Russia was intensely religious, and in their hearts the older people are yet. They say there's about fifty churches in Moscow holding services—but, there used to be about two thousand. Lots of them have been changed into clubs; lots of them have been torn down, or changed into anti-religious museums.

Due to seventeen years of steady work on the younger people with anti-religious propaganda, they have weaned a large proportion of the young away from the church. The elders—no. If you are a believer in some supreme being, no matter what religion, you don't give that up as easy as you change your government. And you can't replace religion with nothing—so they have built up their own religion. It's the religion of Lenin, or of Leninism, rather. They have built him up into almost what might be their God. Statues by the millions of him. I'd rather have the Lenin statue building contract in Russia, than to have the Ford automobile building rights in there. Everywhere you go there's a statue of Lenin, and pictures of him. His tomb in Red Square in Moscow is the show place of all Russia.

They try to keep their patriotic enthusiasm continually going. Russia works just like a football squad, with a pep talk all the time. You're either working, or listening to some guy lecturing all the time, it's going all the time. And to the young folks, this Lenin is the only great man they ever heard of. Now we have our heroes—and there's many of them—and we know all the heroes of every other country, because we have been allowed to read all the literature in the world. But they know of only one. So you can see how he's been built in a religion in their system.

It's always called a system over there. Everything is a system. Now here's one. They put a lot of people to death in Russia, and they are still doing it for doing something against the system. But they say there's never been a one of them that didn't—just before being executed—offer up some kind of prayer. Now you know, the big members of the Party—to be a member you've got to declare yourself an atheist—every one of them offered a prayer, or made the sign of the cross, or made some manifestation of faith. So this system sort of works up to the time when something's going to happen to you, and then religion seems to kind of come back to you.

That's what President Roosevelt told me over in Honolulu, when we had dinner with him when we were going to Russia. The President was talking about Litvinov, Russia's Commissar for Foreign Affairs who visited over here. And they were talking about religion, as you'll

249

understand, before we recognize Russia, we reserve the right to have our church for our people to worship in Russia in any way they want. That's in our treaty of recognition with Russia. So the President seemed to know a good deal about Litvinov—that he was a Jewish person, and he was raised to be a rabbi—and so the President said: Now just before you're going to die, you're not going to tell me Litvinov, that you're not going to do something religious. You've already professed atheism, and believe there is no God, but wait till the time comes. You're going to do something.

Then I said: Well, what did he say? And the President said: He changed the subject, and started talking about borrowing some money, or something, and he got back into regular business again.

Then there is the building that's going on. Los Angeles in the boom days wasn't doing as much building as they are. The buildings all looked to be a kind of a cheap nature—five or six story apartment houses. Now when you say you got a room in Russia, that don't mean you've got a room like we know about a room. You got one corner of a room. And a partition ain't a partition like we know it. A partition is a sheet between you and the other folks in the same room. And there might be four people—four lay-outs all living in the same room. The housing problem is something tremendous.

Then we went down to where everybody wants to go, and that's the Divorce Court. Mrs. Rogers got kind of itchy in there. I even got a little scared after I got in there. Boy, I behaved myself while I was in Russia, I'll tell you that. Well, we were sitting in there, with a girl interpreter. And the first thing you know, a fellow come in with a brief case. He put his things down on a desk, and he was in there a minute, and they asked him a couple of questions, wrote down something—then he got up and went out. I said—I'd been watching—I said to the interpreter—what did that guy do that just come in here?

She said: he got a divorce. I said: huh? That guy that just went out got a divorce already? He wasn't in there longer than I've been telling you about it. And sure enough, yes. I said—my Lord, where was the girl he got the divorce from?

She said: well, they'll send her a card tomorrow, saying: you ain't with us any more.

I asked: Is that the way they get married, too? I can come in here and marry somebody, and announce that I am married and then send Miss Greta Garbo a card, and say: Miss Garbo, you're married to me?

She said: No. You've got to bring the girl when you get married.

Now that sounds awful easy, but wait a minute. Divorce ain't like right here in Hollywood, where we are now. Say listen, here you come in with three or four of those marriages and divorces. But they got a limit on them over there. Out here there's no limit to what you can do, but over there, they do. You come in on about your fourth marriage, and they've got all your records down there, and they'll say: Wait a minute! This thing has gone about far enough. See? This is a Communistic country, and we believe in dividing up, but you ain't going to get all the women in Russia. Now you better go back and make up with the old one.

There is many more things to talk about in Russia. So let me know. Write and let me know your questions, I'll be glad to answer any question. Anything I don't know about the country, I can make up. For Russia is a country that no matter what you say about it, it's true. Even if it's a lie, it's true.

1935

A plebiscite in the Saar favors reunion with the German Reich by a ratio of nine to one over union with France. Hitler also repudiates the Versailles treaty clause limiting German military armament, and he openly announces formation of the German Air Force. Until now Germany has had an air force, but it existed in the guise of "private flying clubs." Full conscription is restored.

Germany establishes a state-controlled news and propaganda bureau and begins a drive to eliminate the non-Nazi press. The Nuremberg Laws are formulated, depriving Jews of German citizenship. Heinrich Himmler, head of the SS (Black Shirts), starts project Lebensborn ("Life Source") to produce a pure Aryan race.

To counteract the rapid emergence of a militarily strong Germany, a conference is convened at Stresa. Britain, France, and Italy try to establish a common front, hoping to contain the Nazi threat, if only by the appearance of unity. But Italy is a less than ideal partner, also bent on expansion. Her general mobilization fills barracks; munitions output is at an all-time high. Preparations for a military adventure are obvious everywhere as Benito Mussolini alerts the nation that "hard times are ahead." Two full divisions are sent to East Africa.

Emperor Haile Selassie of Ethiopia appeals to the United States for support. President Roosevelt rejects the plea, claiming: "The U.S. is loath to believe that either Italy, or Ethiopia, would use other than pacific means to settle the dispute." In October, Italy invades Ethiopia.

Conditions inside the Soviet Union can best be judged by Stalin's edict that henceforth, Soviet children above the age of twelve would be subject to the same punishment applying to adults. Examples: eight years in a labor camp for the theft of corn or potatoes, five years for stealing cucumbers.

Only the business of signing pacts seems to be flourishing. The Soviet Union and the United States sign a trade pact. France and Russia sign a five-year treaty of mutual assistance; in the fourth year of that five-year pact, Russia and Germany will sign a mutually more advantageous pact, so France will find herself in 1939 with a meaningless pact on her hands. Russia and Czechoslovakia sign a pact to help each other. Russia will use that pact later to help herself—to Czechoslovakia.

In Japan, a company manufacturing automatic textile looms, Toyoda, tries diversification, and turns out its first motorcar, bearing as its name a slightly changed version of the parent company— Toyota.

The United States Supreme Court declares the NRA (National Recovery Administration) to be unconstitutional. Despite the setback, President Roosevelt asks that Americans voluntarily observe the spirit of the NRA, which is fairness and common sense.

In an address to a joint session of Congress, President Roosevelt says: "We must quit this business of relief!" His remedy: By executive order he creates 3.5 million jobs through WPA (Work Projects Administration).

In August, the Social Security Act passes Congress. It will be a system that provides old-age benefits and unemployment insurance.

Disunity in the ranks of American labor causes a wide rift. The dissident splinter group forms the Committee for Industrial Organization (CIO), walking out on the parent American Federation of Labor (AFL). John L. Lewis, president of the United Mine Workers, is elected president of the new organization.

There is general unrest in Louisiana, with demonstrations against the "dictatorship" of Senator Huey Long. Martial law is declared in January, after five hundred national guardsmen force one hundred demonstrators to surrender, and then fire tear gas into a group of unarmed sympathizers. Forty protesters are seized and held incommunicado. In September, Huey Long is assassinated.

The dust storms in the western states show no sign of abating. Highway traffic is stopped and schools have to be closed as day is turned into night.

Bruno Richard Hauptmann is tried for the kidnapping slaying of the Lindbergh baby. After thirty-two court days, the jury of eight men and four women deliberates for eleven hours and finds Hauptmann guilty. He is sentenced to die in the electric chair the week of March 18. Because of delaying maneuvers by the defense, he will be executed April 3, 1936, still protesting his innocence.

A German chemist, Gerhard Domagk, discovers the first sulfa drug, called prontosil; it is used to treat streptococcal infections. Englishman Robert Watson-Watt builds the first practical radar defense system for detecting aircraft. The S.S. *Normandie* wins the symbolic "Blue Ribbon" denoting the speed record for crossing the Atlantic, taking only 107 hours and 33 minutes. Amelia Earhart flies alone from Honolulu to California in 18¼ hours, finding the airfield in Oakland despite a heavy fog.

Among the books of the year are: *Studs Lonigan,* by James T. Farrell; *The Stars Look Down,* by A. J. Cronin; *Tortilla Flat,* by John Steinbeck; *Goodbye, Mr. Chips,* by James Hilton; *The Postman Always Rings Twice,* by James M. Cain; and for the younger readers, *National Velvet,* by Enid Bagnold, and *Mary Poppins,* by Pamela Travers.

Popular songs are: "Begin the Beguine," "Red Sails in the Sunset," "The Music Goes 'Round and 'Round," "Just One of Those Things," and "I Got Plenty o' Nuthin'."

In the theater, the big hits are: George Gershwin's *Porgy and Bess; The Petrified Forest,* by Robert Sherwood; *Night Must Fall,* by Emlyn Williams; and Maxwell Anderson's *Winterset.*

With the country's mood somber, and reality hard to bear, the movies are an escape. And Hollywood is making films bigger and better. *Mutiny on the Bounty,* with Clark Gable and Charles Laughton, will win the Academy Award as best picture of the year. *A Midsummer Night's Dream,* with James Cagney, Olivia de Havilland, Joe E. Brown, and Mickey Rooney, will win the Academy Award for Hal Mohr as the best director of photography, as a write-in candidate. Others: *The Story of Louis Pasteur,* with Paul Muni; *Anna Karenina,* with Greta Garbo and Fredric March; *The Thirty-Nine Steps,* directed by Alfred Hitchcock, with Robert Donat and Carole Lombard; and *The Informer,* directed by John Ford, which wins its star Victor McLaglen the Academy Award as best actor.

This is a glimpse of the demand on Will Rogers' time: On January 15, Will delivers a speech, which is broadcast at Notre Dame University; the following night he appears at a benefit for the blind, at the request of Helen Keller. On the seventeenth, he is in Philadelphia, where he speaks before the Poor Richard Club. On the eighteenth, he is in Indianapolis at a benefit for the James Whitcomb

Riley Hospital. On the nineteenth, he is in Washington, to appear for the Alfalfa Club. On the twenty-second, Will is in Austin, Texas, at a benefit for crippled children. On the thirtieth, he is in New York at the baseball banquet. While in New York he also speaks at several benefits.

Back to the West Coast and the movies. On June 15, Will speaks to the bar association in Los Angeles. In July, he is master of ceremonies at the dedication of the Los Angeles Times building. For July Fourth, he flies to Stamford, Texas, to attend a cowboy reunion and a small-town rodeo.

In late July, Will has completed his film commitments for the year. Already released are: *Life Begins at Forty,* with Rochelle Hudson, Richard Cromwell, Jane Darwell, Slim Summerville, and Sterling Holloway, and *Doubting Thomas,* with Billie Burke, Alison Skipworth, Sterling Holloway, Frank Albertson, and Gail Patrick.

Two films are already made but are yet to be released: *In Old Kentucky,* with Dorothy Wilson, Russell Hardie, and Bill ("Bo-jangles") Robinson, and *Steamboat 'Round the Bend,* directed by John Ford, with Anne Shirley, Irvin S. Cobb, Eugene Pallette, Berton Churchill, Francis Ford, and Stepin Fetchit, based on the book by Ben Lucien Burman.

Fox Film Corporation will decide to release these two films in the reverse order in which they were made.

On the spur of the moment, as he does so many things, Will flies with Wiley Post to Vermejo Park, New Mexico, for a visit to Waite Phillips' ranch. It is really a test flight for the plane Wiley has assembled. The plane is a hybrid combination made up of unrelated parts and, in fact, has only a "restricted" license. It is excessively nose-heavy, especially at slow speeds, such as at landing and taking off. Adding floats, as Wiley plans, will increase the "drag," adding even further to the problem.

On August 3, Will Rogers makes out his will and has it signed by two friends visiting the Santa Monica ranch.

The next evening, Betty and Will, Jr., accompany Will to the airport. He is off "to see that Alaska."

The Congressional Record

I received a wire from a Congressman friend of mine, who wants a copy of some fool thing I wrote, to read into the Congressional Record. Now I feel pretty good about that. That's the highest praise that a

255

humorist can have, is to get your stuff into the Congressional Record. Just think, my name will be right in there, alongside of Huey Long's, and all those other big humorists.

You see, ordinarily you have got to work your way up as a humorist, and first get into Congress. Then you work your way up into the Senate, and then, if your stuff is funny enough, it goes into the Congressional Record. But for an outsider to get in there as a humorist, I'm not bragging, but, by golly, I feel pretty big about it.

Did I ever tell you, I don't know whether I did, or not, about the first time I ever had any of my stuff in that daily? Well, I had written some fool thing, and it pertained to the bill that they was arguing—I mean, that they was kidding about in the Senate. So some Senator read my little article, and anything that a Senator reads, goes into the Record. So another Senator rose, and said, as they always do, if you have ever seen them: "Does the gentleman yield?"

They always say that. They call each other gentlemen in there, but the tone that they put on the words, it would be more appropriate, you know the way they say "gentleman," it would sound better if he come right out and said: "Does the coyote from Maine yield?" That's about the way it sounds, you know; he says "gentleman," but it kind of sounds like "coyote."

Then the man says, "I yield." For if he don't, the other guy will keep on talking anyhow. So the "coyote" from Maine, says: "I yield to the 'polecat' from Oregon." He don't say "polecat," but he says "gentleman," in such a way, that it is almost like "polecat."

Well, anyhow, that's the way they do it. They are very polite in Congress, but I must get back to my story. When this Senator read my offering, the other Senator said—after all the yielding was over— the other Senator said, "I object to the remarks of a professional joke maker being put in the Congressional Record!"

You know, meaning me. Taking a dig at me, see? They didn't want any outside fellow contributing.

Well, he had me wrong. Compared to those fellows in Congress, I'm just an amateur. And the thing about my jokes is that they don't hurt anybody. You can take 'em, or leave 'em. You know what I mean. You can say they are not funny, or they are terrible, or they are good, or whatever it is, but they don't do any harm. But with Congress, every time they make a joke, it's a law!

And every time they make a law, it's a joke.

Deficit Spending, Taxes, and Pilgrims

Let's talk about taxes. Boy, when you talk about taxes you're going to hear a howl like a pet coon. This money that the government is throwing away, just where is it coming from? Everybody says: Where's it coming from? Well, I don't know, but just off-hand, I'd say it was coming from those that got it.

Of course there is the government printing press, you know, a press to print money. First you have to buy a press, then you have also got to have plenty of paper, and a lot of ink. Now the government has got all of these. But there is two different schools of thought in this country on this. People who have money, are against the printing press, they are against printing any more money. And people who haven't got any, why, they are in favor of it, see? Both schools, mind you, are equally honest and it's awful hard to reconcile two views like that. The only way I see for folks to ever view the money question the same way, is for everybody not to have any. Then they'll all look at it the same way. Or go the other way and let everybody have some, then they'll all look at it the same way too.

But the big yell comes nowadays from the taxpayers. I bet you, when the Pilgrims landed at Plymouth Rock, and they had the whole of the American continent for themselves, and all they had to do to get an extra hundred-and-sixty acres, was to shoot another Indian, well, I bet you anything, they kicked on the price of ammunition. I bet you, they said, just like we are doing today, What's this country coming to that we have to spend a nickel for powder?

Of course we know our government is costing us more than it's worth, but do you know of any cheaper government that's running around? Do you? If you do, they'll sell you a ticket there anytime. You can try Russia! There's no income tax in Russia, but there's no income.

So the question is: How can we make such a holler on what the government wants to collect back from us? But I don't know what it's all about. I don't know any more about this thing than an economist knows, and God knows, he doesn't know anything.

I referred to the Pilgrims landing on Plymouth Rock and you should have heard what I got from New England. I split New England just wide open. It seems there's a town up there, called Provincetown, and they have adopted a slogan which says: Don't be misled by history, or any other unreliable source. Here's the place where the Pilgrims landed. This is by unanimous vote of the Chamber of Commerce of Provincetown. Provincetown has been made the official landing place of the Pilgrims. Any Pilgrim landing in any other place, was not official.

Now in the first place, I don't think that this argument I have created up there, is so terribly important. The argument New England has got to settle in order to pacify the rest of America, is: Why were the Pilgrims allowed to land anywhere? That's what we want to know. There has never been any comparison between the Pilgrims and the Indians. Now I hope that my Cherokee blood is not making me prejudiced, I want to be broad minded, but I am sure that it was only the extreme generosity of the Indians that allowed the Pilgrims to land. Suppose we reverse the case. Do you reckon the Pilgrims would have ever let the Indians land? Not a chance! Why, the Pilgrims wouldn't even allow the Indians to live, after the Indians went to the trouble of letting them land.

Well, anyhow, the Provincetown officials, they sent me a lot of official data, that when the Pilgrims landed, they found some corn that the Indians had stored, and that the Pilgrims were about starved, and that they ate the Indian corn. They claim that corn was stored at Provincetown. So you see, the minute the Pilgrims landed, they got full of the corn, and then they shot the Indians. Perhaps because they hadn't stored more corn.

Of course, they would always pray. That's one thing about a Pilgrim, he would pray—mostly for more Indian corn. You never in your life, any one of you—you never saw a picture of one of these Pilgrims praying, that he didn't have a gun right by the side of him. That was to see that he got what he was praying for.

To Read or to Write?

Well, all I know is just what I read in the papers, or what I see as I try to look down through the wings of an aeroplane. If you want to see something, don't go up in the air and try to see it. Just as you glimpse it, why, the wing of the plane will cover it and before the wing passes over it, it's too far back to see. I flew East and back here a couple of weeks ago, and it was when the dust storms were going, and in lots of places where the real dust storms was not operating, it was dark and looked like rain, and I said to my sister in Oklahoma, it's going to rain today! and she said, no, it's been this way for days and days. It's just the very fine dust that's in the air.

I just been reading tonight some reviews. I have the autobiography but haven't had time to read it—but will, of John Hays Hammond, the great engineer, who has operated all over the world. He used to come out here to my place, and we would talk about South Africa. We would talk about the Jamieson Raid. He was mixed up in it, and it's what started the Boer War. He was down there before the war, and I got in just before the end. Not in the fighting. I was breaking horses, and at the close, working with a little Wild West Show. (My very first show experience.)

He has had a great, colorful career, has John Hays Hammond. Eighty years old the other day. I was going to send him a wire, but like everything else I am going to do, I forget it before the time comes. Like about ten days ago, Dorothy Stone, my little pardner in Fred's show one time, why, she opened here as the big star in *As Thousands Cheer,* and while I went myself, I plum forgot to send either wire, or flowers. Now I mean well, but I get off to talking to some old guy about the N.R.A., or some cowpuncher about who won the roping at Ft. Worth at their big show, or maybe knocking the ball around on the polo field, or roping at some old, gentle calves that are trained to stick their heads in the loop. I get to doing all this foolishness, and plum forget to do what I ought to do. I sometimes wonder if the Lord is going to make the proper distinction between the fellow that means well, and the one that does well. I don't believe He will blackball us just because we don't remember.

Now some people are so wonderful about things, and they remember, and they do and say just the right things at the right time. My desk right here before me now, is piled higher than Postmaster General Jim Farley's, of letters from friends, and folks that should be my friends, if I would show them the least courtesy of answering. But, do you know, I will keep putting it off. I carried some of them clear to New York and back. Now I knew in my own heart darn well, that I wasn't going to sit down and write any letters while I was on the planes, or in hotels, but I meant well. I intended to answer 'em, but I knew darn well I wasn't going to. There ain't a thing in the world to lay it onto, but laziness. I could have quit talking, and boring somebody long enough to answer a lot of them. I could have stayed up an hour or so later, and answered another dozen, or so, but no, I was too darn lazy, and I get sleepy early, and then the darn reading. I want to read everything in the world that is in a paper. No sporting writer ever wrote anything that I didn't read it all.

Why, you know what I do, and I bet you I am unique. I even read the editorials. Yes, sir, now you can't beat that for miscellaneous reading. That's what you call exploring in reading. Course I forget everything I read. I haven't got any more memory than a billy goat, and I forget about nine-tenths of what I read, and get the other tenth wrong. But it makes me think that I am sorter doing something when I am reading. Then too, I can fall to sleep and never drop the paper. My closest friend can't tell when I am reading, or sleeping. They are pretty near always wrong. They say: "You read a lot!" and I say, "No, I sleep a lot over my reading."

If they would just quit printing newspapers for about a year, I could get some books read, but by the time the daily papers are read, I am sound asleep.

They send me books, they autograph 'em to me, sometimes with some very kindly and much more than fair inscriptions, but do you know that I am that lazy and ornery, that I don't acknowledge 'em?

Now that is terrible, but I just get out of it by letting the impression go around that I am just so busy that I haven't the time. Well, I haven't got the time because I am out on a horse somewhere, or asleep somewhere. If it wasn't for riding, and reading newspapers, and dozing off, I bet you I would be writing to more people than Mrs. Roosevelt. Lord, I would like to borrow that lady's energy for a month, and I would wind up with some friends, instead of a lot of unintentionally-made enemies.

Now here lay all these important letters here tonight, and I could answer at least a tenth of 'em, but here come the morning papers—they come out the day before. Now will I answer these letters and maintain my friends? No, I will take the papers and go to bed, and go to sleep holding it out at arm's length, the lights burning, and the glasses on.

Off on a Sightseeing Trip

I am off on a little sightseeing trip with Wiley Post. Went out to the flying field at midnight in Los Angeles, to catch the plane for Seattle. You see, day or night means nothing to 'em now. With courses all lighted, they run schedules in the night time the same as in the day. When my wife knew it was with Wiley, it didn't matter where it was we was going, and she was mighty fine about it.

Well, she is about everything. You can't live with a comedian long without being mighty forgiving. She is no mean aviation enthusiast herself. In fact, she was flying the next night after I left on this trip, clear back to New York, and to Maine, to see our daughter Mary.

From the same field in Los Angeles, she had seen me off a couple of years, or more, ago, off to Vancouver to catch a boat to go to the Japanese Manchurian war, and then fly on around the world and meet her in Geneva, Switzerland, at one of those Disarmament Conferences, where I used to always go for my amusement. Come to think of it, that was back in 1931 and 1932.

Anyhow, now I drop off in Frisco and tend to some business early the next morning, and then to Seattle at five in the afternoon. That's a pretty trip. The pilots in the big Boeing just scraped Mount Shasta. Snow all over the old ant hill. We flew right up and over what I think they call the Redwood highway. Lots of pretty little towns nestled back in little valleys and canyons. First stop out of Sacramento was Medford, Oregon, where a few days before some ambitious reporter had sent out a dispatch that he had seen Wiley Post and me flying over there, when we were at that time crossing Arizona. So this time he is liable to report that I arrived there by horse and buggy.

Say, there is some mountains over that route. South of Medford, and north of Medford. That's the town where they raise the fine pears. I was forced down there on my previous flight to Vancouver, and they kept telling me about the fine pears, and I afterward wrote about them but said they never did offer me any, they just kept telling how great they was. Well, sir, when I returned from around the world, they sent me practically all they raised in the valley that year—I think. Every time a box would come, it would be more pears, and better pears, (if possible).

Looked down and saw a big forest fire in the mountains. Pilot said it had been burning for days. Lots of great timber going to waste. Beautiful country, northern California and Oregon and Washington, everything green, rivers galore.

Into Portland, Oregon, a beautiful air field on an island, and a beautifully located city. I asked for Tex Rankin, a flyer that had hauled me around over that country in the early days. He was a fine flyer, and is yet, which means that he is good. "You ARE a fine flyer" means a lot more than saying "You WAS a fine flyer." Girl stewardess come along somewhere in the story here with a fine lunch. It had more dainty little sandwiches, and knickknacks than I had ever seen in any lunch in my life; it was arranged lovely. They say it was made up at the St. Francis Hotel in San Francisco.

Then into Puget Sound country, beautiful bays and islands. Tacoma, who had the first slogan that I can ever remember; it was when I played there in vaudeville about 1908: "Watch Tacoma Grow!" I have never watched it much since, but it did.

Seattle? That's a whole story in itself. The Gateway to Alaska! To the Orient, to Canada. Seattle is a real city, New York in miniature, boats for China, Japan; Los Angeles seven hours by plane, Spokane, Minneapolis and Chicago by plane. Sixty lakes are in sixty minutes' drive by car from City Hall. Saw the world's greatest bombing plane being finished. If we don't want it, Abyssinia does.

Yes sir, a plane is a great place to see anything, only the wings are right under where you want to look, and you can't see anything. But I did really see Mount Shasta. They couldn't hide it under the wings.

It's a beautiful morning in Seattle. Wiley and Mrs. Post have been here a few days getting the ship from wheels to pontoons. I have had a mighty pleasant and lovely 24 hours here.

AUGUST 7TH. Mrs. Post and Wiley and I drive out to the field. It's a combination land and water airport, called Great Lakes Airway, right on beautiful Lake Washington. Mrs. Post decided at the last minute to go up to Alaska a few days later by boat, so it's only Wiley and I that are taking off. The plane looks mighty pretty. It's a Lockheed body, Sirius wings, three-bladed pitch propeller, big Wasp engine. It's a bright red with a few trimmings of white stripes. Wiley calls it "Aurora Borealis," I call it "Post Toasty."

The pontoons are awful big looking things, but Wiley says "None too big." Wiley is kind of a Calvin Coolidge on answers; none of 'em are going to bother you with being too long. Mrs. Post asks me to take good care of Wiley. I said, "Of course you mean in the air, after we get on the ground he is able to look after himself."

There had been an extra single seat ahead of a double seat. Wiley took it out, and there is left a world of space, as there is this comfortable double seat; it could be possible to be a six-passenger job.

Take-off in Seattle. Well, she took off like a bird, with an awful short run and with about 260 gallons of gas. Seattle is awful pretty from the air—well from anywhere, but with a sea plane that takes off from the water, you are nearer the city and not so high as you would be if flying over it in a land plane. Then you start above those channels, and islands, and lakes, and then out and up the coast. If there is a prettier trip in the world than from Seattle to Alaska by what they call Inland Passage, I never saw it.

Victoria, British Columbia, over on the left, the place that is the most English of any place outside England, and even more English than 90 per cent of England. Beautiful gardens, beautiful flowers, a lovely dignified old city. It's England.

Then up the coast. Big timber coming right down to the water edge.

I don't know where they would ever get any shortage of timber.

Did you ever pay much attention to a map of Alaska? Well, there is some astonishing things about it. Now we have a long, narrow strip of land that I don't think is but 30 miles back from the ocean to the top of the ridge of mountains, and then comes Canada. We cut Canada off from the ocean for five or six hundred miles. I don't know just how that come about, well, I do too, you see we bought it from Russia in 1868 (I think it was). Seward was secretary of state, and he bought it from the Russians and the ambassador at the time from there was a Count Von—somebody, or other. There is a big picture of it in the wonderful museum in Juneau, and it shows the signing of the bill-of-sale. We paid $7,200,000, the two hundred thousand extra was the Count's commission, I guess.

Anyhow, that was some trip! A thousand-mile hop from Seattle to Juneau. We was going to stop at Ketchikan for lunch, but mist and rain and Wiley just breezed through there, never over 100 feet off the water. We had pretty weather for about the first three hundred miles, but then it began to kinder close in. I guess Wiley figured that if he stopped at Ketchikan, we would get closed in and wouldn't get any further up the coast. So he flew low over the very pretty little city right along the water edge, with the high mountains to the back of it.

Talk about navigation! There is millions of channels and islands and bays, and all look alike (to me), but this old boy Wiley, he turns up the right alley all the time. Nothing that I have ever seen is more beautiful than this Inland Passage—by either boat or plane—to Alaska.

I still don't know how Russia, or anybody else, ever got England (or Canada rather) cut off from the sea like that. England is kinder crazy about her seas and oceans, and when you let her get 30 miles away from one, and then don't let her to it, why, it's almost a miracle. Anyhow, this may make you look at your maps and see just how Alaska lays. Do you see that the Klondike is in Canada, and not in the United States? Well, that's enough geography for now.

AUGUST 8TH. This is Juneau, the capital of the whole of Alaska. The governor is a nice fellow, a Democrat, but a gentleman. In their government there is sixteen congressmen and eight senators. Fifteen of the congressmen are Democrats, and all the senators. It's about the nearest to an ideal existence you can get.

The Chamber of Commerce will shoot me for this, but I have been buying raincoats since early morning.

We are flying to Skagway now and see the famous Chilkoot Pass.

We will do it in ten minutes, and it took the pioneers two and three months.

AUGUST 9TH. Juneau. Bad weather. Not a plane mushed out of Juneau yesterday. Not much news of Congress, and what we do get is mostly bad news.

Had a great visit last night with Rex Beach, the great writer, who is a mighty dear old friend. Rex seems to know everybody and everything about Alaska. He come to Nome in about 1901, that was when she was really "hot." You see, the miners that come in '98, they went for Dawson and the Klondike district, a thousand and more miles from Nome. Then the Nome strike took it away from the old Klondike district.

Did I ever tell you that Rex Beach and his wife Greta (that's Mrs. Fred Stone's sister) are responsible for me being in the movies? They was making a great Alaskan picture, and the character was *Laughing Bill Hyde*. It was one of Rex Beach's short stories, by that same name. I was playing that summer in the Ziegfeld Follies, and Rex and Greta got the "nut" idea that I could play the part. We made the picture while I was working in the show. It was made at the old Fort Lee studios in New Jersey, just across the river from New York City. They used to make an awful lot of pictures there.

It was made for Mr. Sam Goldwyn, the famous producer. With producers coming and going, he has held his own right at the top. He was my first picture boss, and we have remained friends all these years—a rare combination.

I learned what little I know about mining, which is practically nothing, from that picture we made. Rex supervised the picture, and he made 'em make all the details as to the actual mining scenes, exactly correct, you know, "sluice boxes," and "panning" gold. Then Rex wrote all the subtitles—the picture was silent—and they were great.

I went to the barber and got a hair cut right in the middle of the picture, and like to spoiled it. I didn't know what I was doing—here I was going in one door with long hair, and coming out with a hair cut. They all like to had a fit. But I think yet it was the best picture I ever made, for I hadn't learned to try to act. There ain't nothing worse than an actor when we act.

I tell you these little towns and cities in Alaska have mighty fine newspapers. They take all the big news and whittle it down till you can read it and understand it. And they have a splendid radio service for messages all over this vast country, and brother, it's vast—and vaster still. A distance of 500 miles is just about a jaunt down to the post office and back. They speak of being visiting over to some town 7 or 8 hundred miles away, like you would be going to your next door neighbors, and those trips might be a thousand, or fifteen hundred miles.

AUGUST 10TH. Get your map out and look this up! Aklavik, North West Territory! The mouth of the Mackenzie River, right on the Arctic Ocean. Eskimos are thicker than rich men at a "Save the Constitution" convention. We are headed for famous Herschel Island in the Arctic. What, no night? It's all day up here!

That Yukon River that you have read about, that is formed away in the Yukon Territory of Canada; we flew down it from the head, and it winds and twists till it comes out away down near St. Michael, in the Bering Sea, 3,000 miles away. It was interesting to be flying where the trip took you over land where one river went on to the Arctic Ocean, while a few miles away over a divide, the waters of another river would be headed for the Pacific.

At Herschel Island, in the Arctic, we couldn't land on account of the ice in the water, but we circled it a time, or so. There are only half a dozen houses, but it's a noted place, where the whalers, the real old sailing ships used to land and spend the winters. They would come up from America, or the various Scandinavian countries, in one summer, get in there and winter. That would give them an early start the next summer, when the ice went out. Then they would hunt all summer, which was about three months, then back into Herschel for the second winter, and then out with the whalebone the next summer. A whale used to net 'em about 18 or 20 thousand dollars, when whalebone was selling, but the minute the women started with rubber corsets, the old whalers were pretty near put out of business. The blubber and oil had to make up for the old whalebone corset stays.

AUGUST 11TH. We saw old Captain Peterson's big old boat. He comes and trades generally for the month of August. They are strict about who they let come and trade. For instance in Canada anywhere, they don't allow just any trader to take a dog team, or a boat, or any conveyance, and go out and trade for furs. It's against the law.

They have to let the Indians or Eskimos bring the furs in and trade at the posts. Canada has a great system of dealing with their native population, away up in the far north. In all that country that is north of the real mainland of Canada, all those tremendous islands and gulfs up there, a white man is not allowed to fish, hunt or trap. It's entirely for the support of the Indians that live up there. Now we had never thought of that.

Well that's one thing I don't believe I could ever be, a hunter or trapper. One thing, I haven't got the nerve to stand the gaff and go through the great physical hardships and I can't go for that trapping of animals, although I know that it has to be done. These Eskimos have one of the most regulated lives there is, almost to the day of the various months or seasons they will go from hunting or trapping of one animal to the other. White fox takes up just so many days, then they will move to another place to take up other game. Muskrat, then white seals, then fishing for their supply of dog food. Then polar bear takes up so much of their time. He is pretty hard to get and is worth real money to 'em.

It's a great country, is Alaska and the Canadian North West, where you have to live off the country, hunt, trap, kill and live. Four mails a year into that place, two and a half months of the year when it's not frozen. The hospitality and generosity of those trappers that live out there would put us to absolute shame. Here we pass folks every day, every hour, that we could help, but don't go to the trouble of doing it, when we can well afford the time and money—but we don't do it. Yet up here, they would mush through the winter, 50 degrees below for days, to help a friend. We think they punish animals. We punish humans, only we don't think so.

AUGUST 12TH. Aklavik, North West Territory. Was you ever driving around in a car and not knowing, or caring, where you went? Well, that's what Wiley and I are doing. We are sure having a great time. Friday and Saturday we visited the old Klondike district, Dawson City, Bonanza, Eldorado.

When Wiley or I hear of whales or polar bears in the Arctic, or a big herd of caribou or reindeer we fly over and see it. Oh, yes, they got caribou to hunt. There is literally thousands of caribou all over Alaska and the Yukon and North West Territory. They say they pass in great herds, like the old timers say the buffalo used to do.

Say, I want to tell you the great story some time, of the big drive of 3,000 reindeer from away over in the very north-west tip of our country of Alaska, clear along the very banks of the Arctic Ocean for 2,000 miles to this place, Aklavik, the very mouth of the Mackenzie River. They was five years getting them there. It's the greatest story in animal driving I ever heard. The Canadian government had bought them from the Loman Brothers, the big reindeer men of Alaska.

You ought to see the marvelous works of art by the Indians and Eskimos. Those Eskimos are really a mighty high class bunch of folks, and plum proud. They won't mess at all with the Indians, and not much with the whites. They think they are superior to the whites, and it don't take much to tell that they have kinder got it on us.

An Eskimo dog, from the time he is just a half sized pup, is never untied. He is always tied with a chain, and he don't bark at all, he howls. They call all Eskimos "Huskys." I always thought that it was the dogs that were called "Huskys," but it's the Eskimos, themselves.

And say, there is a horse here; the furthest north of any horse, and he eats fish and travels on snowshoes. But that's enough northern knowledge for one lesson, especially when some of it maybe ain't so. Maybe Pt. Barrow today.

AUGUST 13TH. Fairbanks, Alaska. This Alaska is a great country. If they can just keep from being taken over by the U.S. they got a great future. This is the greatest aviation-minded city of its size in the world. There is only 30,000 white people in Alaska, and there is seventy commercial planes operating every day, in winter on skis.

There may be some doubt about the Louisiana purchase being a mistake, but when Seward bought Alaska, he even made up for what we had overpaid the Indians for Manhattan Island.

AUGUST 14TH. Anchorage, Alaska. Well, we had a day off today, and nothing to do, so we went flying with friend Joe Crosson, Alaska's crack pilot, who is a great friend of Wiley's and who had helped him on his difficulties up here on his record trips, and Joe Barrows, another fine pilot. In a Lockheed Electra we scaled Mount McKinley, the highest one on the American continent. Bright sunny day and the most beautiful sight I ever saw.

Crosson landed on the glacier over half way up the mountain, in a plane and took off. Flew right by hundreds of mountain sheep, flew low over moose and bear down in the valley. Now out to visit Matanuska Valley, where they sent those 1935 model pioneers.

Joe Crosson has a mine and we went out there, and he has a partner, a Swedish fellow that runs it, and he had just killed a bear— right at his house door. Ernest, that's the Swedish fellow, told us how Mickey, a wirehaired fox terrier, went out one night and run the bear in. Well, as a matter of fact, Mickey went out and the bear chased him in, and Ernest had to shoot the bear to keep him from running Mickey under the bed. They say there is more fellows been caught by a bear in just that way. An old pet dog jumps the bear and then they hike straight for you, and the bear after them, and the first thing you know, you got a bear in your lap, and a dog between your feet.

So there is two kinds of bear dogs: the ones that drive 'em away, and the ones that bring 'em in. Little Mickey thought he had done it, as Ernest said, and he chewed the hair off the bear, after death.

AUGUST 15TH. Fairbanks, Alaska. Leaving Fairbanks, we was trying to get off, and the river was sorter narrow and many bends, and Wiley was afraid that with a full load of gas, we might have some difficulty in taking off. So we had some gas sent out to Harding Lake, a lake about 50 miles out. And then we flew there and loaded up. Now we will be headed for Point Barrow, the furthest north piece of land on the north American continent.

Well, Wiley's got her warmed up. Let's go.

Less than six hours after leaving Harding Lake, at 8:17 on an Arctic summer's evening, the little plane crashed into Walakpa Lagoon, twelve miles south of Barrow, Alaska. Will Rogers and Wiley Post were killed instantly.

Index

Index